MORE MESSAGES
FROM
MICHAEL

Twenty-fifth Anniversary Edition

MORE MESSAGES
FROM
MICHAEL

Twenty-fifth Anniversary Edition

Chelsea Quinn Yarbro

Cælum Press
an imprint of
Writers.com Books

http://www.caelumpress.com
publisher@writers.com

Manufactured in the United States of America

Trade Paperback Edition: ISBN 978-0-9766544-4-5
Hardcover Edition: ISBN 978-0-9766544-5-2

Published by Cælum Press
a division of Writers.com Books
Akron, Ohio

Original version first published in 1986
by Berkley Publishing Group

A Note From the Publisher:
Our edition of the first Michael book, *Messages from Michael*, was, indeed, published about twenty-five years after the first. We would have liked to have published this edition to coincide more closely to a twentieth anniversary, but by the time this volume reaches the shelves it will be about twenty-four years since its first appearance. So, for the title, we chose to "round-up" as that rather nicely matches our first Michael publication:
Messages from Michael: The Twenty-fifth Anniversary Edition.

For the mediums "Jessica Lansing" and "Camille Rowe"
as well as the two mediums represented
in this book as "Leslie Adams"

Author's Note

The material in the following pages has been compiled from transcripts of mediumistic sessions over the past decade, as well as from special sessions during the writing of this book in order to fill in the gaps and clarify certain parts of the material. Michael's dictations are set off in sans serif typeface (as with this example) to differentiate them from other comments and text. I am grateful to the mediums Jessica Lansing and Camille Rowe and the two mediums incorporated as Leslie Adams for their generosity with their material and their time as well as their very special gifts. I would also like to thank the many members of the Michael group who gave me access to their transcripts and supplied me with the other material for this volume. As in the first book about Michael, *Messages From Michael*, all names and many descriptions are fictitious. Michael's statements and opinions do not necessarily reflect the opinions or beliefs of anyone but Michael.

Additional Note for This Edition

Special thanks to Libba Spencer for her excellent work in catching mistakes and reconciling varying styles of capitalization from differing sources and eras.

Contents

Introduction
Opening Words From Michael
(Revised for the Twenty-fifth Anniversary Edition)

We offer this teaching unconditionally. You are not expected nor are you required to accept what we say, to agree with it, to "believe" in it, to uphold it, to embrace it, or manifest any other response to what we impart. We do not offer the one true way, for each Fragment in each life has many paths to the goal, and each of you is capable of finding your way. In this regard you are, of course, free to change your mind at any point, to pursue your Life Plan or not, to decide to pursue any teaching or no teaching. If we serve any purpose, it is as an information service to travelers, and as sign posts. We do not say this lightly: no one is required to "believe" in sign posts, or even to read them. The information we provide is valid—we have no reason to distort information, for that would impose conditions on what we teach—and we make a gift of it to you. Note that we do not say bribe. We do not require or expect anything in return.

In the intervening years since we first dictated these comments, we have seen the consequences of many choices manifest not only within our little group, but among many of your species, and have often been asked to comment on our perceptions of these changes: Typically of Young Soul planets, the tendency toward extreme political positions, justified and enhanced by religious zeal, has escalated all over the world. While this is not uncommon on a Young Soul planet and in a Young Soul country such as yours is, it has served to bring about profound societal disruptions throughout a great number of societies, and not only to those actively involved in disagreement. While there is no "wrong" in this, we are aware that the turn from seeking transparency in social institutions to demanding opacity in the same institutions has led to a policy of obfuscation and mendacity as a matter of course, which, we would wish to point out, has impacted the choices of individual Fragments for no more reason than because social institutions choose to ignore the reciprocity that is usually the hallmark of societal institutions in technologically advanced societies; such social policy is more typical of what are sometimes called "developing" nations, where societal institutions are most apt to operate on a system of patronage, usually linked to families or regions. The degree of martinet-style administrations among many of the social institutions active in technologically advanced societies has tended to subvert the society in general, which weakens the society and inclines the societal members to distrust, schadenfreude, smugness, and other signs of burgeoning Chief Features. In the long run, this will incline the society toward despotism, if previous experience is any indication of the possibilities here. It is, of course, a matter of choice on the part of the society's members to what degree of this policy will be allowed to endure. Given the nature of Young Souls, it is unlikely that these, or any other conditions, will last "perpetually," no matter what efforts are undertaken to ensure that perpetuality. We have no direct concerns with these machinations, and, of course, the choice to endure the policies in place are equally valid as all choices are, but we do perceive a profound distortion in the matter of perceived choices and that, while as valid as any perception, nonetheless tends to "slow" the rate of validated evolution.

We have also been asked to comment upon the climate change underway: We will reiterate what we said when we were first asked about this phenomenon, more than thirty years ago: This planet periodically undergoes a shift in weather patterns that are the nature of the planet itself, which is why this is not a prediction, merely the observation of a cyclic pattern. The current, ordinary shift that began in the late 1970s has been exacerbated by the presence of atmospheric carbon dioxide in greater quantities than in the mammalian past, and the level of hydrocarbon particulates in the atmosphere.

While a degree of weather-pattern change may prove inconvenient, the possibility of a more profound climacteric change is not "beyond the pale" and therefore we would agree that reducing the human additions to the planetary climate conditions would not be amiss, we must also remark that there will be a shift in climate—and we remind you this is not a prediction, for we do not predict, but a comment based upon the history of the planet and long-established weather "adjustments"—the degree to how much that shift impacts your species may well be, to a degree, in your hands. That is not to discourage you in your efforts toward improving the atmosphere. We did not say that nor did we mean to imply it, but we do wish to point out that the change, with or without your participation, is underway. Failure to act to contain the human contribution will tend to redound to the disaccommodation of the humans more than other creatures. You are, of course, free to do this, as you are free to do anything, but for those concerned about the world you will come back to in your subsequent lives, you might choose to work toward minimizing the scale of the shift. But as we say this, we also remind you of that very typical Young Soul law: the law of unforeseen consequences.

Those of you reading this book may choose to hear the words we provide and to validate this teaching for yourselves. If you decide to explore this teaching, we would wish that you do not accept it "on faith" but question it and test it to determine if its approach and "message" is useful to you, for that is the most direct means to validation accessible to you on the physical plane. Nothing we say is intended to be dogma, or interpreted as "scripture". Let us point out that all validation is a Personal Truth: what is true for one Fragment may not be true for another, yet both Truths are valid for the individual Fragment doing the perceiving. Therefore attempting to fit our teaching into a religious context obviates our "purpose" in offering it. There is no "one right way" to experience spirituality, nor can such a schematic lead to recognition and validation. Let us reiterate, we would hope those who choose to pursue this teaching would exercise skepticism in dealing with the material given, so that validation may come, as it most often does, through testing.

Let us point out that one of the most easily validated aspects of this teaching is the differentiation between Personal and World Truths. Some of the Personal Truths are yours to accept or change, for choices are of a personal nature. You may, for example, learn to overcome a stammer, should you choose to do so, but you are pretty much stuck with eye color and bone structure. On the other hand, you cannot change gravity or the radiation from the sun, a World Truth, although you can make hybrid crops or dam rivers, impacting World Truths. That time means age and aging—which are Extended World Truths, in that they happen throughout the Physical Plane, your personal age, either in the chronological or the evolutionary sense—is a Personal Truth. The Physical Plane offers a variety of Truths to those extant upon it, and it is part of the evolution of the soul that brings students to this and many other teachings, valid and not valid, for the purpose of sorting out the Truths.

We impart our knowledge to you. That is our purpose. Your use of it, or lack of use of it, does not change the teaching, nor does it change us. No matter what your opinion of us may be, we, and you, will continue to evolve, which is the validation of what you have called perfect love. The evolution does not require anything of you or us, for that is the Tao, which is complete in itself because it contains all things and all happening in all Planes of existence. It is no more a deity than the laws of motion are deities, and seeks no worship or other sign of notice—that would be similar to adoring your corpuscles, which you may choose to do, of course, but it would not contribute much to most Fragments to do so. The Tao is more omnipresent than DNA and subatomic particles, and all life and all physicality "interacts" with the Tao, as do all aspects of all Planes of existence.

Some have described the evolution through incarnations as the voyage from primate to Buddha. While this is a glib and superficial statement, nonetheless it contains elements of the truth. Very young souls, in the Infant Cycle, are more deeply in the grasp of the species in which they are ensouled just as a human infant reflects more "animal" patterns than the acculturated adults around it. At the end of a single life, even the very youngest souls will have learned something. At the end of the Cycles of lives, the Fragment, or, if you prefer, the individual, with or without awareness, will understand the nature of life of a Fragment incarnate on the Physical Plane. One student put it this way: you come back again and again until you get it "right" and when you get it "right", you can go. This does not mean that there is a right or wrong way in which to "get it," but that self-realization, recognition and validation, and all-inclusive evolution will lead to the comprehension that all of life, and all lives, are equally valid, and that the totality of experience is, in fact, the final goal.

Of course, there is evolution at all Levels and all the lessons of the Physical Plane are brought to bear in further evolution on the Astral Plane, the Causal Plane, the Buddhic Plane, the Akashic Plane, and the Planes beyond until all returns to the Tao. We do not mean to suggest that there is a "right" and a "wrong" way to live a life, for that is not the case. There is life and life is what it is, and the response to it, positive and negative, is the lesson of living. Just as belief is not required to work an electric light switch or to operate a pasta-making machine, so belief is not required to evolve. Essence will choose the lives that bring about evolution, and the personality will choose to live or not to live that life. Whether or not the chosen life is lived during a life, the life is always valid and whatever is learned will contribute to evolution.

Of course, there is evolution at all Levels and all the lessons of the Physical Plane are brought to bear in further evolution on the Astral Plane, the Causal Plane, the Buddhic Plane, the Akashic Plane, and the Planes beyond until all returns to the Tao. We do not mean to suggest that there is a "right" and a "wrong" way to live a life, for that is not the case. There is life and life is what it is, and the response to it, positive and negative, is the lesson of living. Just as belief is not required to work an electric light switch or to operate a pasta-making machine, so belief is not required to evolve. Essence will choose the lives that bring about evolution, and the personality will choose to live or not to live that life. Whether or not the chosen life is lived during a life, the life is always valid and whatever is learned will contribute to evolution.

Nothing is wasted. What we would wish to communicate to you is the sovereignty and responsibility of choice. All in life is chosen. Some choices are under duress, some are open, highly varied opportunities, but all aspects of life entail choices, and choices decide the life. That is true for all extant on the Physical Plane. Every life is chosen, every personality is chosen. Barring karmic interference and exigencies of the Physical Plane, the life that you live is the life that you choose, and the living of it brings lessons to bear that contribute to the growth and understanding of every Fragment. Aside from the Fragment that is the core of your self, no one—and we stress no one—is keeping score. You answer to your Essential self. And your self does not accept excuses, nor does it need any, for Essence perceives without distortions, and all that you do and have done is known and understood by Essence, untrammeled by fear and the impositions of the Physical Plane.

We have remarked before, but we will reiterate: fear is a "necessary" part of the Physical Plane, the response that is an admirable aid to survival for all species, ensouled or not. But once ensoulment occurs, then fear takes on resonances and complications, projections and enlargements, so that acts that are not intrinsically dangerous—giving a speech, arranging a dinner party, going on a "blind" date—take on the same degree of dread that crossing a crocodile-infested river would entail. Once ensoulment has occurred, the Fragments develop the capacity to anticipate, and to worry, both of which involve the creation of suppositions, which is where the fear becomes entrenched and fixates as Chief Features. It is not the fear itself that is "hazardous," but the compounding of responses that extend fear into all aspects of life, most of which have little to do with the problems of physical survival. And while the unensouled creatures of this planet are capable of fretting, of nervous alertation, of anxiety, and of panic, they do not and cannot project imagined possibilities, and do not tend to "embroider" the fear they feel with an accumulation of fearful experiences to enhance the fear they feel. Animals habitually in danger can become habitually fearful, but even that does not entail the kind of amalgamated terror that Chief Features produce.

Our little group has chosen to provide this teaching, and their questions which spurred the answers, to you for a second time. They were not compelled or instructed to do so, for we do not teach that way. That the group has chosen to remain anonymous and closed does not invalidate what we have answered, nor does it limit what the Fragments in our little group have learned. Neither criticism nor praise is appropriate to their decisions in this, or any other, matter.

Although we are now a reunited Entity of the Mid-Causal Plane in what you perceive as the fifth Level of the Mid-Causal Plane, we have all lived as you are living now. We were of your species, on your world, and passed all our lives in "human" bodies. Since valid communication beyond your immediate species is rudimentary at best, incarnation for all of you will continue to take place only in your species. Only when complex communication with ensouled species beyond your own is routinely achieved will you choose to incarnate in other ensouled species. We know all that you know—and in this instance we mean you as the collective mass of humanity—from experience and observation. We perceive each of you both as the Fragments you are, the Essence within, and as the Entity you each are part of. We have shared all that you can share—food, shelter, thoughts, feelings, courage, urbanity, rurality, isolation, cowardice, social position, economic "realities", dread, war, travel, weather, fashion, illness, health, stasis, opposition, support, ostracism, lionization, politics on all levels, "beneficence", "malice", natural disasters, famine, plague, youth, age, grief, joy, affection, alienation, hope, despair, sex, the rearing of children, tending crops, harvest, hunting, the creation of art, esthetic perception, mathematical perception, practical craftsmanship, construction, destruction, civic responsibilities, civil rebellion, unearned advantage, undeserved neglect, wealth, penury, lawfulness, criminality, devout religiosity, apostasy, atheism, philosophy, depression, exaltation, industry, fame, lethargy, honor, glory, disgrace, all manner of gender manifestations, conformity, nonconformity, talents, skills, appreciation, derogation, "sanity", "insanity", loyalty, betrayal, domesticity, wildness, exploration, limitation, and all the rest of the entirety of life—and now experience that sharing as integration. We regard you with compassion and utter understanding. For those on the Physical Plane, perceptions are, by their very nature, distorted. We, on the Mid-Causal Plane, are without the blinders that hamper contact and integration. Our perspective is different from yours and as such we are able to aid in lessening the illusions that surround each of you shutting out much truth. You may choose to recognize these truths or you may choose to reject them, you may choose to accept part of what we say and discard the rest, you may choose to reinterpret what we impart—it will no longer be our teaching, but you are free to choose to do it—you may choose to try to refute what we say, but the truth of what we impart remains, as your many, many lives serve to teach every one of you.

Should you decide to avail yourself of the information presented here and in the previous publication, much insight may made available to be brought to bear in your life, should you choose to recognize it. However, the insights will come, with or without this or any other teaching. As bodies inevitably age, so do souls, but, of course, on a different time scale. Let us add that Older in evolution is not "better", it is only more experienced.

Those who see Old Souls as in some way superior to Younger ones are indulging in "wishful thinking" and scripting, which you may choose to do, but such assumptions will tend to block recognition and validation on many levels for all concerned. Every Fragment in your species and all species extant upon the Physical Plane were once First Level Infant Souls and will eventually be Final Level Old Souls. The Cycles cannot be abbreviated beyond the occasional transition of one Level during a lifetime, usually the result of trauma and/or extreme stress. The necessity of Internal Monadal Transits makes "leaping over" Levels and Cycles an invalid concept and incompatible with the nature of evolution: Just as a raptor dinosaur does not suddenly hatch a chicken, so an ensouled Fragment cannot "bound" from Fifth Level Young to Fifth Level Mature, nor can a Mid-Cycle Young Soul be "sent back" to "do over" First Level Young, or any other Cycle and Level already transited.

Let us encourage each of you to question his or her life, to examine your experiences and perceptions, so that you may recognize and validate your perceptions, if you wish to seek self-awareness. Not all lives are chosen for self-awareness, just as not all persons wear the same size shoes. Essence will indicate the path you have chosen if you care to give attention to those inner promptings, if it is your desire to know. There is no "error" in whatever choice you make. Your decision on this, as in every other issue, is yours to make. There is only choice and the consequences of choice. Let us point out that every one of you is growing and evolving, as Fragments, as members of Entities that are themselves evolving. All choices contribute to this evolution, and there is no way that you cannot choose: saying "I will not choose" is, of course, a choice.

Our information is given with unqualified love.

Dictated January, 1985
Revised June, 2009

CHAPTER ONE
At a Michael Session

Jessica Lansing is thinner now than she was in 1978, and her hair is shorter. A greenhouse window has been added onto the foyer, just off the living room. Her daughter, a teenager when *Messages From Michael* was written, is now in her twenties and married.

"We've had ups and downs, like everyone else," she says, nodding to the half-dozen people sitting around the coffee table. "I guess the worst was Walter's illness, at least for me, but everyone else has had their difficulties, too." She indicates the others. "Camille Rowe, who's been our second medium for the last five years, has had a series of family crises, David Swan has taken a post in Cleveland at one of the museums there—every now and then he comes to a session when he's in the area, but otherwise we don't see much of him, though we get phone calls—and Marjorie Randall and Kate O'Brien have left the group entirely. Lucy North comes occasionally, but is much more active in church work now than she was five years ago. She remarried last year and I don't think her husband has much liking for the Michael teaching. On the other hand, there are new faces, not all of them here today. Alex Squire, the tall chap with the pewter-colored hair, has been in the group a couple of years. He's done special work with Milly— Camille Rowe, that is—and with our other back-up medium. And there's John Verano. Alex and John are both Scholars, by the way."

"She's packing the court," Camille Rowe laughs. "On the other hand, we have added a few others. There's another Old Sage, to keep me company now that Lucy isn't around much, and a couple more Warriors. Not too bad a group if you don't mind all the Scholars."

"The interesting thing is that we seem actually to have two divisions of the group at the moment," Jessica remarks. "Milly's more interested in personal development, and when she's in charge of a session, we all spend a lot more time on that. When I'm in charge, then it's more on issues and specific information on events, past and present. Lately

Michael's been saying a fair amount about world Cycles. We'll get into that later."

She pours herself more coffee and adds a low-calorie sweetener to it. "I've been channeling Michael for more than a decade now, and there are times it amazes me that it still has a great attraction for me." She looks around the group in her living room. "We don't meet as regularly as we used to; there's so much going on in all our lives. My new boss has been making changes in my work, which has limited my time, and Milly has had to deal with all the hassles that are part of family troubles, so there hasn't been as much opportunity."

"Well, there's also been the other consideration: we've all grown cautious because of some of the responses to the first book," Camille says thoughtfully. "The trouble is, you want to help, really. It's hard not to want to help. But there's only so much time and, well, there are a lot of weirdos out there, and material like this brings them flocking. It's hard; everyone insists that they're sincere and, by their lights, they are, but I end up very worried about what I read and hear."

Alex Squire nods. "I'm a psychologist, and I know what Milly's talking about. It's a shame that we have to be so circumspect, but there isn't a workable alternative, not if either Jessica or Milly is to have any kind of privacy at all. The work that Milly's done with me has been a great deal of help, but I hesitate to reveal too much about her mediumship. Between my colleagues' conservatism and the attitude of the public at large, I know that it's wisest to keep a very low profile where Michael material is concerned. It's amazing the variety of responses information of this sort can evoke."

"That's one of the reasons the group voted to take nothing from outside," Jessica says with a shake of her head. "For one thing, when we tried to answer the questions we were sent—and we did try for a little while—we'd have another request for even more information in addition to all the new requests. We'd get what we call shopping-list letters, asking for Overleaves for everyone in the person's family as well as anyone they had had any dealings with at all. Then there were those who were convinced they had been someone very famous or notorious and wanted Michael to agree with them. So far we've had seven Cleopatras and nine Abraham Lincolns. And then, there were looney letters, and religious denunciations, and some very unpleasant threats. I think those were the worst: the threats. So, in the last five years, we've become very, very careful about new people in the group as well as refusing to take any and all questions from outside the group. Because Quinn is visible, we never put her answers in the transcripts and she is not allowed to pass on inquiries to any of us. It may seem hard-hearted and unreasonable, but it has become necessary." Jessica sips her coffee and looks out her picture windows, to the tree-covered hillside. "Walter didn't approve when the group voted to take no outside questions. At first he said that we didn't have the right to turn down anyone, but he's changed his mind in the last three years. And since he's been in the hospital, I'm relieved that I didn't have anything more impinging on my thoughts than my job and his health. If we'd had to contend with outside letters and phone calls as well as his surgery and then his recovery, I think I'd have gone round the bend, and I know that Walter wouldn't have been able to handle such pressure."

Camille agrees. "You know that Jessica has done a very good job of keeping her anonymity, and I'm trying to do as well, but with my consulting with Alex, it isn't quite so easy. I'm a junior executive with a brokerage firm, and I know they'd take a very dim view of my mediumship, those who know about it at all."

The others concur. "It's been hard, sometimes," Emily Wright says. "I hear people talking about Michael teaching and they obviously know nothing about it. There are times I want to . . . preach at them."

"You are a Priest," Jessica reminds her with a smile.

"And that makes it more difficult, I think, to remain silent. We Priests," she goes on with exaggerated prissiness, "take a very dim view of heresy."

"It isn't heresy," Camille corrects her in an easy tone that suggests this is an old game with them. "No one has to believe this, or get it"—she makes quotes signs with her fingers—"right. And insisting that they do isn't—"

Emily finishes with her "—Good Work. [*March, 1988:* Good Work, according to Michael, is that which contributes to the Life Task, not that which is "beneficial".] Yes, I know, and I accept it, most of the time. But when an officious and obvious Young Slave comes up to me and informs me grandly that he's a fifth Level Old King;, it's all I can do to hold my tongue. The trouble is, when I argue, it doesn't do any good, it just creates hard feelings."

She sighs and reaches for some of the strudel that John Verano brought to the session. "God, this is good. I wish I could afford the calories." Since Emily is tall and willowy, no one takes her protestations too seriously. "I will say this," she goes on, licking her fingers between each word, "thanks to Michael, I'm more willing to accept heresy. I've come to realize that there is a place for heretics in the world, and that they're good for Priests."

"The way that lions are good for gazelles?" John suggests.

"Or for Christians?" Camille adds.

"You're all making fun of me," Emily protests, laughing. "It isn't easy for Priests to come to terms with heretics."

"I wouldn't know," Camille remarks blithely, "I'm a Sage, myself."

"And you know what we say about Sages," Jessica goes on, then explains. "We have a joke about Sages in the group: that if you have a large foxhole with seven guys in it, one of each Essence, and the enemy is advancing on the foxhole and there are bullets and bombs all around, the one standing up saying 'And another thing' is the Sage."

Although this is clearly a familiar joke, everyone in the room laughs, especially Camille. "I have my way for getting back at Scholars," Camille says with a show of calculated innocence. "When they need something explained, or a little diplomacy, they come to me."

"That is something I've learned from Michael," Lizzy Roarke tells the others, more seriously. "When I had to do some negotiations on the job, Michael gave me some useful suggestions, including that I avail myself of the knowledge of the Sages in the group."

The others agree. "I've been told to talk to Warriors about strategy," Camille says, elaborating on what Lizzy began. "And I really appreciate it. Sages are lousy at strategy; it comes naturally to Warriors."

Tracy Rowland chuckles. "And Warriors—speaking from personal experience—are awful at negotiating. It goes against our grain as much as strategy goes against Sages' grain." She looks around the room, gauging the reaction of the others. "Michael has helped me to be more tolerant, in a very odd way. I know its all right that there are people doing things I think are wasteful and foolish, and I've realized that it's not only impossible, it's inadvisable for everyone to like everyone else. I'm an Old Warrior and one of my aunts is a Baby Priest. I used to try to settle things with her, just to know where we both stand. I don't do that any more. I can see that she and I are doing very different things with our lives, that our perceptions and priorities are entirely different—I used to think they were at odds, but they're just going to dissimilar places and for different reasons. And that's all right. I don't say I like her any better, but I do dislike her less. Does that make any sense?"

Alex fumbles for his napkin. "That's the sort of thing I've noticed about this group, and it's one of the things that keeps me coming back. Curiosity would be enough, but there's more to it, and a large part has to do with this sort of understanding and tolerance that Michael seems to promote."

Lizzy concurs at once. "As a Mature Scholar in Passion, I've had to work through some puzzling problems over the years. One of the lessons I've been able to inculcate—seventh Level is for inculcation, if you're doing it right—is that what's appropriate for me is not therefore the norm for the whole world, and that my ability to take risks is not shared by everyone. Passion loves to take risks."

Jessica shrugs philosophically. "When I'm working the board, there are times I know that I, that is me, Jessica Lansing, will not agree with what Michael is saying, but part of my job as a medium is to let them say it their way. I can still get very mad at the greed and stupidity I see around me, but I realize that there is no way that anyone will avoid learning something during his or her lifetime, even if you seek to avoid it."

"Michael gave us a lecture on that not long ago," Camille adds.

We would seek to remind all here gathered that nothing in life is wasted: all choices and actions in life are means for lessons to be brought to bear. You cannot avoid the lessons. A life in which every Agreement, Monad, karmic ribbon, Essence contact, Entity Mate, Cadre Mate, Configuration Member is deliberately avoided only serves to teach the Fragment what such avoidance brings. We have said this many times and in many ways: all is chosen. There is no right or wrong choice, for Essence is not "moral" in any way that you understand the word, although we would say that Essence is ultimately ethical, and at the same time innocent. You speak of unimportant choices such as "Shall I skip lunch?" "What color should I wear?," but we do not find these choices as insignificant as you do. All choices are important. Those made on minor matters provide practice for choices made on more major matters: "Shall I end my marriage?" or "Am I willing to shoot the armed burglar in my house?" certainly these latter choices have a greater bearing on the life, but they are no more or less important than the matter of skipping lunch. That is one of the reasons we encourage parents to permit their children to make choices early. Every one of you needs all the practice you can get to deal with the major decisions in your lives. [*From August, 1997:* As tides move in the ocean, so choices move in the life; the motion itself is part of the nature of choice, and therefore whether the choice is for a china pattern for a bride, or whether to bomb "enemy" targets, the "energy" of choice impacts the life, and will continue to impact it for all of your evolution. The "significance" of every choice is part of the "ebb and flow" of all lives, and what is "minor" in one instance, can recur as "major" in another. (This last was a bad pun, since the person asking the question is a musician.)]

"That's variation number twenty on the Choice Lecture," Jessica remarks with a hint of exasperation. "Sometimes I feel as if we ought to hang up ten-foot banners saying 'All is chosen.'"

If it would help you to remember this truth and to accept it, we would see no reason not to, although there are occasions when it might be awkward to explain such banners, should you choose to do display one.

Camille is laughing. "I can just imagine trying to explain to my strict Lutheran parents what it meant. So far as they're concerned, God has a plan for everyone, and to depart from that plan in the most minuscule way, is to court damnation. They worry about damnation a lot."

"Do it as a pillow," Lizzy suggests. "You know, like the ones that say, 'You can never be too rich or too thin or have too many silk blouses,' or 'Never mistake endurance for hospitality,' or 'Nouveau is better than no riche at all.'"

John grins. "Hey, you might get yourself a little sideline going there, Lizzy: inspirational pillows from Michael."

"God, you're irreverent," Jessica says with mock severity. Lizzy puts her hands on her hips, trying to look indignant as her blue eyes sparkle.

"We're irreverent? What about Michael? They're more irreverent than any of us."

There is a honk from the street below and Jessica's old dog, an unlikely cross of Doberman and Bassett hound, trundles over to the window to bark. "That's enough, Trudi," Jessica says, turning to John. "Can you see who it is?"

"Larry, by the looks of it."

Camille grins and throws her hands up in a gesture of relief. "Another Sage. Thank goodness."

Emily pours out the last of the coffee and offers to make another pot. "We won't be getting started for a little while, will we?"

"Probably not," Jessica says. "You know where everything is, don't you?"

Emily nods. "Sure. By the way, I think you're out of milk."

"Use the non-dairy stuff, then. I know we've got that." Jessica leans back in her rocking chair.

"I sometimes think one of the nicest things about sessions is the talking we do. Michael is very stimulating, and what he says can really help us to find ways to talk about what is going on in our lives. Camille did a lot of channeling for me while Walter was in the hospital, and it made a lot of difference, not only in how I felt about his surgery, but in my understanding of myself. That was the best part of it, I think, the insights Michael provided at a time I needed them."

"Well," Camille responds, "when my family started having difficulties, you did the same for me. I think that without Michael and all the help, it would have been a lot more painful and much more prolonged than it was. I feel that I understand what it is that went wrong, not that I could have done much about it. My husband reached a crisis in his life, and things weren't the same after that. I did what I was able to, and when he left, I tried to make it as clean a break as possible for both of us."

Alex Squire agrees. "A few of my clients have had difficult relationships that were clearly more than the usual kind of mismatching that happens all the time. I asked Michael about them when more standard methods weren't getting results, and most of the time, there were Agreements or Monads or other compelling factors at work. Finding a way to pass this on to the client was always the trickiest part, but in a few cases, it turned out to be much easier than I would have thought. In fact, in one case, the client said that it sounded like something he'd read in an intriguing book a friend had loaned him. You can guess what book that was."

Camille adds, "I went to a lecture not long ago that purported to be about the Michael material, given by someone I'd never heard of, and he didn't do too bad a job of presenting the basics, I'll say that for him. I asked him what his sources were, and he mentioned the book and a couple of the people who had been in the group some time ago."

"Did you tell him you were in the group?" John asks, his interest piqued.

"Yes." Her hazel eyes brim with mischief. "He got very quiet after that, and his answers to my few remaining questions were . . . subdued, to say the least."

"Doesn't that make you furious?" Emily asks from the doorway to the dining room. "I can't stand to hear Michael used that way."

"It irks me," Camille admits.

"It more than irks me," Jessica says, "but I try to put it in perspective. For a little while, about a year ago, I stopped doing sessions altogether because I was getting so much static from people who had been to what were billed as Michael sessions, and seemed to have . . . unlikely information; the kinds of things Michael has never said to this group." She falls silent for a moment. "I know that there are other teachers out there, and I know that much of what some people are getting is valid. But I also know that the instant you're told what to do, then you do not have a Mid-Causal teacher on the line. They simply don't do that, because it is contrary to the whole choice thing. Michael will make suggestions or recommendations, but always with the understanding that each of us has to choose what to do, and that the choice is the crucial part, at least from Michael's point of view. We had one person who said that she had been in a Michael group in L.A. and Michael had told them whom to associate with and what to eat and where to live and what sorts of fibers to wear, and described the punishments for sins. I don't know what the medium was hooked into, but I can tell you right now, it wasn't Michael."

We have said before that there are many who would prefer to be spoon fed than to have to learn to eat for themselves. Many of them are drawn to all sorts of teachings in the hope that someone will give them a blueprint that they can follow and never again be troubled with choosing for themselves. Choice is a frightening thing, for it implies responsibility, which is a valid insight. As you are aware, many Fragments will do anything in order to avoid being responsible for their lives. These credulous Fragments are no exception, and rather than be angry with them for their credulity, we would suggest that it is not inappropriate to see the lesson in the rule of maya here, for there is no greater illusion—which is the rule of maya—than the assumption that you are not responsible for yourself. [December, 1988: When maya is embraced, then the Chief Features have access to all the poles of all the Overleaves, and this makes it possible for fear to permeate every aspect of the life, which increases the chance of the Fragment in question choosing to validate fear rather than to avail him- or herself of the experience of self-intimacy which is the first step toward validating love. When such choices are made to limit love, then the "vacuum" created tends to fill rapidly with fear. In the face of such a development, it is likely that all choices will be influenced heavily by fear. There is, of course, nothing "wrong" in such experiences, but they are often not without "peril," for actions undertaken in the throes of fear are inclined to suborn the efforts of the Fragment to recognize the validity of such experiences.]

"I love Michael's syntactical backflips," John says as he reads back the comment. "'It is not inappropriate.' Beautiful!"

There is a sharp knock at the front door, and then the sound of the latch being lifted. Three sets of footsteps come up toward the living room to the chanting of "We're sorry. We're late. We're sorry. We're late."

Larry Heron is the first into the room, a tall, fair man in his early thirties. Behind him are Kim and Henry Ingvesson, a couple in their forties, both Mature Scholars.

Camille throws her arms wide and gazes up at Larry. "My Sage!" she exclaims.

He takes up the game immediately. "My Sage!" He drops on one knee beside her chair and kisses her hand.

"Cut it out, you two," Lizzy says laconically, but she holds out her hand to Larry as she says it.

"I'm making a fresh pot of coffee," Emily says to the newcomers. "Do any of you want some?"

"Please," Larry answers, and Henry asks, "Is there any tea?"

"That's one of the differences between sessions at Jessica's and sessions at Milly's," John explains. "At Jessica's we meet in the afternoon, have strudel and coffee. At Milly's we meet in the evening and have wine and cheese."

"Is that the difference between Sages and Scholars?" Tracy inquires.

"I think it's more a question of time of day and the fact that with the medication he's on, Walter can't have anything alcoholic, and so I don't get any wine."

"Is anyone else supposed to be here?" Lizzy asks, looking around the room as the others settle themselves.

"Brad Sturgis said he'd come after the concert," Jim Verano says, cutting another sliver of the strudel.

"We've brought some cookies," Kim Ingvesson says, holding up a cloth bag. "I took them out of the oven just before we left."

"Yummy!" Lizzy says, getting up from the couch. "Where do you keep the plates for this, Jessica?"

"The cabinet in the dining room," is the answer while a scramble is made for another bit of strudel and to get mugs for coffee.

"We've tried to be formal, once in a while," Jessica says to Kim, "but it's a lost cause. And I think we get more done this way, no matter how chaotic it is."

"There's more fun this way, too," Camille says. "Sessions at my house are just the same. We talk and joke, and then ask a number of questions, then we talk about the answers we get, if they're the sort of thing that needs answers."

"Overleaves don't often need much explanation," Jessica goes on. Overleaves are Overleaves: Essence, Level, Cycle, Mode, Goal, Attitude, Centering, Chief Feature. Camille gets them in a slightly different order, but it's the same information, and there isn't much to talk about unless there's something strange about them, such as a Chief Feature of Self-Destruction, which often doesn't show up except through its underlying fear until the person finds a way to . . . well, destroy himself, just the way it implies."

"That's pretty cut and dried," John agrees, "but there are other things, such as questions about relationships, and we all end up discussing Michael's answers, and adding our own observations, which Michael says is Good Work and part of the validation of the lesson. That's fine with me, whatever he—they—mean by that."

Emily has returned with a fresh pot of coffee and as she puts this down on the trivet, she says, "The water's hot on the stove if you'd rather have tea."

"Does anyone have anything pressing for this session or do we just go around the room as usual?" Jessica asks as the various group members get their hot beverages and settle down with strudel and cookies along with their pens and notebooks.

"Tell Michael to go slow," Lizzy says to Jessica. "I'm out of practice and they've been going too fast for me the last couple sessions."

"I'll try," Jessica says dubiously. "But you know what it's like when they get going." Everyone nods, and the attitude becomes more serious.

"All right, John. Do you want to start?" Jessica says, choosing the person on her right.

"Uh . . . sure," he answers, pulling out a sheet of paper with his scribbled questions on it. "I've got a question about the guitar I'm making—"

"Not again!" Lizzy protests, chuckling. "And I'd like it if Michael will tell me about the best source of material for the bridge, given the design I'm working from."

"All right," Jessica says, taking the planchette in her left hand and putting it on the glass surface of her custom-made board.

First we would think that the Fragment who is now John would want to consider what it is he wishes to achieve in terms of the quality of sound. If a sharp and penetrating sound is desired, then one of the best substances, given the design of the bridge, is the shinbone of wild deer. Let us emphasize that the deer in the wild state tend to denser bones and therefore the material is slightly but significantly different than the bone of deer raised in captivity, such as those to be found in zoos. If a more flexible sound is what is desired, then we would think that the ribs of whales would be more to your liking and will produce the results you are seeking. In the case of whales, we would think that a professor of ceatology at the local university might be the best place to inquire in order to obtain the bone.

John begins to read back what has been dictated, and pauses. "I lost some of this," he says. "Can anyone help me out. What comes after 'more flexible sound'?"

Between Kim Ingvesson and Lizzy Roarke, John is able to get the rest of his answer and to mull it over. "Do we get two questions?"

"That's usual," Camille says, a bit dryly.

"Well, this is for a friend, who has some sort of health problem which hasn't been responding to treatment. Can Michael tell me what's wrong and what, if anything, can be done?"

[Note: At this time we were not routinely being given Secondary Chief Features.—CQY]

This Fragment is a fifth Level Mature Slave in the Repression Mode with a Goal of Acceptance, a Realist in the Moving part of Emotional

Center with a Chief Feature of Stubbornness. The Overleaves support the ill health from the negative poles, and it would be of some worth to examine these polarities to understand the way the body responds to the various attempts to heal it. As to the disease itself, this Fragment has ingested harmful chemicals in his drinking water that are the results of toxic substances from a local industry which have seeped into the general water supply. These chemicals have caused an adverse reaction in the gastro-intestinal—

Jessica speaks the last word. "You're not going to believe how Michael was going to spell 'gastro-intestinal,'" she says before continuing with the board.

—tract, and the tissues are "stripped" of their normal flora. There are several patches of "raw" intestine, very much irritated and subject to a variety of infections. Because there is no one bacteriological basis for the infections which continue to reoccur and to spread, the treatments are not likely to have any lasting benefit for this Fragment. Let us suggest that along with continuing with his physician, this Fragment consult a competent homeopathic practitioner with a good traditional medical background in order to balance out the bodily chemistry more effectively. We would also think that using bottled or well-filtered water for consumption, even in tea and coffee would do much to alleviate the condition. Let us point out that cooling off bottled water with ice made from tap water will not do much to improve the situation. This Fragment is likely to require some time to heal, and it may be that surgery to remove the damaged tissue will be a wise course if there is no significant improvement over the next six months. In general we are reluctant to recommend something so permanent as surgery, but where damage is real and chronic, it is often the most prudent course. We would think that in this case, the advice of the physicians can be valuable when making such a decision. It would be of some interest to this Mature Slave to know that there are others in his community who have had similar reactions to the contamination and there is Good Work in alerting the community to the danger at hand, should he choose to take action on the issue.

"He hasn't said anything about toxic-waste sites in the area," John muses when the comments have been read back. "Thanks, Michael. I'll make sure he gets this information soon."

"I like what Michael says about the ice," Larry Heron remarks as he reads his page and a half of scrawl. "That's exactly the sort of thing I'd overlook. I don't know about the rest of you."

There is general agreement that it would be very easy to use ice that had been made from tap water.

"So, Alex, you're next," Jessica says as she adds artificial sugar to her coffee. "Two questions, as usual."

"Good; I hope we can get a second round, because I've got quite a little list." He whistles a few bars of Gilbert and Sullivan tune about making a list from *The Mikado* through his teeth as he consults a neatly typed page on his clipboard.

"Haven't we all?" Kim Ingvesson asks the air.

"I tell you what: let's start with this one." He sighs once, not too deeply. "I've been asking about relationships for the last six months or so, and I think I've boiled down my areas of interest to one or two spheres. First, what is the basic area of dispute with couples?"

As you are well-aware, Alexander, there is no one basic area of dispute in anything. However, we would say that the first misunderstandings arise out of a lack of common definitions. When one partner says, for instance, "I'll take care of the bills this month," what is meant is that this partner will make out the checks and mail them, or so the volunteer assumes. The other partner hears the words in another context and assumes that means that the volunteer is offering to pay the bills. When the volunteer asks for money from the other partner, that partner reacts with distress, feeling that the volunteer has gone back on his or her word, or has deliberately set out to "embarrass" the partner with this action.

Of course, this is not only true of couples, but of businesses and nations, and communicating species, for that matter. When large issues are at stake, it is often the practice of creatures of reason to be at pains to define themselves for the benefit of others. When what would appear to be minor considerations are the issue, there is a tendency to assume that the other automatically "knows" what is meant, and therefore no definitions are necessary. This is where scripting can be most detrimental to valid communication, for it is not a very long reach from assuming to scripting. [*July, 2001:* In answer to a question about the difference between planning ahead and scripting, Michael said: When a Fragment assesses the possibilities of coming events without "clamping down" on one particular scheme for those events, this is not an unusual kind of preparation and allows for many kinds of interactions. However, when the Fragment decided upon a single acceptable course of events, complete with lines and business, a perception allowing for no variation from the course expected, then that is scripting, and it is "doomed" to disappoint all concerned.] These small misunderstandings build up until, to take an extreme case, one partner hacks the other up with a cleaver for putting liverwurst in the picnic lunch.

Let us digress a bit on this subject. Because your species is independently mobile—that is, each of you can move and live without the necessary presence of any other Fragment—you live in more isolation and loneliness than any other sort of species. For what interest it may be, this degree of isolation is not as common as you might expect. You perceive it as "normal" and assume therefore that it is the standard for all species of creatures of reason. This is not the case. There are whole species of creatures of reason that require almost constant contact with other Fragments in order to ensure physical survival. You would have trouble recognizing some of them as being alive, let alone creatures of reason like yourselves. However, this isolation imposes great burdens on you, including a much higher opportunity for misunderstandings. We would think that it would be of benefit for all of you, and we do not limit this to those here present, to be aware of what you mean when you express a thing, and if there is apparent doubt, choose to define your terms. Obviously there are circumstances more conducive to such assessment than others. You are more likely to take time to define your terms when you are at leisure than when you are, for example, in an automobile heading downhill without working brakes. We would wish to point out that if there has been a good level of understanding while at leisure, you are less likely to have difficulty in the runaway automobile.

That does not mean that each and every word must constantly be weighed and defined. We did not say that, and we did not mean to imply it. It is your choice to define or not. There are occasions when such definition would be more of a "hassle" than it would be worth in gained understanding, and there are other occasions when the attempt to attain one level of understanding would lead to greater misunderstandings on other levels. It is for you to choose, of course, and to deal with the results of your choice, but it is not trivial to think of what you are saying, since your primary means of communication is speech.

"Can we have a break?" Jessica asks as she looks up from the board. "There's a lot more there, but I need a minute . . ."

The others are glad for the opportunity to stop transcribing.

"Michael was really tearing through that one," John says, looking at the scribbles on his page. "I don't think I've got very much of this. What about you, Lizzy?"

"Some of it, but not all. We can probably piece this together if everyone works at it." She glances at Jessica. "One of the fast ones, wasn't it?"

"You know it," she says, shaking her head. "You've really tapped into something, Alex."

"So it would appear," he agrees, his expression a bit sheepish. "I didn't mean to pull out the whole file."

"Well, we'll get a little more of this, and then, if you don't mind, we'll move on. I have trouble channeling something this intense and fast for too long."

She helps herself to a little more coffee. "It's not that it isn't exciting—it is. But it wears me out."

"I know the feeling well," Camille confirms.

Henry Ingvesson gets up and pounds the cushion on the back of the sofa. "Excuse me, but . . ."

"I know; there are some uncomfortable spots. Go right ahead. I like the extra time," Jessica says, dawdling over her coffee. "Better get ready for the next moving van," she says, reaching for her planchette once more. This time the pens are poised more tensely.

"Try to hold it down if you can," Alex suggests. "I'll try, but Michael's on one of their binges about this."

She puts the planchette on the board again.

It is rare that any two Fragments have precisely the same definition of anything, but there are many areas of agreement, and it is the agreement that leads to understanding. It may not appear to be important to have such understanding on, for example, what the color red is unless you are planning to paint your house red, in which case, it could be crucial.

There is another aspect to examine, which is the tendency for Fragments to talk simply to fill the silence. There is nothing wrong in this, but again, it is more beneficial if it is understood that all that is being done is filling the silence. We are aware, Alexander, that you are worried about a couple currently consulting you, one of whom says what she means, the other of whom speaks to fill the silence and to "entertain". There is much confusion for both Fragments, since she assumes that he speaks to say what he means, and he assumes that she is filling silence at least half the time. There is no ill will between these two Fragments, but there is massive misunderstanding, which as you are aware, arises from their Overleaves. That is often where the difficulties begin, for the Overleaves are what orient the Fragment to the conduct of his or her life.

"I think that's it for the time being," Jessica says, leaning back in her rocking chair and rubbing her eyes with her free hand.

"That's a lot more than I expected," Alex tells the group at large. "I'm sorry I took up so much time. And energy."

"Will someone please read that back to us?" Camille asks. "I've got most of it, but I want to be certain I've got it all."

It takes some time to get the whole message read back. Michael's speed had not decreased; if anything, they had been faster in the latter part of the dictation than in the former.

"I think I'll pass on a second question, this time," Alex says, still adding the few words he lost while Michael was dictating.

"Self-Dep acting up?" Lizzy chides him affectionately. "Go ahead. You didn't know you'd tapped the Grand Coulee Dam on the last one."

"That's right; go after that old Self-Dep," Camille urges him. "Actually, the question has to do with my Self-Deprecation."

He looks down at his fist again. "I want to have some insight, Michael, on how I came to get this Chief Feature in the first place."

"Uh-oh," Lizzy says, "sounds like another biggie."

"If it is, I can wait until the next round," Alex offers, although no one pays much attention.

"Go on: ask the question," Jessica prompts him.

"All right," Alex sighs. "Michael has indicated that the Chief Feature is taken on at the time of the Third Monad, the point when the individual separates from the identity of the family and is 'out of the nest' whether he continues to live in the family or not. This usually happens around eighteen to twenty, Michael has said, although there is a lot of variation. I have a hunch that mine got hold of me when I was about sixteen, while we were traveling extensively. I felt like such a clod, so incapable and awkward, and so unprepared to deal with anything around me." Even now—and Alex is in his late forties—he squirms at the unhappy memories. "Was that the time it got me?"

We would agree that the insight is valid, and that the Chief Feature did assume control at that time. The event which triggered its full domination was on the occasion of a visit to an elderly lady who had been a friend of your grandfather. This woman was a grande dame of the old school, very proper and imposing, and she was, in fact, very baffled by teen-aged boys, and so took on her most formidable manner. Since you, Alexander, had been treated to a constant stream of such reactions, this seemed like more of the same. In other instances, you had reacted a number of ways, but with this particular woman, you took on the outward humility that appeased this old woman, and therefore, you were rewarded by being praised rather than looked down upon, since you were already "looking down" on yourself and we would have to say that at the time the device worked. Of course, that is the lure of the Chief Feature, that when there is much stress and the circumstances are difficult, it will, in fact, get you through. Chief Feature, we remind all here present, is a survival device, and one of its strongest hooks into the personality is the instilled conviction that you cannot survive without it.

"Thanks," Alex mutters after the response is read back. "You're next, Lizzy."

"Glad to be off the hot seat?" she asks Alex. "Well, yes. And no." He smiles warmly. "How 'bout you?"

"Hell, I can take it," she says, deliberately bragging. "But then, I have Arrogance, not Self-Dep."

"What's the question?" Jessica asks.

"First, I'd like two sets of Overleaves for a couple new students. I get along very well with one, but the other baffles me. The first is named Carla Preston, she's about sixteen, and she has already had about three years of flute. The other is Gina Huntsberger, fourteen, very bright and defensive. Let's do Carla first."

This is a first Level Mature Warrior in the Observation Mode with a Goal of Growth, a Skeptic in the Moving part of Emotional Center with an emerging Chief Feature of Impatience.

"That figures. She's got the walk," Lizzy says as she reads back what she has on the page. "What about Gina?"

This is a mid-Cycle Mature Artisan in the Caution Mode with a Goal of Acceptance, a Pragmatist in the Intellectual part of Emotional Center. No Chief Feature yet, but Stubbornness is a good bet for this Fragment.

Lizzy studies these Overleaves for a long time. "You know, I never spot the Artisans. I must be Artisan-blind. Well, this might be a little tricky. Why does she want to play the flute?"

She does not want to: her parents are eager to have her display her talents, and the Goal of Acceptance gives her no means to resist or the inclination to suggest that her gifts might lie elsewhere. We would think that it might be possible to explore her ambitions with her while teaching her the flute, Lizbeth. This Fragment has been cowed by the more aggressive Fragments within her family and has not yet developed a sense of the best means to realize her own talents. Let us add that she truly has talents, and there are many lessons in her life that can be brought to bear through the expression of her talents. If you choose to encourage her, we remind you that she may choose not to respond, but anything that aids in breaking the stranglehold of fear, acknowledged or unacknowledged, is Good Work, and does much toward the evolution of the soul.

"Does that count as two questions? I guess it does," Lizzy says. "I'll wait until the next time around."

"Minoring in Self-Dep, are we?" Alex teases her gently. "Larry? It's your turn."

Larry fiddles with his glasses. "Warriors you know by the walk; Sages you know because they simply can't remain still," Camille observes.

"I'm guilty of it, too, Larry." He chuckles. "Well, it's true. Ever since Michael pointed it out, I've noticed that I am always moving a little, shifting focus here and there. Comes with territory, I guess."

He looks around the room. "I'd like to know the Overleaves of my friend Pat Jensen, and I'd like a comment on why he's so afraid of mice. They terrify him, and he has no reason for it."

This is a sixth Level Young Slave in the Observation Mode with a Goal of Growth, an Idealist in the Emotional part of Intellectual Center with a Chief Feature of Stubbornness. In the immediate past life, this Fragment was a cabinetmaker in what is now Poland. He died of lack of food and heat in a cellar where there were sacks of rotted grain which had attracted many mice. As this Fragment was dying, the mice ran over him in their attempts to get to the grain. He now associates these creatures with his last death, which is hardly surprising. Many such phobias are the results of traumatic deaths.

"Aren't all deaths traumatic?" Larry asks, a little surprised.

Not at all. When the life is complete and the Fragment has done most of what was on the path for the life, death is not unpleasant. It is similar to the feeling a farmer has putting down his tools at the end of a good harvest day. That may sound a bit romantic to some of you at first glance, but we assure you that it is not. Harvesting is hard work, and there are many strains and difficulties and choices that are part of the process. When it is done well, it gives great satisfaction and an affection for the harvest. There is some of the same feeling at the end of a completed life. If you prefer the image of a mariner leaving a ship after a long voyage and returning to dry land, that is also apt, in its way. Both, of course, are metaphors and for that reason are not to be taken literally. Remember, that by your very nature, your species makes you creatures of the land, yet for a time, a boat permits you to be riders of the water. Please note, we do not say that you are therefore creatures of the water, for you are not adapted to live in it continually without certain unpleasant repercussions. Yet you can love the water and love the craft that carries you over it while you remain a species that is of the land. There are similarities with the Essence and the body, for the Essence is not of the Physical Plane, although while it has a body, it is on the Physical Plane. The ship, if you would wish to regard it that way, is the true personality, the body and the Overleaves, and the skipper is Essence, if there is good validation. In time, the Essence returns to the higher Planes, although the body cannot, being finite. The Physical Plane is the only Plane on which Fragments can experience being Fragments as well as being finite, at least in any sense that you can grasp. While we would agree that many deaths are unpleasant, it must be remembered that there are lessons to be learned, and there are times that it becomes necessary for Essence to choose to manifest the lessons in difficult ways.

"Okay," Larry says. "I have more questions on this, but I'm not ready to ask them yet, even if I had another turn." He turns to his right.

"Tracy? You next?"

"I guess I am," she says. "Milly, would you mind getting this? Jessica knows some of the people involved and she's already told me that she'd prefer you get the answer."

"Fine," Camille says, casting a quick look at Jessica. "Is this a touchy one?"

"For me, yes," Jessica allows. "I'm not sure I wouldn't interfere with the answers I get. It's not as bad as trying to get an answer about myself for myself, but at the same time, there's a strong emotional tie here and I'm afraid that would influence me." She picks up her coffee. "Besides, it's nice to have a break."

"Okay," Camille exclaims. "Everyone, please be very quiet. I can't do this if there are distractions, okay?" Camille, unlike Jessica, does not use the board, but writes directly onto her legal-sized pad. She writes quickly, making no spaces between the letters, very much the same way everyone in the room writes when taking the dictation Jessica provides from the board. The room is very silent as Tracy asks her question.

"I recently visited a friend in the hospital and was given a lot of gobbledygook from the staff about his condition. When I visited him, I didn't like the way he looked or sounded. His former wife has been visiting him and she's satisfied that he's getting good treatment, but I'm worried. Will Michael comment on Ed's condition, please?"

We would agree that all is not well with this Scholar, but at the same time, we wish to point out that this Fragment has contracted a serious disease and the message that he wishes to be taken care of is very clear. Remember that this Scholar has a Chief Feature of Greed and it is fixated on respect. There is no such thing as enough respect for him. In obtaining the divorce, the Young Slave showed him what he regards as a lack of respect, and the conditions of being a patient also contribute to his sense that no one respects him "enough". We would suggest that there is nothing that you can do directly, although it might be wise to ask the Young Slave if either she or the Fragment who is now Edmund has thought of having some form of therapy. Since the Fragment who is now Edmund teaches mathematics at the community-college level, he feels frustrated and longs to be the very finest mathematician in the area, or the country, or the world, and while we agree that he is quite intelligent, his reasons for desiring this recognition have more to do with his Greed than with his innate abilities. If there is no change in his treatment or the attitude around him, we would think that his condition will deteriorate seriously unless the Fragment who is now Edmund chooses to arrest the process for himself. There is already permanent muscle damage in his left side, and the longer he persists in his current state of mind, the less chance he will have of making a reasonable recovery. If the Young Slave is willing to seek a means to help the Mature Scholar regain some of the respect he longs for, then it might be possible for him to regain his health. As it is now, he is determined not to respond to the medicines and treatments because everything being done only serves to reinforce his perception that no one respects him, which strikes at the heart of all his fears.

"Is this man a math teacher?"

Camille asks as she hands the sheet to Tracy to read.

"Yes," she replies, frowning as she goes over the message. "Not very encouraging, is it?"

"Well, it's not discouraging, either," Camille is quick to mention.

"I just don't know how much they'll listen to me," Tracy says in an abstracted way. "Jessica, you know Amy better than I do. Want to give her a call in the next couple days? I'll go see Ed tomorrow and suggest that he might want to talk to someone about his illness."

"We can give it a try. But not push," she adds.

"Yeah, I know. No matter how tempting, it's not Good Work to push. The negative pole of Warrior is coercion, and that includes pushing." She sighs as she looks at the answer.

"Okay. My other question is about the problems I've had sleeping, which isn't usual for me. I don't think it's anything bad, by the way, just that there's something going on that keeps waking me up."

"Are you sure it's not your cat nibbling on your toes?" Camille suggests. "Jessica can get this one, can't she?"

"Fine with me," Tracy says, adding, "No, it's not my cat. The cat finds it almost as disruptive as I do."

Often emerging Entity activity disrupts the patterns of the person and the personality. We remind you that the Essence does not live in the biological sense, but transcends it, and therefore is not bound by the limits of the Physical Plane as you are. Essence is often most active when the personality and person is most quiet. That often means when the Fragment is asleep, and for that reason, sleep is disrupted. For most, the experience of Entity activity is dissipated by the rationalizations that explain such as a fantasy of sleep. When there is recognition and validation on all levels there is also an increased function of Essence in what you call the conscious personality, which is, of course, a misnomer. When this occurs, sleep patterns are often disrupted. As to getting more rest for the body, which is important, we realize, we would think that increased physical activity would be of assistance here and it would also be easier if you were able to accept more of the insights without resistance to them. Where there is resistance, the struggle is greater, for it not only involves the problem of reduced rest, but of the fatigue of holding insights at bay. You have all seen those who are prepared to fail by doing what they must to succeed. We would hope that you would look beyond the usual applications of the self-sabotage to see how it can influence you by other means, such as blocking insights.

"All right," Tracy says slowly as she reads back the answer. "Blocking insights can disrupt sleep, Essence activity can disrupt sleep, and I guess I've been doing more than my share of both. Thanks, Jessica."

"Good luck with it," Jessica says, nodding now to Henry. "Your turn."

Henry rubs at his short-trimmed, reddish beard. "I was wondering... Does anyone here have a compilation of all the basic terms and their definitions? We've been wanting to have one place that we can get all that material without plowing through Messages every time we need to figure something out.

"I've got the material," Alex says. "It's pretty long, but you're welcome to a copy if you want one." He reaches into his book bag at his feet and brings out a couple dozen photocopied pages stapled together. "Here," he says, handing it to Henry.

Lizzy grins, and paraphrases T.S. Eliot. "'The naming of parts is a difficult matter,/ It isn't just one of your holiday games./ You may think at first I'm as mad as a hatter/ When I tell you a part must have three different names.' I don't think I can make it work any longer," she apologizes.

"Thanks. We appreciate it," Henry says.

CHAPTER TWO
The Naming of Parts

We use terms specifically, and for that reason, we will define them for you. We would urge you to look upon these terms without the usual cultural or social biases that are often associated with the terms, but to look beyond them to the function of the term.

Overleaves: By this we refer to the ways in which a Fragment manifests itself and its work toward a Life Goal in a specific life. The Cycle, Level, Mode, Goal, Attitude, Centering, and Chief Feature are all factors in the Overleaves. The Essence, while included in description of the Overleaves, is not truly part of them. Essence is the body, the Overleaves are the clothing. As you change your garments, so Essence changes Overleaves from life to life in order to evolve.

Role in Essence: there are of course, seven. They are Slave, Artisan, Warrior, Scholar, Sage, Priest, and King. Slaves constitute roughly twenty-five percent of the population, both on this planet and throughout the cosmos. Artisans constitute roughly twenty-two percent of the population. Warriors constitute roughly seventeen percent of the population. Scholars constitute roughly fourteen percent of the population. Sages constitute roughly ten percent of the population. Priests constitute roughly eight percent of the population. Kings constitute roughly four percent of the population.

Slaves: The ordinal of the Inspiration Polarity, the Slave Essence seeks to serve the common good, whatever the Slave determines that to be. The common good is a choice made by the Slave. As such, they are often drawn to the educational, medical, diplomatic, bureaucratic, and serving professions. The positive pole of the Slave Essence is service, the negative is bondage.

Artisans: The ordinal of the Expression Polarity, the Artisan Essence seeks the structure and its realization. Artisans often drawn to engineering, fine arts, genetic and botanical sciences, carpentry, all sorts of crafts, dance and poetry. Many athletes are Artisans. The positive pole of the Artisan Essence is creation, the negative is artifice.

Warriors: The ordinal of the Action Polarity, the Warrior Essence seeks a challenge. By nature the Warrior Essence is intensely loyal, both as friend and foe, supportive of comrades and protective of those assigned to Warrior care. Warriors are drawn to professions that encourage activity and provide challenges, including armed services in the Young and Mature Cycles. The positive pole of the Warrior Essence is persuasion, the negative is coercion.

Scholars: The neutral position, the position of Synthesis and as such more capable of understanding all the others more fully. The Scholar Essence seeks knowledge and tends to regard life as an experiment. They are drawn to informational occupations, and to the contemplative life. The positive pole of the Scholar Essence is knowledge, the negative is theory.

Sages: The cardinal of the Expression Polarity, the Sage Essence seeks communication in all things. As such, they are drawn to all forms of entertainment, including politics and the law, as well as religion. The positive pole of the sage Essence is expression, the negative is oration.

Priests: The cardinal of the Inspiration Polarity, the Priest Essence seeks to serve the higher good, whatever the Priest conceives the higher good to be. The Priest desires to succor, counsel and uplift, as well as to preach, and seeks work that will permit such service, or can be used to that end. The positive pole of the Priest Essence is compassion, the negative is zeal.

Kings: The cardinal of the Action Polarity, the King Essence seeks to lead, mandate. Other Essences will often seek out Kings to be given orders, for the word of the King carries great impact. As such, most Kings seek positions of authority, whether it be as corporation presidents, intensive-care-unit nurses, or orchestral conductors. The positive pole of the King Essence is mastery, the negative is tyranny.

There are five Cycles experienced on the Physical Plane, the Infant, the Baby, the Young, the Mature and the Old, and each has seven Levels.

In the Infant Levels, the Fragments have little experience and therefore often seek simple lives in limited surroundings until the experience of being on the Physical Plane is no longer as strange and frightening as it is in the beginning. The motto of the Infant Souls is "let's not do it," a feeling born out of the newness and fear that is all around it. The youngest Fragments extant on your world at this time are third Level Infant Souls.

In the Baby Levels, the conservatism continues but in a wider arena. The Baby Souls are often active in the world and upon occasion attain high position, although they tend to lack understanding. Their rigidity of perceptions are limiting not only to them, but to those around them. The motto of the Baby Souls is "do it right or don't do it at all".

By far the greatest number of souls on this world at this time are Young Souls, the time when the desire to act, to bring about the transformations, is uppermost in the minds of the Fragments. It is often the desire of Young Souls to make others like them or to reject them out of hand. There is much energy at this Level, at least in the sense of energy on the Physical Plane. The motto of the Young Soul is "do it my way," emphasis on the "my". The average age of a Soul on this world is fifth Level Young.

The Mature Soul is more inward-looking, and is concerned with understanding. It is not unusual for the Mature Soul to grapple with emotions and perceptions all through the Cycle. While we would agree that all other Fragments have similar experience, it is rare that any Fragment outside the Mature Cycle will spend an entire lifetime seeking understanding with the intensity of the Mature Soul. The motto of the Mature Soul is "do it anyplace but here".

The Old Soul Cycles are concerned with being, with accepting the dichotomy between the World Truths of the Physical Plane and the Universal Truth of the Tao and the Essence, which comes from the Tao and returns to it as part of the Logos. The Old Soul is drawn to those areas of endeavor that will permit it an opportunity to be, with as little interference as possible, which is why many Old Souls toward the end of the Cycle will live almost as simply as Infant Souls. The motto of the Old Soul is "you do what you want and I will do what I want".

Each Cycle has its merits, and it is not appropriate to assume that any Cycle is "better" or "worse" than any other. Every Cycle can attain Intimacy, Essence Contact and Evolution, and every Level can advance the Fragment if there is recognition on any Level. To take the attitude that "older is better" or "wiser" or "superior" is to turn from the lesson of the Cycles and the experiences themselves, which is not Good Work.

Within the Cycles are Levels, and each of the Levels has significance and direction that shapes the tasks and emphases of the Levels. In order to understand the focus of the Levels, we will discuss their polarities now.

The first Level has as its positive polarity purpose and as its negative simplicity. It is possible at the first Level for the Fragment to set out, with deliberation, on the new journey through the Cycle, and that is achieved through the positive pole, of course.

The second Level has as its positive polarity stability and as its negative balance. The difference between balance and stability may be easily discerned.

The third Level has as its positive polarity enterprise and as its negative versatility. While we have nothing against versatility, this is often the Cycle where the Fragment is the "jack of all trades and master of none".

The fourth Level has as its positive polarity consolidation and as its negative achievement. There is also the mid-Cycle, which incorporates elements of both the third and fourth Level, so that the enterprise of the third Level is part of the consolidation of the fourth Level. This is the only time that this overlap occurs between Levels, and the similarities of function are what make the overlap possible. Let us point out that Fragments at the mid-Cycle have the outward thrust of the third Level along with the gathering together of the fourth, often making them appear inconsistent or contradictory in their behavior.

The fifth Level has as its positive polarity expansion and as its negative adventure. The average Soul on this planet is a fifth Level Young Slave, as the patterns of behavior should reveal when examined.

The sixth Level has as its positive pole harmony and as its negative connection. Those at the sixth Level often have several different circles of acquaintances or friends who meet through the sixth Level Fragment.

The seventh Level has as its positive polarity inculcation and as its negative eclecticism. Fragments at the seventh Level must bring all the previous lessons to bear before going on to the next Cycle, or leaving the Physical Plane entirely.

Cardinality and ordinality also have polarities, of course. The positive polarity of cardinality is lucidity and the negative is activity. The positive polarity of ordinality is responsiveness and the negative is passivity. If you wish to think of cardinality as will and ordinality as muscle, although this description is vastly over-simplified, there is some validity to it, nonetheless. Remember that in polarity fear and desire operate together, so that what you wish for, you also fear. You can choose to overcome the fear and "go for" what you desire, or reject the whole thing, both the desire and the fear, and do something that is less disturbing. You are also capable of "settling for less" or "coming to terms with reality" or "being sensible," which also reveals the unwillingness to confront the conflicts inherent in polarities. You can then be free to think of yourself as a victim of fate or circumstances, thwarted from attaining all that you could because of "destiny". It is much easier to blame fate instead of realizing you chose to act in this way and avoid the question of polarities. This is not to say that it is "wrong" to avoid the conflicts of polarities, merely that it does not often lead to much advancement in the life.

Fragment: the individual soul, which truly is a Fragment, a part of an Entity. We do not use the word Fragment lightly, but with great accuracy. Each of you is a Fragment of your Entity, which is a part of its Cadre, and as such, the illusion of separateness is only that—an illusion.

Entity: a group of Fragments, usually numbering between one thousand and one thousand two hundred Fragments, and generally consisting of two to four Essences. While we are not aware of any Entities consisting of only one Essence, we are aware of some consisting of as many as five Essences. The Entity is part of a Cadre.

Cadre: a group of seven Entities, all cast at the same time, and therefore "linked". The Fragments in a Cadre will usually spend a good portion of their lives on the Physical Plane interacting with one another. Within Cadres, all Essences are represented, and in the percentages already described.

Agreement: An arrangement made between lives, not unlike an appointment for lunch, that offers aid, support, introductions, or other benefit, either mutually or directly. These are not binding and while they can have an impact on the life, are not as compelling as either Monads or karma. For that reason, most Fragments have a number of secondary Agreements to "take up the slack" if the primary ones are abdicated. Incidentally, Agreements may be abdicated for many excellent reasons. For example, a Fragment may have a minor facilitating Agreement with another Fragment which would be accomplished by introducing one of the Fragments to another. That introduction would constitute the entire sequence of the Agreement. But the Fragment who has agreed to facilitate might have broken a leg on a ski slope the week before the introduction was to occur and is still in traction when the introduction was to be made. There are two solutions. One is simple abdication, the other is postponement. Agreements of this sort can easily be postponed. Sometimes, however, abdication of Agreements may result in distancing of the Fragments, such as when two Fragments have had a partnership Agreement, and to complete the Agreement, they have married: one of the Fragments decides to abdicate. At that point it is likely that the marriage will not be successful and at the least an estrangement will develop between the partners.

Monad: An experiential unit that is experienced from both sides of the relationship. For example, the Parent/Child Monad, or the Teacher/Student Monad. This does not mean that every child and every parent is doing this Monad, or every teacher and every student are actively involved in the Student/Teacher Monad. Monads are more involved than that. Fragments caught up in the Parent/Child Monad will spend most of their lives in dealing with the relationship, which may not be entirely pleasant. The bond of parent and child will extend far beyond the Third and Fourth Internal Monads, and often continue until one of the Fragments has died. It is not unusual for the Parent/Child Monad to interfere significantly with the private lives of both Fragments, to the extent that the parent not doing the Monad will be shut out of the lives of the parent and child caught up in the Monad, and the child of the Monad might never have a successful sexual relationship while the parent is alive. This does not mean that every "mama's boy" is doing the Parent/Child Monad, but that is one form the Monad can take, although not very successfully. There are two sorts of Monadal configurations: by far the most common is the reciprocal, where the Fragments exchange roles in the Monad. The other, and rarer variety, is the tandem, where both Fragments pass through certain experiences together, such as going from tranquility to stress in one life, and then through similar difficulties from stress to tranquility in another life. These lives are rarely sequential, by the way, so that the lessons have been brought to bear before the Monad is completed.

The Seven Internal Monads: These are experienced in various degrees of success by all Fragments who live long enough to accomplish them. The First, obviously, is birth, or more precisely, taking the first breath, which is when the soul enters the body in almost all cases. The Second Internal Monad is the individualization of self, the point when the Infant recognizes that it is a separate being. This usually occurs before the age of two, although there are cases when it can take longer. The Third Internal Monad is the "out of the nest" Monad, when the Fragment differentiates itself from the family. This is marked by the emergence of the Chief Feature and usually takes place between the ages of eighteen and twenty, at least in occidental civilizations, and is more easily accomplished by males than females due to various social expectations. The Fourth Internal Monad takes place generally between the mid-thirties and the early forties in technologically advanced societies, and is similar to what has been called the "mid-life crisis." In this Monad, the Overleaves will either manifest themselves and the true personality emerge from what has been learned, copied, programmed and taught, or the False Personality will take over entirely. This Monad is a particularly difficult one and it is not unusual to require two or three years to pass through it. The Fifth Internal Monad we would wish to call the "Senior Citizen's Monad," when the life is reviewed in terms of what the Fragment set out to do as compared to what was actually done. This tends to occur in this society between the ages of sixty-five and seventy-five, depending on the nature of the activity that has taken up the Fragment's life, which does not necessarily have anything to do with the Fragment's employment. The Sixth Internal Monad is the onset of whatever it is that will be fatal to the Fragment. This need not be unpleasant, as we have already indicated, but the more attached the Fragment is to the body and the Physical Plane, the more difficult such a Monad is likely to be. The Seventh Internal Monad is, of course, death.

Karma: As we have said many times, a Fragment does not incur karma for bad manners. Karma results when the life choices of another Fragment have been abrogated without prior Agreement. Killing karma is, of course, the most traumatic. Karma is also the result of unlawful imprisonment, which includes selling a person into slavery if that is not part of the Life Plan. Karma is the result of desertion when the Fragment being deserted cannot manage alone, such as leaving a six-month-old Infant without food, clothing or shelter, or abandoning a large and poor family of which the deserting Fragment is the only means of support. Karma results also from what you call "mind-fuck," that is to say, the deliberate disruption of the mind and/or personality through manipulation and deprivation. This covers everything from the extreme conversion methods of some religious groups to psychological terrorism to brain-washing, as it is called. Karma is without doubt the most compelling tie between Fragments, although it is often unpleasant. There is another form of karma, considerably less common than the one already discussed, and that is what we call philanthropic karma, where a Fragment, out of "the goodness of its heart" creates a choice in the life of another Fragment that would not have been possible otherwise. As an example, a Fragment hears another Fragment perform in an amateur musical entertainment and realizes that this particular Fragment has an unusual gift. The first Fragment decides to aid the second with some form of support, no strings attached, and from that, the bond of philanthropic karma is created. This bond is very pleasant and it is not unusual that once a Fragment has done this, that it will, whenever possible, do it again, because it is not only one manifestation of agape, it also "feels good".

Modes: To return to the Overleaves: Modes are the manner in which the life is expressed, the way the Fragment goes at living. There are, of course, seven Modes.

The neutral Mode is Observation, and it has as its polarities clarity in the positive and surveillance in the negative.

The ordinal Goal of the Expression Polarity is Caution, which has deliberation as its positive pole and phobia as its negative pole. Almost eighty-five percent of all Fragments on the Physical Plane have Modes of Observation or Caution.

The ordinal Mode of the Inspiration Polarity is Repression, which has as its positive pole restraint and as its negative pole inhibition.

The ordinal Mode of the Action Polarity is Perseverance, having persistence as its positive pole and immutability as its negative.

The cardinal Mode of the Expression Polarity is Power, and it has as its positive pole authority, and as its negative pole oppression.

The cardinal Mode of the Inspiration Polarity is Passion, and it has as its positive pole self-actualization, and as its negative identification.

The cardinal Mode of the Action Polarity is Aggression, and it has as its positive pole dynamism, and as its negative pole belligerence.

Goals: The Goal can be regarded as what the Mode is aimed at achieving. The Goal indicates also the use the Mode will be put to. Obviously, a Fragment in the Repression Mode will manifest the Goal in a different manner than a Fragment in Passion Mode. There are, of course, seven Goals.

The neutral Goal is Stagnation, which has as its positive pole suspension and as its negative pole inertia. Incidentally, we would wish to point out here that stagnation does not mean that the Fragment will do nothing with the life, for there are those in stagnation who have achieved much in life, but usually of a transitory importance, such as becoming a major sports champion or the president of a law firm.

The ordinal Goal of the Expression Polarity is Rejection, and it has as its positive pole discrimination, and as its negative pole prejudice.

The ordinal Goal of the Inspiration Polarity is Retardation, and it has as its positive pole atavism and as its negative pole withdrawal.

The ordinal Goal of the Action Polarity is Submission, and it has as its positive pole devotion, and as its negative pole subservience.

The cardinal Goal of the Expression Polarity is Acceptance, which in many ways is the highest and therefore the most difficult Goal. Acceptance has as its positive pole agape and as its negative pole ingratiation.

The cardinal Goal of the Inspiration Polarity is growth and it has as its positive pole comprehension and as its negative pole confusion.

The cardinal Goal of the Action Polarity is Dominance and it has as its positive pole leadership and as its negative pole dictatorship.

Attitudes: The Attitude indicates the way the Fragment will look at life, the point of view it will have in regarding itself and those around it. The Attitude will often show itself in the way the Fragment relates to others, for that will be based on the perceptions of the Attitude.

The neutral Attitude is Pragmatist, which has as its positive pole practicality and as its negative dogma.

The ordinal Attitude of the Expression Polarity is Skeptic, and we must observe that most of the intellectual advances of your species have been made by Fragments with this Attitude. The positive pole of Skeptic is investigation and the negative pole is suspicion.

The ordinal Attitude of the Inspiration Polarity is Stoic, which has as its positive pole tranquility and as its negative pole resignation.

The ordinal Attitude of the Action Polarity is Cynic and it has as its positive pole contradiction and as its negative denigration.

The cardinal Attitude of the Expression Polarity is Idealist, which has a positive pole of coalescence and as a negative pole abstraction.

The cardinal Attitude of the Inspiration Polarity is Spiritualist, which has as its positive pole verification and as its negative faith.

The cardinal Attitude of the Action Polarity is Realist, which has as its positive pole perception and as its negative pole supposition.

Centers: We have noticed that Centering is the most difficult concept for those seeking this teaching to grasp. We will try to explain it more cogently than we have before to aid in ending the confusion. Centering determines how a Fragment reacts to situations and how that reaction is expressed. There are those when put into an unknown situation will want to discuss or argue about their feelings. This is the result of the Centering, which in such a case will be the behavior of someone in the Intellectual part of Emotional Center, that is, the Fragment's first reaction to events is emotional—it feels—and the means of revealing the reaction is to talk about the feelings which is the function of the intellectual center.

We have stated before but we will reiterate that for your species the Higher Emotional and the Higher Intellectual Centers are not often experienced except during moments of great stress or extreme elation. We are unaware of any Fragments extant on the Physical Plane who are habitually Centered in the Higher Intellectual or the Higher Emotional Center who are independently mobile, although we would also say that most Fragments will have brief moments when these Centers are engaged. [April, 1991: For independently mobile species, access to the higher Action Center, the Moving Center, is almost essential for survival, for it is what allows the Fragment the responses for individual survival. All ensouled species have habitual access to one of the Higher Centers: for individually mobile ones, Moving Center is it. For various kinds of "cluster" ensoulments, the Higher Intellectual or Higher Emotional is necessary to maintain the integrity of their collective consciousness.]

All Fragments have all Centers present within them, but habitually manifest in a certain way, due to being fixated in that Centering, often the result of how the Fragment was socialized as a young child before the Second Internal Monad, but may very occasionally shift, the result of compensation. For example, a dyslexic child might become fixated in the Moving Center for the simple reasons that the Intellectual Center is the source of embarrassment and frustration because of what is basically "faulty wiring" in the brain. Incidentally, children who have been permitted to draw early in their lives—and by that we do not mean in books with set lines and patterns to be filled in, but simply to invent their own shapes and areas—have less tendency to become dyslexic when reading and writing is being learned, for the eye/hand coordination has already been intuited by the young child. So, rather than trying to learn to do three things at once—identify the shape and orientation of the letter, perceive the sequence of letters, and remember what the resulting word means—the young child need only do two things: perceive the sequence of letters and remember what the resulting word means, which is by far the easiest part of learning to read, for most of it has to do with simple rote memorization.

To return to the Centers. The neutral Center is the Instinctive Center, with a positive pole being atomic, the negative pole being anatomic. Those whom you identify as "idiot savants" are often in the Instinctive Center. Those with remarkable facility with numbers are in the Intellectual part of the Instinctive Center, those with artistic abilities are in the Emotional part of the Instinctive Center. Often the Fragments known as feral children are in the Moving part of the Instinctive Center.

The ordinal Center of the Expression Polarity is the Intellectual Center, which has as its positive pole thought and as its negative pole reason.

The ordinal Center of the Inspiration Polarity is the Emotional Center, which has as its positive pole sensibility and as its negative pole sentimentality.

The ordinal Center of the Action Polarity is the Sexual Center, which has as its positive pole amorality and as its negative eroticism. We will remind you all that we do not limit sexuality to copulation and peculiar clothing, but to an entire aspect of reaction, just as with the Emotional and Intellectual Centers.

The cardinal Center of the Expression Polarity, though not often attained, nor for very long, is the Higher Intellectual Center, which has as its positive pole integration and as its negative pole telepathy.

The cardinal Center of the Inspiration Polarity is the Higher Emotional Center, again, very rarely attained. Its positive pole is empathy and its negative pole is intuition.

The Moving Center is the only Higher Center which Fragments have habitual access to, and it is the cardinal Center of the Action Polarity. The positive pole is enduring, the negative pole is energetic.

As you are aware, Fragments are described as being in a particular part of a particular Center. The second word identifies the actual Centering, the first word indicates how it is expressed. For example, those in the Moving part of Intellectual Center are those who must take action on the things they think about. On the other hand, those in the Intellectual part of Moving Center have been described as those who "shoot first and ask questions later". If the Fragment is in the Emotional part of Moving Center, then it would feel about the shooting after it was done. We should point out that those who are not Intellectually Centered, either primarily or secondarily, often have trouble expressing themselves in words, since words are the tools of the Intellectual Center.

If you desire to reach a Center which is not often attainable, but not the Higher Centers, it often helps to distract part of the Centering. Let us give you an example to clarify. Let us say that a Fragment is in the Moving part of Intellectual Center and wishes to have a better understanding of his or her emotions. Taking a long walk—nothing too rigorous or involving—distracts the Moving Center so that the Intellect can reach the Emotional Center. If the Fragment is in the Emotional part of the Intellectual Center and is having trouble getting going on a project, then listening to pleasant music might distract the Emotional Center so that the Moving Center could get into "focus". Of course there is no certainty that the Fragment would do the project, it is just as likely that the Fragment would express the movement by dancing.

Chief Features: We come now to Chief Features, and we will say again that there are no good Chief Features. All Chief Features are based in fear, and fear is the driving force behind all negative poles in the Overleaves and in the cosmos, for that matter. All Chief Features are present to some degree in all Fragments, just as all Centerings are, but only one Chief Feature actually gains control of the Fragment and distorts the function of the Goal, which is the way in which the Chief Feature manifests its control of the Fragment. [*November, 1989:* In regard to Secondary Chief Features, it is the Attitude that the Secondary impacts, as the Primary impacts the Goal. After the Third Internal Monad, ninety-eight percent of all Fragments have a Primary and Secondary Chief Feature. The term Secondary does not in any way describe a diminished "importance" or "power," but it does indicated which of the Overleaves it most affects.] In attaching conditions and expectations to the Goal, the Chief Feature "colors" so that it cannot be recognized or is acceptable only under certain very limited circumstances, often circumstances that are impractical at best, such as a young woman with genuine back problems who feels that the only way she can be worth anything in life is if she becomes a ballet dancer. We would have to say that while such things are not impossible, they are unlikely, and will tend to blind the Fragment to other genuine potentials and accomplishments because of the firmly held belief that it only "counts" if she is a dancer.

The neutral Chief Feature is Stubbornness, and it is far and away the Chief Feature most often encountered in your species. The underlying fear of Stubbornness is the fear of dealing with new situations, and for that reason the Fragment will tend either to make the new situation as much like those with which it is already familiar or it will find inventive ways to avoid the new situation. The positive pole of Stubbornness is determination, the negative is obstinacy. While it is tempting to say that determination is a useful quality, let us point out that coming from fear, it is likely to be the determination born of panic or other less obvious forms of fear.

We would wish to caution all Fragments against becoming "fond" of their Chief Features, as one would embrace an "ugly duckling". There are no potential swans in Chief Features. This is also like the story of the princess and the frog. Except where the Chief Feature is concerned, the princess is more apt to become a frog, too, rather than turn the frog to a prince.

The ordinal Chief Feature of the Expression Polarity is Self-Destruction, which has as its underlying fear the fear of loss of control. Fragments with this Chief Feature are often terribly well-disciplined Fragments, and we do not use that word lightly. The positive pole of Self-Destruction is sacrifice, the negative is immolation.

The ordinal Chief Feature of the Inspiration Polarity is Self-Deprecation, which has as its underlying fear a fear of inadequacy. Those with Self-Deprecation are prone to informing others not to expect too much of them, often because they are too busy doing other things for other people, or have a variety of "irons in the fire," all of which demand time and attention. Occasionally, this is revealed when a Fragment takes on far too much and then either exhausts the Fragment in an attempt to "deliver the goods" or causes massive disappointment all around, which, of course, only serves to reinforce the Self-Deprecation. Those with Self-Deprecation will sometimes lavish praise on others not only to demonstrate their fear of inadequacy but in the hope that some of it will be returned and shore up the sagging confidence of the Fragment with Self-Deprecation. The positive pole of Self-Deprecation is humility, the negative pole is abasement.

The ordinal Chief Feature of the Action Polarity is Martyrdom, which has as its underlying fear a fear of worthlessness. Those with Martyrdom will find myriad ways to "tempt fate" in order to do something that will establish worth once and for all. Martyrdom can bring on thankless families, wasting diseases, sabotaged careers, destructive personal relationships, and an almost constant search for the illusive "grail" of worthiness. Many times the Fragment is convinced that if it only suffers enough, someone will assure it that it was all worthwhile. The positive pole of Martyrdom is selflessness, the negative pole is mortification, sometimes in the most literal sense.

The cardinal Chief Feature of the Expression Polarity is Greed, which has its underlying fear a fear of loss or want. Whatever the Greed becomes fixated on, there is no such thing as enough of it, even if the Fragment has all that there is in the world. If the Greed is strong, there is no price, literally or figuratively that the Fragment is not willing to pay to acquire more of its fixation. Greed, of all the Chief Features, is hardest on those around it, because where the subject of the fixation is concerned, the Fragment is likely to be completely ruthless. The positive pole of Greed is egotism, the negative pole is voracity.

The cardinal Chief Feature of the Inspiration Polarity is Arrogance which has as its underlying fear the fear of vulnerability. Fragments with Arrogance, as we have often observed before, are truly shy, although their behavior might not appear so to those encountering them casually. Those with Arrogance are often determined not to reveal any aspect of their vulnerability and will, in fact, deny that it exists, or that they have been "wounded" or, if that is undeniable, that they can "take it." The positive pole of Arrogance is pride, the negative pole is vanity.

The cardinal Chief Feature of the Action Polarity is Impatience, which has as its underlying fear the fear of missing something, along with the assumption that whatever is being missed is more important than whatever the Fragment is currently doing. Fragments with Impatience often have difficulty finishing things, from filling out forms to dealing with crises of major import. As Greed is the most difficult Chief Feature for others to live with, so Impatience is the most difficult for those possessing it to live with, for it causes constant restlessness and dissatisfaction. In your society, Impatience is often regarded as an attractive trait in men, and it can serve as a stimulus in relationships, although they rarely have the opportunity to develop if the Impatience is strong. The positive pole of Impatience is audacity, the negative pole is intolerance.

We would wish to caution you that it is a habit of occidental thought to see polarities as extremes and ignore the mean, which we would think would delay understanding for many Fragments. We emphasize the Polarities as much as we do because the negative Polarity is always controlled by fear: it is the fear that makes it negative.

The positive polarity is always part of love—we do not say controlled because it is not in the nature of love to control—and it is through the positive poles that Essence has access to personality. In the negative poles, Essence is blocked. Where it is possible for the positive poles to be operative, then there is growth and evolution. It is the desire of Essence to evolve, and it can do this through the positive poles and no other way while on the Physical Plane. It is not a question of "right" or "wrong" but how much Essence can be functional that will determine growth.

Perhaps it would be wise for us to take time to digress again on the subject of love. Most of the Fragments on the Physical Plane define love as a syrupy sort of sentimental territoriality, but this is not what we mean. Love is not possessive. Nor is it conditional. If there is love, it is without expectation. That does not mean without hope, but hope and expectations are two different matters. Love is the strongest force there is, and we say this as a Universal Truth. There is nothing that is stronger. Fear weakens and distorts and subverts it so that it is regarded with suspicion and disdain, but that does not change the strength of love—it only points out how seductive fear can be. Love is the source of true intimacy, which is the most binding experience that can be had on the Physical Plane, and we do not limit intimacy to sexual contact, which is often about as intimate as purchasing shoes. Intimacy is validation and recognition at once, and can happen under very unlikely circumstances, as many here gathered are aware from experience.

Essence Twin: One of the two Fragments to whom a Fragment is "bound" from the time of casting until the Entities and Cadres reunite in their evolution back to the Tao. The Essence Twin is the most intimate bond that is possible. The Fragments are truly twins, that is, equals. They are six times out of seven the same Essence, and they are never in the same Entity. The bond of Essence Twin, if recognized and validated, remains unbroken throughout the life. We will add that often the bond is too intense and is rejected for that reason alone, for fear is never more threatened than in the presence of the Essence Twin.

Task Companion: The other Fragment to whom a Fragment is "bound" from the time of casting until the Entities and Cadres reunite in the evolution back to the Tao. Task Companions do the complement of each other's True Work, and although it is possible for them to go through every life without actually meeting, the work will be done. This is generally an easier relationship than the one with the Essence Twin, since it is outwardly rather than inwardly focused. Six times out of seven Task Companions are in the same Entity. They are never the same Essence. One Fragment is in a cardinal position in casting, the other in an ordinal one. When Task Companions work together, they accomplish significantly more than they would do apart.

Configuration: Triads, quadrates, pentates, sextants, septants, octaves, and so on. These are working arrangements agreed upon by Fragments usually after several life experiences together, and usually not agreed upon until the late Baby or early Young Cycles. The configuration makes a good "team" and can function with as much as half of the configuration missing. Occasionally two configurations will agree to work together, but this arrangement rarely lasts for more than two lives, and is ended when the specific task is finished.

Magnetic Old King: Usually very cardinal in casting, Magnetic Old Kings draw their kingdom to them to accomplish the mandated task. Those in the presence of their Magnetic Old King will feel "inspired" and "encouraged" to take on new tasks. at this time there are fifty-seven Magnetic Old Kings in the world. [*January, 2008:* That number is now sixty-one.] There is one Magnetic Old King in the United States of America. There are two in the United Kingdom. There are three in Europe. There is one in Egypt. There are two in Northern Africa. As we have said, these Fragments are very rare and those who answer the mandate often discover that many of their difficulties have been cleared away as if by magic, or so it would appear to those not responding to a mandate. The Magnetic Old King for any given Fragment is not necessarily one living in the country in which the Fragment resides. For example, among this group of students, only one of you is part of the kingdom of the Magnetic Old King residing in this country. The rest of you are part of other kingdoms, in other places in the world. Let us point out that it is rare for such powerful Old Kings to be in positions of specifically political power, since such positions are no longer attractive to them. All Magnetic Old Kings are at the sixth Level of the Old Cycle, and once that Level is completed, the tremendous draw of their magnetism ends, although they still have the natural King power, of course.

Let us give some information about the Astral and Causal Planes. There are three Levels to the Astral Plane: the Lower, Middle, and Upper. At the Lower Level, there are often Fragments from the Physical Plane, such as those who assume that they are dreaming, are under the influence of drugs or other mind-altering techniques, and the recently dead. Many of those with advanced occult abilities have routine access to the Lower Astral Plane. The Mid-Astral Plane is where the Essence "resides" between lives, where the experience is reviewed and the new choices are made. Those on the Mid-Astral Plane may occasionally have contact with those on the Physical Plane, particularly those with whom there are karmic ribbons or strong bonds, such as Essence Twins and Task Companions. The Upper Astral Plane is where the Fragments of Entities go when they have finished with all their lives on the Physical Plane, but members of their Entity are still finishing up theirs.

The Lower Causal Plane is where the Entities reunite completely and "blend" again. It is not incorrect to think of the reuniting of Entities as the merging of Task Companions, since six out of seven task companions are in the same Entity, and this of course spurs the Entity on to more work. At the Mid-Causal Plane, the Entities become teachers, such as we are. There are literally countless Mid-Causal teachers, but they are all teaching the same lessons. The "style" may be different, but the lesson is the same. Above the Mid-Causal Plane, those Cadres whose Entities have not yet finished teaching wait to be reunited. That reuniting binds the Essence Twins together.

As far as Essence is concerned, the Astral Plane experiences are the Sixth Cycle of growth, and the Causal Plane experiences are the Seventh Cycle, finishing out the five Cycles begun on the Physical Plane. At the time the Cadres reunite, all sense of Fragment—that is, individual—identity is lost and each experience becomes the entire experience of all the Cadre.

Life Task: The work Essence assigns itself for a life, usually defined with a great deal of leeway, so that the Fragment may adapt to changing conditions in order to accomplish it. Life Task may carry over through several lives if it is a complex one.

Life Plan: The manner in which the Fragment plans to complete the Life Task. Also not rigidly defined in almost all instances.

The Three Sizes of Truth: There are Personal Truths, World Truths and Universal Truths. Seven is a Universal Truth, as is the all-encompassing strength of love. There are many ways in which this can be expressed, but as long as it is at least in some part genuine, then there is some sense of the Universal Truth that is the core of love.

A Personal Truth is something that is true for a particular Fragment and body. For example: "I have myopic vision" is a Personal Truth for the Fragment who has certain distortions in the shape of the lens of the eye. Personal Truths, while "true" in their way, change often throughout life. "I cannot read" may be true of a Fragment all life long, or it may change when the Fragment acquires the skill. Those things which are valid for the person can be interpreted as Personal Truths, including such things as "I have a weakness for blondes" or some other evaluation based on body-type attraction. Body-type attraction can be both a Personal and a World Truth, since the specific attraction is personal, but its existence—that there is such as thing as body-type attraction and compatibility—is a World Truth.

World Truths: Things that are true for this world and the Physical Plane in general. The gravity you experience is a World Truth. The radiation from the star that is your sun is a World Truth. The conditions of atmosphere are World Truths. We remind you yet again that the Physical Plane contains all of interstellar space in its bounds, although to all intents and purposes from your point of view, space is truly "infinite," for the limits of the Physical Plane far exceed any capacity you have at present to measure it. Your species is a World Truth, but not a Universal Truth. That there are species of creatures of reason is a World Truth, but closer to Universal Truths than some others, just as a number of mathematical equations, while describing the World Truths of mathematics, come closer to Universal Truth than others.

Creatures of Reason: Any member of a species that is ensouled. On your planet, that means human beings and cetaceans. No others species is ensouled. All others have hive souls. Let us describe something of the nature of a hive soul. It is the central wiring for a species, a program on which the species is run. That program dictates almost all choices made by any animal belonging to the species, and choice is possible in very narrow parameters. We wish to point out that creatures of reason, by their very nature, are dealing with choices, but creatures of nonreason have had almost all of their choices made for them.

We will give you an example on choice and "wiring" which is sometimes called instinct. A person in a burning barn has the choice to find a way out, even if it means taking the risk of running through fire. It can mean the risk of burns, but it may also save the life of the Fragment. A horse in the same burning barn is not able to choose to run through fire; the wiring of the horse does not permit that, and the only way it will be able to take that method of escape is if some person, preferably a person the horse knows and trusts, comes and first blindfolds it and then leads it through the fire. Otherwise the program of the species will compel the animal to burn to death unless it can kick the side of the barn out before it starts to burn.

Another difference between creatures of reason and creatures of nonreason is that creatures of reason can be acculturated and creatures of nonreason cannot. Those living "domestically" with human beings may learn certain sorts of behavior from their owners, but they will never truly be acculturated. Creatures of reason, on the other hand, experience acculturation as part of the Seven Internal Monads and the results of the chosen life.

To return to the nature of creatures of reason, let us comment that the bond of Entity is a strong one, especially among members of the same Essence. It is very much like the familial bond of cousins, in that it is a valid link even when individual Fragments clash, either through abrading Overleaves, past experiences or simple personality dissimilarities. Within the Entities and the Essence groupings are what we call Cadences. The Entities are cast, all of one Essence in an Entity and then all of another. the Essence groupings are, of course, in groups of seven. Those groups of seven are known as Cadences, and that bond, as those of you who have experienced it know, is particularly strong. Often members of the same Cadences will have extensive past life experiences together, and in some case, Cadence members will spend as much as eighty percent of their lives in each other's company. Occasionally two or three Fragments of the same Cadence will find some means or other to be in each other's company for every life, as a touchstone.

Let us try to clarify some of this casting for you. We will use a metaphor that is not to be taken literally, or even picturesquely. Let us say that a baker is making many flavors of cookies. He rolls the dough out into long tubes and cuts off those lengths he needs, flavors those tubes appropriately, then slices them into the individual cookies. Each cookie is still part of the tube of dough, although it is now artificially segmented, and has a particular flavor. Entities are like three or four tubes of dough being cut and baked at the same time, and the Cadres are like the other sorts of cookies and combinations of cookies on other shelves in the oven. As we have already warned you, this is not a literal description, but it gives something of the sense of Entities and the matter of order in casting which results in Cadences.

Evolution, on the Physical Plane as well as all other Planes of existence, is through the manifestation of love, which is the contact of Essence with Essence. There is no other way. Let us emphasize that: Essence Contact is the only means of evolution of the Physical and any other Plane. Love, in the sense of agape, is the means of Essence Contact. No matter how fleeting this may be, it is valid and the Fragment does advance. It is uncommon for such contact to be prolonged, in part because it is frightening, and in part because few of you are willing to take the time and risks that are necessary to bring about the prolongation. As is obvious, the Chief Feature will do its utmost to block or deny such contact, but if the contact has occurred, then even denial cannot change it.

Often this recognition of contact comes about indirectly, and the process is through what you on the Physical Plane call art, or the arts. True art, as compared to craft or artifice, stems from a perception or "vision" of validation, and the attempt to express that "creatively" is what brings about the power that arts have to bring about insights so that the lessons are brought to bear. What you on the Physical Plane call art provides a link for personality and Essence, not only for the artist, but for those who perceive the link in the art. The recognition of the "vision" that is beyond the art, whatever form that art may take, is often a direct link from personality to Essence, and as such, is a source of growth, not just for those doing the art, but those perceiving it.

Two last definitions: the **false personality**, which is the "trained" or acculturated self, the "you" you were raised to be, which may or may not have much resemblance to Essence or Overleaves. False personality is the ultimate bastion of the Chief Feature, and is the source of much resistance and denial. The false personality often remains in force throughout life if the Third and Fourth Internal Monads are not completed, recognized, and validated by the Fragment.

True personality is the manifestation of the Overleaves in the life, and the progress toward the completion of the Life Task, that overall goal that is established for any given life. True personality is what is expressed after the successful passage through the Fourth Internal Monad, and gives the Fragment the opportunity for true work on the Life Task.

We would wish to remind all those here present that we neither require nor desire belief in what we say to you. If you choose to question and validate for yourself, the progress will be accomplished with knowledge and recognition. But progress will occur whether you perceive it or not and the choices made are "good" choices no matter what they are, for the choice itself is the lesson, and its ramifications and outcome bring the lessons to bear. There is no "right" or "wrong" way to decide—getting out of bed in the morning is a choice not to remain there—but if we would urge you to anything, it is to the understanding that all of life is choice: you cannot not choose; as we have pointed out before, to say "I will not choose; I will do nothing" is a choice to do nothing. Rather than regard choices as terrible burdens and impositions, you would release much of your fear if you would realize that you are making choices all the time, and the process, rather than overwhelming you, is in fact the means to freeing yourself from the bonds of fear. Of course, you may choose to deny or ignore this, as well. That is as much a choice as anything else in life.

CHAPTER THREE
Continuing the Session

"Thanks," Henry says as he looks over the pages in a perfunctory way. "I'll want to sort this out later." "Whose turn is it?" Jessica asks, gazing longingly at the pastry which is not quite gone. "Somebody ask a question before I do something caloric." Kim fusses with her pencil. "I think I'm next." She appears nervous and slightly embarrassed. "I hate to ask this, but it's been driving me crazy, and I can't figure it out for myself." She takes off her glasses and cleans them. "I know I'm procrastinating. All right." She heaves a quick sigh. "Michael: I've been clumsy most of my life. I hate being clumsy, but I can't seem to help it. Is there anything I can do about it? I don't mind going to some expense if I have to, but . . ." Her voice trails off and she looks hopefully at Jessica. "There's a lot in his answer," Jessica warns, and everyone readies their pencils and pens.

First we would wish to say that this Fragment is not what is called clumsy, which would indicate a poor control of muscles. This Fragment does not lack for muscular control and there is no neurological reason for this dysfunction, which has far more to do with eyesight than with muscles. You will note, Kim, that when you are looking straight ahead through your glasses, you do not behave in a clumsy way. You are what you call clumsy when you cannot clearly see that which is around you. For that reason we would recommend that contact lenses would be an excellent investment, and then a class in ballet for beginning adults, which would develop a better sense of physical orientation and cause less difficulties for you. We would think that this would also do much to aid your confidence as well as developing a better sense of movement, all of which is of use. Let us also recommend adding a full complex of amino acids in tablets taken between meals, and an increase in the B vitamins. You will find that you will benefit more fully from the nutritional value of your food which aids in the sense of well-being that is part of improving the perception of the body, and not simply as a tool or an object of desire or repugnance. Of course, changes do not occur overnight, but reasonable perseverance should bring about the results you seek.

"Contact lenses and ballet lessons," Kim says after she has read back her notes.

"And amino acids and B vitamins," Henry adds, shaking his head. "Who do we know who can recommend a ballet teacher?" Kim flushes at his eagerness. "I'll . . . make a few phone calls when we get home." She coughs once. "I get another question?"

"Go ahead," Jessica says with a warm smile. "It's so hard to choose. I've got . . ."

"A little list?" Lizzy prompts.

"I've got a huge list," Kim corrects her, ignoring the reference. "And I don't want to miss any of it." She reads briefly. "All right; I know the one I want to ask. My boss—you got his Overleaves for me last session, Jessica; he's a Young Slave in Observation and Submission—is pressing me to take on more of running his office. It's not that I don't want to, but I feel annoyed at being pressed this way. Will Michael please give me some suggestions as to how I can best handle the situation?"

"Don't say best," Camille reminds her.

"Okay: comments on how I might choose to deal with the situation," Kim corrects herself.

In dealing with this very officious Young Slave, we would think that resistance as such would bring poor results. This Fragment will respond more to your statements of the common good you wish to serve. Since this is a young soul, we remind you that his motto is "do it my way," and he is eager to believe that he has awakened the social conscience of all those around him. He sees himself as the wise and guiding servant who selflessly expounds great truths to a world of unappreciative beings.

"He sure is," Kim mutters.

For the most part, this Fragment will respect what he sees as dedication equal to his own. In your work, you have many areas where service can be rendered in a way that he would recognize and accept as valid. What is apt to convince him of your dedication is your assurance that you can perceive how great his service is, and make it plain that he has inspired you to give service in your own area of endeavor. This will be more gratifying than any other answer, and it is not untrue, although you neither perceive nor define your work in terms that this Young Slave would agree with.

Kim looks up. "Who got that? I don't know why it is, but I always have trouble getting the answers to my questions."

"Everyone does," Camille tells her. "It's probably because you've got a higher level of interest in those answers, and you're trying to hear words instead of just writing down letters."

"I botch my answers all the time," Lizzy seconds. "That's why I'm glad we have more than two or three people at a session; it means that I won't lose material."

"I'll try that approach," Kim says to Jessica. "It can't go any worse than it's been going."

"Well, for what it's worth," Camille says, "when I've done what Michael recommended, I've found that things usually worked out better. Sometimes it's just a way to make the best of a bad situation, but it does keep things from getting worse."

"Do you think they would have gotten worse if you hadn't followed Michael's suggestions?" Alex can't help asking.

"I don't know," Camille admits. "I do know that there have been times when I've resisted the urge to try to explain my position in circumstances that were tricky, and when I've managed to keep my Sagey mouth shut, I've been able to get out of awkward situations more gracefully than I probably would have done otherwise, judging from some of my past experiences."

"Your turn, Henry," Jessica says, glancing at the clock on the wall.

"Okay," Henry declares, pulling his chair a little closer to the coffee table. "I'd like to know if Michael can tell me how I should handle the current controversy in my department."

"I don't think you want to phrase it that way," Jessica warns. "Michael will only give you the Choice Lecture if you ask them what to do."

"Well, what would get me a good answer? Besides, I wish Michael would tell me what to do. I wish someone would tell me what to do." His expression is exasperated and he clicks his pen a few times in emphasis.

"But Michael will only make suggestions," Jessica reminds him. "What about phrasing it so that you can get some insight, or some suggestions as to what is going on. Will that work for you, do you think?" She is holding the planchette loosely in her left hand, her head slightly cocked to the side.

"That's fine with me," Henry sighs.

It is difficult for the Fragment who is now Henry to realize that there are circumstances in which his participation is not central. His position as department head complicates the situation currently troubling him because he is perceived as being in charge and therefore in some way responsible for the conflict that has arisen between two of the teachers who work "under" him. Let us clarify one or two things for you, Henry. First, it would be useful to realize that you are not, in fact, focal to this conflict. The actual difficulties are between a Young Scholar in Caution and Rejection with a Chief Feature of Impatience and a Mature Artisan in Observation and Dominance with a Chief Feature of Arrogance. These two Fragments have several past associations, not all of them pleasant, and they have "unexplainable" animosities about each other that they do not know how to deal with, and cannot stop indulging. We would think that your willingness to listen to their complaints would do much to clear the air, but if you do so, you will not be able to get away from the pressure of being caught between them. You will do well to weigh the various advantages of action and inaction before making up your mind, although, of course, we remind you yet again that anything you do is your choice. It is not likely that these two Fragments will become fast friends or even tolerant pals, and to deal with them in any way with that expectation will bring you little but disappointment. Learning to release expectations is Good Work, but may not be in accordance with your role as head of your department.

Henry sighs. "That's great. A real damned if you do and damned if you don't game."

We would not describe it as a game, and of course, there is no validity in the concept of damnation.

Larry laughs aloud. "Michael's doing his one-liners again." Lizzy chuckles.

"I wrote it down wrong," she says, referring back to the quip. "I had 'There is no salad'."

Even Jessica laughs at this. "I wonder what kind of dressing a Michael salad would have?"

"Caesar or Green Goddess?" Camille ventures, grinning. "That's awful," Alex groans.

"You have another question, Henry?" Jessica asks, not quite seriously.

"I was thinking it might be worth it to quit while I'm ahead, but I know I'd kick myself later." He runs his thumb over his beard, which he often does when making decisions. "Michael discussed rest last session, and talked about what is rest for various people here. I'm curious to know what is restful for me."

We have said that rest is something more complex than the body being inactive or the brain being stupefied, and we would wish you all here gathered to be aware of that distinction in pursuing this matter. What is restful for the Fragment who is now Henry is pottering about in a rowboat—and we mean a rowboat, not something as potentially difficult as a canoe—on calm waters, a gentle tending of gardens, and reclining in hot tubs. This Fragment has much need of "unwinding time" for like most Scholars, he has a noisy mind and it is not easy to quiet it.

"I do like to garden," Henry says reflectively. "I haven't done any rowing since I was in high school."

"Maybe you should take that up when I take up ballet," Kim suggests, the hint of a mischievous smile at the corner of her mouth.

"I'll think about it," Henry promises her.

"Emily?" Jessica says.

"Oh, is it me already?" she asks, wide-eyed. "I guess it is," she adds, looking around the room. "Will Michael comment on the life before last? He said some time ago that I had a number of unfinished lessons from that life, and I didn't follow that up at the time, but I think that it would be useful to know more about it now."

"Do you recall what it was that Michael said about it?" Jessica asks.

"I brought my notes from that session. I'll read it to you." Emily flips through an old pad of paper, filled with well- scribbled pages. "Here it is: Much of the difficulties currently before you stem from the life before the immediate past one, when you were engaged in highly competitive trade in rare stones and metals. At that time, the Life Task was abdicated in favor of increasing the material opulence of the family as well as the social betterment of your seven children. Michael didn't say anything more than that."

"And you'd like Michael to elaborate on it and indicate what bearing it has on this life?" Jessica asks, making sure she has Emily's inquiry right.

"Yes; that's about right."

This Fragment was of Spanish heritage, living in the south of France, where the family had long been involved in trade. This Fragment was determined at an early age to better himself and his family by any means possible without flagrantly breaking the law. Many of the bargains struck were "shady" and did not make the Fragment who is now Emily any friends in the business world. On the other hand, the determination to realize great wealth did result in his acquiring a sizable fortune, which made it possible for him to marry five of his children to those who offered social and economic advantages far beyond what would have been attainable in his youth. He was sincerely devoted to his family and convinced that he had—

"That's not a word, Michael," Jessica interrupts herself as the planchette moves aimlessly over the board. "It's as if they're trying to show me three or four slides at the same time." The planchette moves more vigorously, and Jessica resumes dictating.

—an obligation to them to improve their lot, though it meant depriving others of needed material and social advantages to accomplish this goal. At that time the Fragment who is now Emily lived to the age of sixty-seven and died suddenly of a stroke brought about by chronic high blood pressure and stress. This life not only did little to advance the evolution of this Fragment, but it caused hardships to many, including three of his children, who were disastrously miss-mated in their lucrative marriages. Working with those needing special instruction and guidance in this life is one way you have chosen, Emily, to avoid the limits of that life. We would agree that it is useful for you to explore this life, and it would not be inappropriate to analyze your current relationships with your family in light of the choices of the past.

"Oh, brother," Emily protests as the answer is deciphered for her. "I knew it was something bad, but I thought it was in terms of illegal activities."

There were such activities, of course, but their impact was not as lasting or as far-reaching as the manipulation of family members for "their own good".

"Sounds like that was quite a life," Camille says with a slow nod. "Does it strike any chords with you, Emily?"

Emily flushes. "Yes, it does. That's what's bothering me. I guess I wanted to be told I was some kind of commercial pirate who went out and capitalized on the Greed of others. And I find out that I was the Greedy one."

"We all want to be heroes," Larry says with real sympathy. "I know that I don't like to think I ever did anything that was cruel or unreasonable or harmful, but I know I must have—we all did."

"I remember I went to a woman who billed herself as a psychic about ten years ago," Emily says wistfully. "According to her, I did nothing but lead upright, moral and decent lives from beginning to end. You can't imagine how much I wanted to believe her, but I knew it couldn't be that way. I could feel it in myself, that I'd done things in the past that were not . . . Good Work, as Michael calls it. According to this woman, I should have achieved permanent sainthood sometime in the fifteenth century." She laughs, a touch of sadness in her voice. "If I had really done that well, I wouldn't be here. I doubt I'd need to ask questions of Michael, because I'd have the answers for myself."

"And so you have another question?" Jessica asks.

"I do." She sighs. "I keep thinking that there ought to be a way to just . . . know this material, take it out of the air or something like that. I haven't found a way to do it, and it probably isn't possible, but will Michael please comment on why I can't seem to do it?"

The hold of false personality is strong, and the death grip of the Chief Feature is more powerful than any of you wish to admit. You, Emily, have set yourself an impossible goal, that of achieving perfect understanding. On the Physical Plane, this happens very rarely, and only in those Fragments with the Overleaves that would permit such understanding, and with the Chief Features subdued or extinguished altogether. Let us remind you that you have not yet accepted the negativity of your Chief Feature. You see it as your main protection, and in one sense, of course, it is. As long as you let the Arrogance rule you, you need not face the terror of vulnerability. But that vulnerability is necessary if there is to be understanding, for understanding is not just being aware of the "good stuff," but of all the "stuff," and its ramifications in your choices in this life. Your arrogance is what demands that the understanding be perfect, for that makes it unattainable from the start as well as reinforcing the grip of the Chief Feature. There is no "failure" in consulting a teacher such as we are. Mid-causal reunited Entities have teaching as their tasks in their evolution, as you have the experience of the Physical Plane in yours. Remember, you are on the Physical Plane to experience the Physical Plane, not to avoid the experience. The Physical Plane is obdurate, and it is part of the lesson to recognize that obduracy.

"That's not comforting," Emily says wryly as she copies off of Lizzy's page. "I don't like this obduracy stuff Michael talks about."

"Who does?" Alex inquires.

"Your turn, Camille," Jessica says. "Have you got your questions ready?"

"Reams of them," Camille vows. "However, I have done a little culling, and I've got a few that I think are more important than some of the others. The first is: Michael has said before that the various polarities see relationships in different ways. Would he please explain that, and tell us how the polarities see relationships?"

"That's a big one," Jessica says to the air. "It's gonna come fast. Everyone be ready."

Yes, we would agree that all the polarities and the neutral see relationships in different ways, and these ways often are reflected in the misunderstandings that arise between Fragments in different polarities. We are aware that most of you can discern the differences in the Roles and the things that are important to the Roles, and this is, of course, good work, but the perceptions of relationships are another level of comprehension.

Jessica's face has become flushed; her planchette moves quickly, darting over the board faster than usual.

In the Expression Polarity, that is, Sages and Artisans, the word for relationships is commitment. In the Inspiration Polarity, that is, Priests and Slaves, the word for relationships is dedication. In the Action Polarity, that is, Kings and Warriors, the word for relationships is fealty. In the neutral, that is, the Scholar Role, the word for relationships is involvement. We would think that if you choose to devote some time to the study of these relational words, there may be insights that will be useful to you all.

"That's a big answer," Jessica says as she leans back and rubs her hands together. The color in her face subsides. "There are boxcars of information behind that answer."

"Why would there be so much difference in the relationship words?" Alex asks. "That's not a question for Michael, but to discuss. I know that each Role has a different way of looking at the world, but why this diversity in relationship perceptions?"

John Verano looks up from the page. "It's probably all part of the same thing, the Role and the perception. They'd go together, wouldn't they? If you wanted to do what a Sage has to do, you probably wouldn't want to have a Priest's expectations on top of it, would you?"

"And some of the Roles, by their very nature, have different sorts of relationships in any case. Kings require loyalty; I know how important that is to them, since my boss is one," Henry says. "He puts great store in the . . . well, fealty of his staff. Not that I blame him. The position he's in, he needs that kind of support or he wouldn't be able to do his job well."

"You want to ask another question, Milly?" Jessica asks, with the hint of a wary laugh. "Is it as big as that first one?"

"I don't think so, but it might be—it is related to it." She looks at Jessica with a shrug. "If I could get these for myself, you know I would, but I just don't trust any answer I get to any question of my own. It's too damned easy to influence and edit and cut without knowing it. And when there is a little good material, it's so hard to bring it through."

"I know what you mean," Jessica nods. "I remember what it was like for the three years we didn't have a backup medium at these sessions. I had questions stacked up to the roof, and it was frustrating not being able to ask them."

"I knew you'd understand," Camille says, "but I still feel badly about dropping it all on you."

"Tell your Chief Feature to stuff it," Lizzy recommends. "What's the question."

"Michael has talked every now and then about input, and the problems of what results from it. This is sort of related to my first question: What is the difference between the input of various Roles?"

"Oh, brother," Jessica declares. "You are full of biggies, aren't you?"

Your perception is valid, and we will try to define this for you. What we mean by input is the level or levels on which a Fragment receives information. Those who input on one level are the sorts who concentrate well anywhere, and can think clearly amid chaos. The Scholar, King and Warrior Roles input on one level, or channel. The Priests and Slave Roles input on two

MORE MESSAGES FROM MICHAEL 47

levels, or channels, one always tuned in to the "higher ideal" in the case of Priests, and the "common good" in the case of Slaves. Sages input on three levels, or channels, which is why they find performing stimulating rather than enervating. Artisans input on five levels, or channels, which is what occasionally makes them appear scattered or "spacey" to others. This problem of input is a difficult one, because it is the tendency of all Fragments to assume that everyone else inputs in the same manner that the individual Fragment does, which is of course, not valid. To appreciate this difference of input, you need only examine the artistic work of Fragments of each Essence, and notice the levels operating in their art. There are useful insights to be gained from understanding the levels, or channels, of input, or at least in accepting that they are valid, if you would wish to do so.

"Is that why Artisans often seem so scattered?" Larry asks. "I know it's not my turn, but—"

"Go ahead," Henry offers. "I want to know the answer, too."

For those who do not input on five levels, yes, as we have observed already, it often appears that Artisans are "scattered" and it is true that these Fragments often have more problems than others in learning to "read" others because they are gathering information from so many diverse sources and reacting on a variety of levels. It also appears that such Fragments "tune you out" when they have shifted their major attention to another level, or channel, of input. Such diversification of thought can lead to difficulties because the inputting Fragment is not sure on what level or even if comments and reactions are being processed. The same can be said of Sages, of course, but to a lesser degree. And we would wish to point out that the single mindedness of Scholars, Warriors and Kings can be distressing to those with access to more than one level of input. Recognizing these differences in input is Good Work, we will say it again, and commend you, Camille, for the clarity of your inquiries.

"Commend—hey, that's pretty good," Kim says.

"For Michael, that's high praise." Jessica agrees. "I've been at this a dozen years or so, and that is the strongest language I've ever heard Michael use when saying something approving. They just aren't inclined to pass out bouquets. They've said that too much approval creates competition among students as well as creating the false impression that there are right and wrong questions and insights, which they insist isn't the case." She looks down into her coffee cup, staring at the last of the now-cold liquid. "Michael really is quite impersonal, you know. That's caused some of the people attending sessions to be put off, but most of us are ... well, satisfied with how they impart their information. It keeps us from thinking of it as dogma, and no matter what Michael says about there being no wrong choices, that, to me, is a bad idea. I don't want to see this become dogmatic. There was a time when I was undecided, but since then, I've watched some of the group get really rigid and end up leaving because we wouldn't go along with the idea that we had to live the way Michael 'wants' us to, and refused to believe that there was no specific way Michael 'wants' us to live."

"Yes," Camille says, leaning forward in the high-backed chair she prefers. "Some of the private readings I do are just attempts on the part of the client to get Michael or anyone to tell them what to do. They want rules and regulations and a list of dos and don'ts that will let them have a kind of mental checklist they can measure their performance beside."

She and Jessica exchange exasperated, understanding looks. "It's hard to be patient with clients like that."

"That's why I don't do private readings," Jessica says with a shake of her head. "I tried it, five years ago, for a little while, and I found I couldn't deal with it, especially when the client was someone I knew and liked. It made things much too difficult."

Larry looks up, regarding both Camille and Jessica with genuine curiosity. "What did you encounter that made you so uneasy? Was it just the request for rules and regulations, or was there something more? You're willing to deal with straightening out such questions here—why are private readings different?" Neither woman answers at once. Finally Camille shakes her head. "It could be because when you're doing channeling one on one, the experience is more intense. That's an oversimplification, but it's a factor."

"That's part of it," Jessica concurs. "But I think having to concentrate on that one Fragment and the mass of information that is usually required in a private reading takes more out of you, and a lot of it is . . . oh, routine research, I guess you'd call it. The drain on me, and on Milly, too, for that matter, is pretty hard to deal with."

Alex cocks his head to the side. "I have clients in my practice who always seem to take more out of me than others, and they aren't necessarily the ones with the most severe problems or complex relationships. They're the most . . . needy. They demand a high level of energy."

"Yes, I know that feeling," Camille says at once. "They attach invisible suckers to you and just slurp away." Her pretty, mobile features pucker with distaste, then relax again. "We're getting a little far afield. What are your questions, Jessica?"

Now Jessica grins. "I love this. My turn." She opens a small memo pad and glances over her notes. "I'd like some information on my Task Companion."

"Can Milly get names?" Kim asks, startled.

"No," Camille answers, "but just like Jessica, I can get Overleaves, and some general information. From that, Jessica can start to get her information together and possibly identify the Fragment, if she wants to do it. Everyone, please, remember I need quiet to do this." She bends her head over her large pad of paper and after a moment begins to write. Emily gets up and goes to the kitchen to make a pot of tea. Alex begins to organize his notes. The rest sit patiently and wait for what Camille is writing.

"Okay," she says when she is done. "Here it is."

This Fragment is a first Level Old Warrior in the Passion Mode with a Goal of Dominance, a Pragmatist in the Emotional part of Intellectual Center with a Chief Feature of Arrogance. As you are aware, the Overleaves are complementary. This Fragment is currently thirty- three years old, living and working in Paris, although he is not French. He is involved in the public performance of Modern music. He is the assistant head of his organization. You have had twenty-one direct past associations, but, of course, you have always done the complement of the other's work. The Warrior is cardinal, and you, Jessica, are ordinal in this pairing.

Jessica listens to this thoughtfully. "My public relations firm has had some dealing with French companies. It might be a place to start." She takes the sheet of paper Camille hands her, reading it over before putting it in a large leather folder that lies on the rug beside her rocking chair.

"Do you think you'll follow it up?" Larry asks. "Do you want to?" He leans forward to ask, giving Jessica his full attention.

"I don't know yet. It's something to think about. If the opportunity presents itself, then yes. I do travel to Europe on business occasionally. There may be a way to check around. But then there's always the question of what to say. 'Oh, gee,'" she goes on in an assumed, girlish voice, "'this medium told me that I should meet you because we're Task Companions. I know you don't know what that means, but we're that, anyway,' and then watch him turn green."

"Well, there's no harm in meeting him, if it's possible to identify him. You can always talk about work," Lizzy suggests. "I've seen my TC, but never met him. And the funny thing is, when I did go to hear him lecture, I really knew what he was talking about, and that isn't wishful thinking. When I heard him, I didn't know he was my TC, although I had my TC's Overleaves and knew something of what he did, as Jessica does about hers now. It just struck me that I might learn something from this man that would give me a better handle on what it was my TC's doing. And then, listening to him, I decided that what he was saying made perfect sense, which is what got me to wondering if perhaps the man I was listening to was, in fact, my TC, and not just an expert in the same field. The next session, I asked, and got one of those infuriating of courses that Michael is so fond of."

"Have you been in contact with the man at all?" Larry wants to know.

"No," Lizzy says. "I thought about sending him a thank-you note, but couldn't think of any sensible way to phrase what I had to say, so in the end, I didn't send it. Maybe I should have."

"There is no should," Jessica reminds her wistfully. "It's times like these that I wish Michael would just give a hint or two, but I know that he won't, and that I don't really want him to, in any case. I have to decide what I want to do, and how to do it, if it looks as if we can make some sort of contact."

"Do you want to ask more about that?" Camille prompts gently.

"I do, but not today. I have to think a little first. Let me get out another question, okay?"

"Whatever you want," Camille says, making herself more comfortable in her chair.

"I'd like to know about my life before last. I have the impression that it was spent . . . away from home. My last life had a period of self-imposed exile, I know, but the one before is the one I'm curious about. Will Michael comment on it, please?"

In the life before the immediate past one, the Fragment who is now Jessica was born in what was then Hungary, the third child of a family of lower-middle-class cabinetmakers. At an early age this Fragment became dissatisfied with her lot and determined to improve it by the only means available to her. She ran away to Prague and then to Vienna, where she made her living as a prostitute. She was pragmatic about her life, and sensible with money, and was able to purchase an inn when her most active business life was over. She had a great fondness for music, and often gave free room and board to musicians visiting her tavern. She married her cook at the age of thirty-one and died of cholera at forty-two. She had no children, but she tended a niece and two nephews, paying for schooling through the approximate equivalent of high school. Although her parents and siblings never approved of her way of life, they were aware that her monetary success made her more acceptable than any of the rest of them, and strove to be "sensible" about her, by which they were able to convince themselves that it was proper to accept her money. As you are aware, Jessica, in your next life, the immediate past life, you were a musician, fulfilling a dream of the life before that, although not quite as she envisioned it. We would wish to point out that often when Scholars are female, they seek out either the cloister or the brothel, since those are two of the few areas where women have been allowed, albeit on a limited scale, to study. As we have remarked before, Scholars and Kings are most adverse to being women; Warriors are not fond of it, but it does provide them with the needed challenge. Priests, Sages, Artisans and Slaves enjoy their female lives and often prefer them to the male ones.

"Well, that sounds like quite a life," Jessica says after she reads what Camille hands her. "At least I didn't do anything too dreadful."

"What would strike you as dreadful?" Emily asks, frowning a little.

"Oh, being one of the ringleaders of the French Revolution, I suppose. They were so competitive and sent so many people to their deaths. Being a slaver would be another horrible thing to do. I've probably done that, I think, because I have such a sense of repugnance about it."

"Michael has something more to say to you about that," Camille tells Jessica. "Please, everyone; quiet."

In the early part of the eighteenth century, the Fragment who is now Jessica was of mixed Turkish-British descent, born in Turkey, and apprenticed to a slaver at the age of nine. He rose to be the first officer of this captain and made a small fortune in the slave trade before being murdered by Moroccan business rivals at the age of thirty-eight. The revulsion that you experience now, Jessica, at the notion of slaving is the result of the karmic ribbons you have had to burn as a result of that life. We would say that the lessons have been well-learned. Let us say to all here gathered that such strong reactions to fear-driven activities is often the result of paying debts incurred by such actions in past lives. Those who have been slavers will have, as Jessica has, a profound aversion to slavery in all forms. Those who have been assassins will be repulsed by all forms of murder. Those who have been party to terrorist organizations, whether they be cloaked in political or religious or dynastic trappings, will be apt to loathe all forms of oppression and terrorism.

"Sounds delightful," Jessica says, tossing her head, a bit of color in her face. "It makes being in public relations seem positively tame and sedate by comparison."

"Well, you know that you've also made instruments, been a farmer and blacksmith, written poetry, been a beer-making monk, raised poultry, served as a scribe, been a merchant several times, been a weaver, managed a small bailey, and trained early gunnery men," Lizzy points out, checking through her notebooks. "It stands to reason that you muddied the waters once in a while."

"And that's not all of them," Jessica says, shaking her head. "Well, undoubtedly I learned something from it all." She turns to Camille. "Thanks. One of these days I'd like to do a private session with you and get a full overview of that life. Meaning the life of the prostitute-turned-innkeeper."

"Fine. We'll set up a time in the near future," she promises. "Give me a call in a couple of days, when I've found out what I've got on at work. We're getting in a new computer at the brokerage," Camille explains to the group, "and it's taking up all kinds of extra time. No one knows how to use the blasted thing."

"What fun," Henry says. "Luckily we haven't had that dropped on us yet. It's undoubtedly coming, but with a little planning, we can avoid some of the worst things about transitions." Jessica runs her hand through her hair. "Well, how about round two?"

"Hey! What about me?" Emily protests, sitting up straight on the piano bench. "I haven't got my phone-in questions yet."

"Oh, God," Jessica says, chagrined. "I'm sorry, Emily. I didn't realize . . ."

She laughs. "Serves me right for sitting out of your line of sight. I have a couple of questions from Sally Rogers and I promised her I'd ask them for her."

"You told me on the phone," Jessica remembers. "I know I said to bring them."

"How is Sally?" Alex asks. "I miss having her around."

"She and Ed are both fine. She's got on at the local college and is working with one of the foreign affairs professors on a book about former Peace Corps members. She spent two years in South America in the mid-sixties with the Peace Corps, and she said it's been great talking with other former Corps members. Ed's taken over the practice of a retiring surgeon and they're quite pleased with the way things are working out."

"You'd like Sally," Camille says to Henry and Kim. "She and Ed were in the group for about two years, and then business took them to Arizona. They get back here at holidays sometimes, and then we all get together again. She's a Scholar, he's a Warrior, and they're Task Companions."

"She's a very lively Scholar," Larry puts in. "You'd almost think she was a Sage when she gets going." He winks at Camille.

"I resent that," Lizzy declares. "Just because Sally and I holler and slap each other on the back is no reason to say we're being Sagey."

"It sure isn't very Scholarly," Camille says, picking up Larry's cue.

Kim looks up. "I wonder what it's like being married to your Task Companion?"

"According to them, it's great," Jessica says. "And they get an awful lot done between the two of them."

MORE MESSAGES FROM MICHAEL 53

"She's got tremendous enthusiasm. Craig was the one who first brought Ed into the group, but Sally really got into it, much more than Ed has done, and she keeps in close contact with me. Ed has the same problems Craig does: the job has so many unexpected demands that it's hard to find the time to get to sessions."

"So what's her questions?" Jessica asks. "First, she wants to know if Michael has any suggestions about how she might conduct these interviews in order to get the most out of them. She's trying to find out about what the Peace Corps volunteers expected, what they got, and what influence the experiences have had on their lives subsequently."

"That's a pretty comprehensive order," Alex remarks. "I'm interested in the answer, too. It might give me a few pointers for my more difficult clients."

We would think that a careful preparation of questions, with various phrasings would be a good place to begin. By this, we mean that in order to get the desired information, the Fragment who is now Sally would do well to keep in mind that the responses will be likely to reflect a variety of reactions. Rather than expect the same questions to bring forth a spectrum of answers, let us suggest that a variety of questions might achieve more. For example, if the subject being interviewed is doubtful or hostile, a line of questioning that would reveal the source of the hostility is apt to tell more than trying to break through the hostility with standard questions. If the subject is nostalgic, then a more evocative set of questions can be used to discover why the subject is nostalgic, and for what aspect of the experience. If the subject is dubious or suspicious, then the questions should be geared to deal with this, and not so cut and dried that the subject "clams up" entirely. Incidentally, we would think that participating in this project will provide the Fragment who is now Sally useful insights of her own on that particular episode in her life, and allow her to gain more perspective than she has had in the past.

"Great. She'll love this," Emily exclaims. "She told me she's been stumped by the problem and wants to find out what the trouble is. Her other question is really for Ed. He's interviewing four possible receptionists for his office, and he'd like to get the Overleaves so that he'll have some idea of what he's dealing with. The first name is Anne Caruthers; she's about thirty."

This is a first Level Mature King in the Caution Mode with a Goal of Acceptance, a Skeptic in the Moving part of Emotional Center with a Chief Feature of Stubbornness.

"What's the next name?" Jessica asks.

"Patrick Jennings. He's probably twenty-five or -six."

This is a mid-Cycle Young Slave in the Observation Mode with a Goal of Growth, a Pragmatist in the Intellectual part of Emotional Center with a Chief Feature of subdued Impatience.

"And the third?"

"Elaine White. She's early forties."

This is a fourth Level Mature Artisan in the Observation Mode with a Goal of Submission, a Realist in the Intellectual part of Moving Center with a Chief Feature of Greed fixated on accomplishment.

"Ho-boy," Emily says. "The last is Maria Fisher. Sally says that she's the youngest applicant, around twenty-two, just out of college."

This is a fifth Level Young Scholar in the Observation Mode with a Goal of Rejection, a Stoic in the Emotional part of Intellectual Center with an emerging Chief Feature of Self-Deprecation.

"Poor kid," Camille says sympathetically.

"I know Ed will find this useful. Sally said that he liked Anne and Maria better than the other two, but he wanted to check out his impressions with Michael."

"What did they do about the car?" Lizzy asks.

"What about the car?" Larry inquires.

"Oh, session before last Sally had a phone-in about getting a new car. They were having nothing but trouble with their old one and they wanted to get some suggestions from Michael before buying anything new." Lizzy grins.

"Using Michael to find a car?" Henry blinks, shocked.

"Actually, they did what Michael suggested, and they're very pleased with their purchase," Emily says in a tone that is almost apologetic.

"Here," Lizzy adds, looking through her notebook. "I have Michael's comments right here. I'll read them to you."

First we would recommend that you assess what has gone wrong with your present automobile, and then decide what is needed in its replacement. Then we would think that a serious talk with a competent and trusted mechanic at a repair shop within your city would be the best person to consult to determine which sorts of automobiles of the sort desired do best in the altitude and climate conditions currently encountered. It would be worthwhile to indicate the types of use you anticipate for your automobile, and the range of activities to be undertaken with it. The mechanic would also be a good person to consult in terms of which dealer or salespersons might be expected to offer the best value for your investment. Let us caution you that the more specific you can be, the more satisfied you are apt to be with your final purchase.

"That's good advice no matter what the climate is," Henry remarks. "But I just can't get over their asking Michael about buying a car."

"Why not? People have asked Michael about stranger things," Jessica points out. "After all, Dave Swan always checks out paintings and artifacts with Michael, and Howard Littlecote had all those questions about the dig he was going on, and a raft more when he got back. He's in Saudi Arabia just now, checking out what appears to be an old city with a necropolis attached to it. I know we're going to be inundated with questions about that when he gets back."

"Okay," Henry says dubiously. "Maybe I'll ask Michael next time I need to buy a pair of skis."

"If you want to, go ahead," Jessica offers in her unruffled way. "Now we can start round two. John?"

"Oh, good. My wife and I are engaged in a business venture that we're undertaking with another couple. I got their Overleaves some time ago. She's a Mature Warrior and he's a Young Slave. They're trying to change the time frame we discussed, and that worries me because we're just getting started, and already I feel that it's changed directions in ways . . . I don't really understand. Would Michael please give me a comment on this, and let me have some insight on what's been happening?"

"Do you want to know about any Agreements or other factors?" Jessica asks as she places the planchette on the board.

"If they're going on, I want to know about them." John's expression is a little grim as he speaks, but he does not appear to be anxious.

The Fragment who is now Louise has a facilitating Agreement with the Fragment who is now Amanda. They have had many past associations, most especially as apprentice swordsmiths in China in what you would call the tenth century, and as long-haul carters in the fourteenth century, when they spent the greater part of twenty years in the drayage business together, taking merchants' goods back and forth between Italy and France. This professional association is the basis for the current Agreement, but yes, we would agree that there are misunderstandings that have developed and could lead to disappointment for all involved. As you will recall, the Fragment who is now Louise is an Artisan, and the Fragment who is now Amanda is a Warrior. There are some basic differences in perceptions that have brought about the misunderstandings. It would be of benefit here if all parties would be willing to discuss what they perceive as being the purpose and "thrust" of the venture as well as what level of involvement they intend to have in the work. It might also be helpful if each of you would consider how long and to what degree you expect to devote to this project. In terms of achieving the most satisfactory results, these questions would do well to be addressed before much time passes. The longer the misunderstandings continue, the more complex the resolution of them is apt to be. If you wish, you may choose to set the discussion going, or you may prefer to suggest it to the Fragment who is now Louise and let her approach it as she thinks best. We remind you that her method is likely to be significantly different than the way you would handle the negotiations. Neither is "right" or "wrong," merely a difference in perception and orientation of Essence and soul Level.

"In other words, don't interfere," John says.

We did not say that, nor did we intend to imply it. What action you take, if any, is your choice, as no action is your choice. If you decide to take action, the course of action you take is your choice, and what the others do or do not do about your action or lack of it is their choice.

"Ga-a-a-ah!" Camille bursts out as the comment is read back.

"I know; I know. Really, Michael, I do know that," John says, his brown eyes brightening with irritation. "I wasn't asking to be told what to do, and I didn't mean that you told me to do anything. I was only commenting on what seemed to be the most sensible thing to do for the time being." He leans back, glaring down at the page.

"Do I get another question?"

"Sure," Jessica says. "Why not?"

"All right. I'd like to know how much my Chief Feature is contributing to the problem and how I can recognize its influence at work. I'm not asking," he goes on very carefully, "for Michael to tell me what to do, and I don't expect to get orders. Okay? "

There are understanding smiles all around the room and Camille gives John a thumbs-up sign.

The Chief Feature here is, as you are aware, Impatience. We remind you that the positive pole is audacity, which impels you to undertake bold tasks, often very abruptly. The negative pole is intolerance, which is unforgiving when immediate results are not discerned. You, John, have put energy into this project and are determined to see it thrive at once. You have a fear that if you do not succeed in the venture by the first of next week, you will automatically have failed completely and irredeemably.

John smiles sheepishly as Michael continues.

Let us point out that your involvement in the project at hand is tangential at best, and that your desire to be pivotal to its success reveals the manipulations of your Impatience as much as the more obvious manifestations. You have the fear of missing something and therefore "need" to be part of anything that has gained a certain level of attention. This is often self-defeating, for it not only causes you more anxiety than necessary, it creates ambivalence in others because of your insistence in being part of the project. And often you lose interest before the project has been completed, which is not untypical of impatience, and causes you to move on to another project before the first is finished, leaving others with complex reactions, to put it most mildly. You might wish to ask the Fragment who is now Louise if she actually prefers your participation, and at what level she would like it to be before you undertake to do more. Chief Feature drives Fragments not only to leap to conclusions, but to premises as well, which, as you are all aware, is far more hazardous.

"I got my wrists slapped," John says ruefully as the answer is read back. "It's not that I don't think it was warranted, but, well, it's not easy to have it done in front of everyone."

"No one likes it," Jessica agrees. "Be glad you don't have Arrogance. That is really the pits when criticized."

"Still," Larry says as he goes over the answer, putting in the words and letters he had missed during the dictation, "it helps to have the Chief Feature identified, doesn't it? It has so many disguises that it's easy to think it's not functioning when it really has its hooks in you."

"Yeah," Lizzy agrees. "I hate it when Michael tells me the Chief Feature is screwing up again, but I'd rather know than not know, sort of like having a bad disease—I'd rather know it so I could treat it than not know and possibly make things worse."

"I like that analogy," Kim says, looking up at Lizzy. "That's a good way to look at it, I think."

"So long as you don't depersonalize it," Jessica warns. "Remember, it's part of you."

"That's why I think it's a disease, something inside me, but not really part of the original design. It warps and distorts things, and limits my activities, the way a chronic disease would, like a bad case of arthritis of the psyche." Lizzy reaches forward for the coffee, and makes a face. "I'm going to pour this out and make some fresh; it's got cold."

"That's fine with me," Jessica says. "You know where everything is."

"How many of you want more coffee?" Lizzy asks, pausing to count hands. "Five? All right, I'll make ten cups. That should last us through the cookies."

"Thanks," Jessica calls to Lizzy, who has gone around the corner through the dining room and into the kitchen, with Trudi following after, whining hopefully.

"It's come back to you, Alex," Jessica says, addressing him with a smile.

He adjusts his glasses on his nose. "I've got a couple questions that might be pretty big. You're not getting too tired for this, are you?"

"No, and your Self-Deprecation is showing again," she chides him gently. "I like the big questions. They're tiring, but they're also stimulating. I enjoy them, the same way I enjoy swimming laps."

He nods, accepting this without too many reservations. "In my work, I see a lot of relational problems that develop between couples. It seems to me that there are some basic problems that perpetuate the relationship of men and women. In the past, Michael has recommended various reading material and studies on the problems that develop between men and women, but I'd like it if he'd—they'd—elaborate a little more; or a lot more." Jessica breaths out slowly.

"I'll try, Alex, but it might be hard for me to get. I've got a vested interest in the subject as much as you do."

"If you'd rather not—" Alex begins.

"I'm just warning you that I might block. I'd like to know the answers as much as you would." She glances at Camille. "Do you think you can do any of this?"

"Maybe. If you run into trouble, I'll give it a try. But I'm curious about the answer, too."

Camille straightens in her chair. "I've got a hunch we'd all better pay close attention."

"We all want to know the answer," Larry says, his words echoed by the expressions on the faces in the room.

We would wish to commend you, Alexander, for reaching this point in your explorations, for it is often not possible to grow beyond a problem until the roots of the problem are perceived—please note we do not say understood. What we perceive as the most damaging aspect of the "war between the sexes" is that the unadmitted conflicts often make true intimacy not only threatening to both parties but often impossible. The brutalizing of such relationships is one of the symptoms of this problem. Let us point out that where true intimacy exists, brutalizing is simply not possible, and of course brutalization can take many forms, not all of them as obvious as gross physical abuse. Be aware that Fragments do not brutalize those with whom true intimacy has been achieved. While we do not dismiss or underestimate the very real suffering that has been caused as a result of open and covert brutalization and resentments, we would prefer not to dwell on past injuries, but would wish to see a move toward the healing of wounds that have been inflicted by both sides of the problem. In this case, Sages, by their very Essence nature, are able to express the rewards of trust and intimacy that could result from such actions. It is important to demonstrate to most males and females that the threats they perceive in the "opposite" sex need not be perpetuated and that there can be rewards should they choose to consider taking a chance at bridging the gap and work toward a genuine interrelationship with their partners.

The nature of the conflicts between men and women are the subject of much writing and discussion at present and we would think that much of the writing, when it is not geared to entrench the current and unsatisfactory patterns, contains elements of worth which can be incorporated in many ways into the methods of reconciliation. The need for women especially to admit the need for healing and recovery is of special importance at this time, just as it is necessary for men to understand that the wounds the women perceive in themselves are valid and serious. The rate of sexual abuse of women at the current time should give you some estimate of the vast scope of the problem, yet the resistance of men in general to these statistics or the trivialization of the wounding experiences do much to prolong the current state of affairs. But perseverance is of value here, for when true intimacy is achieved, it is nothing less than Essence touching Essence and it is through this and this alone that the Fragments evolve, for that Essence Contact, with or without the physical counterpart, is what we mean by the fulfillment of love.

We have said many times that where there is great desire there is also great fear, and the unfortunate state of the relationship between the sexes points this up clearly for those who are willing to set aside their dreads long enough to examine the problem with care and an open mind. We would wish to remind all here gathered yet again that every one of you will lead many lives as males and as females, and with every sort of sexual identification: asexual, bisexual, homosexual, heterosexual, nonsexual, ambisexual, as well as those who undergo surgical sexual alterations. You will live these identifications either in harmony or disharmony with the society around you, and through these experiences, learn the lessons that the Physical Plane teaches. It is possible for Essence to do this because Essence is without sexuality or gender. Gender is a Truth of this World, not a Universal Truth. Those who refuse to see beyond the combinations of X and Y chromosomes are condemning themselves to much needless and tragic despair, which is not too strong a word for what so many Fragments experience in regard to the demands and stresses of their sex and sex roles, as well as gender in this and every other culture. We do not say this lightly, but with genuine love.

"It seems to me," Alex says once the answer has been read back and heard out in silence, "that Michael is right, and the most obvious problems in relationships stem from men, at least when the relationship is in certain kinds of difficulties. But also, I think that women make as many—for want of a better word—errors as men do, and often with as much damage to themselves as to their partners. Will Michael comment on this?"

Where hurt, and in this instance we speak of the continual wounding of women which is often unintentional and "enshrined" by the society, has been denied or its pain patronized, it is not unusual for anger, even rage to result, and then often be fiercely denied as part of the attempt to deny the seriousness of the wound as well as the continuing pain. As many of you are aware, this pattern usually begins early in childhood and is amplified and strengthened by what you call your educational system. Where this pattern continues, a need for vindication and/or revenge often results, the determination that since fulfillment and intimacy have been denied them and the resultant frustration and hurt either dismissed or ignored, a price will be exacted, to be paid in a number of ways, such as sexual manipulation, which can take the form of using sexual "payoffs" for certain advantages, or the production of children in the hope that they will not only offer succor but to serve as a goad and attention rivals for and to the male partner; the demand for material goods, especially those with obvious appeal or financial impact; a change in behavior to become "one of the boys" and therefore not a target; constant criticism of ambitions or accomplishments, often accompanied by unflattering comparisons with the partner's contemporaries; disinterest in the life of the partner, or in establishing a partnership with any single individual; compensatory demands for status advancement or power; and many other familiar patterns. Much of the requirements that females substitute for the "hopeless" accomplishment of true intimacy are geared to overcome some if not all of the societally enforced economic inferiority pressed upon them, as well as to convince themselves that their hurt is not "real" and that the intimacy and fulfillment they fear they cannot have does not truly exist. [*May, 2003:* So long as "God" is perceived as male, gender equality is likely to remain culturally impossible. That does not mean that "God" would be assigned female gender to "balance the book," but that no gender, or indeed, humanly modeled form for any deistic figure, would be the only way to bring out true cultural equality for both sexes, and for social acceptance of all manner of sexual orientation to be fully established.]

"I'm sorry, Alex. There's a lot more there, but I can't get much more. I'm really starting to block on this," Jessica apologizes as she moves her glass-covered board off her lap.

"God, Jessica," Alex says softly, visibly impressed by what Michael has told him. "This is so much more than I thought we'd be able to find out . . . I know that's my second question, but I'd love to be able to ask what, if anything, can be done about this mess."

Lizzy nods enthusiastically. "I'd be happy to ask," she volunteers. But Jessica shakes her head.

"Do you mind holding off on that? I'm doing a catch-up session next Wednesday night, and I'll see what I can get then. Camille and I are going to sit down for a couple of hours and go over unfinished business. I'll give you a call after work on Thursday and let you know what, if anything, we got."

Alex accepts this. "I imagine that channeling something this heavy really takes it out of you."

"In more ways than one," Jessica replies cryptically. There is a knock at the door and Trudi sets up a belated howling bark. "It's open!" Jessica calls out.

Two pair of feet are heard climbing the stairs, and then Brad Sturgis comes into the room, carrying a cello case, followed by Katherine Gerrard.

"Look who I found at Benjy's," he says without preamble. He is under thirty, born in Honolulu of mixed parentage, but a resident of the Bay Area for most of his life. His demeanor is reserved yet everyone in the room obviously likes him.

"I got four days off, so I took a chance and drove up," Katherine says to the group at large, then turns to Jessica, beaming at her. "I brought you some more of my transcripts. All this is the relational stuff you asked for."

"Great timing!" Lizzy cries out, waving to Katherine.

"See, that's what I like about Scholars," Jessica says with excusable pride. "They're so good at keeping their information going. Ever since Katherine got her home computer, she's been organizing all the material she has, and cross-referencing it. Last time she was up, I asked her to get the relational material together, and here it is."

"Can I have a copy of it?" Alex says. "You can add the answers we just got to your . . . collection, if you like."

"Sure; fine with me." Katherine looks around the room, realizes that all the chairs and sofa spaces are taken. She tosses her mane of salt-and-pepper hair and points toward the dining room. "Mind if I take one?"

"Go ahead," Jessica offers. "Make yourself at home. Where are you staying while you're up?"

"With Tracy. Give us a call and maybe we can arrange an evening to have dinner together." Her manner is matter-of-fact and she moves with purpose. As she drags a chair in from the dining room, she rummages in her huge purse for a copy of the relational material to give to Jessica as well as a second copy for Alex.

"Sorry to get here so late, but there was more traffic than I expected."

"Where do you live?" Kim asks. And adds, "We're the Ingvessons."

"Hi," Katherine says as if talking to old and comfortable friends. "I live in Malibu."

"And just drove four hundred miles on a lark?" Henry asks. "Well, I was going to come up tonight in any case, and since Eric's still on a shoot, there wasn't much keeping me home except the dog, and the neighbors said they'd feed him for today. So, here I am." She drops into the chair. "I'm sorry. I didn't mean to interrupt."

"If you'd got here ten minutes earlier, you'd have interrupted," Jessica says. "As it is, I'm glad for a short break." She looks over at Brad. "How was the rehearsal?"

He makes a weighing gesture with his left hand. "So-so. The Haydn sounded pretty sloppy." His voice is both soft and resonant.

"Have some coffee," Lizzy offers, rising to get two more mugs. "And there's plenty of cookies left. Kim brought them. They're fresh."

"Christ, don't tempt me," Katherine protests, placing a hand on her abdomen.

"Oh, go ahead," Emily prods. "We all need a little break after that last round of dictation."

"And I want a chance to look over this printout," Jessica adds, thumbing through the pages that Katherine has given her. "Everyone, have another cup of coffee or tea, or get a beer out of the 'fridge. We'll get back to work in a little while."

CHAPTER FOUR
Michael On Relationships

There is clearly no one basis for relationships between and among Fragments, and rarely is a single factor at work, although this is sometimes the case among very Young Souls or short-lived relationships. Tempting though it may be, dwelling on the source or "purpose" of a relationship often defeats the relationship by creating a barrier in the name of involvement. Some relationships are easily understood, others are more perplexing. We are willing to discuss all aspects of relationships as we perceive them with the caveat that we do not encourage or require any of you to share our views or our conclusions.

[*March, 1997:* While many factors contribute to relationships, many of the manners in which they are expressed are, of course, culturally conditioned. The manner in which a farmer in Argentina relates to his wife is noticeably different than such a relationship in Indonesia, or Newfoundland. Every cultural model is tied to the whole fabric of the group expressing that model. This is true for all manner of relationships, not just domestic ones. Friendships, business dealings, instructional relationships, even feuds and rivalries are structured by the culture in which they occur. For those engaging in cross-cultural relationships, more attention is "required" in order to compensate for the lack of commonality of social models. The more fluid and diverse a society, the less problematic cross-cultural relationships are apt to be, and the more monolithic the society, the more difficult cross-cultural relationships become.]

In almost all relationships, even the most brief, there is an element of body-type attraction or compatibility. In other words, your body is comfortable in the presence of the body of the other Fragment. Where this comfort is lacking, difficulties can arise due to simple physical ill-feeling. No matter how minor this may appear, it is hardly insignificant. Let us give you an example: a man is small and very slight. He is required to interview another man who is both very tall and heavily built. It is not likely that either Fragment will be comfortable in this situation, no matter how many other factors of a positive nature are present because there is so little physical commonality. This is one of the lessons of the Physical Plane, and, of course, the Physical Plane is literally the only place this lesson can be learned, since it is the only place where Fragments are clothed in flesh.

Not surprisingly, body-type attraction can be and often is a large factor in sexual relationships, as well as in many simple friendships. It has been noted that the two Fragments in a couple appear to "look alike," and this is no accident. Some of the attraction comes from vanity, but much of it comes from body-type attraction, which enables other recognitions to occur more easily and more directly. We do not "disdain" this level of attraction and relationship, incidentally. Much worthwhile experience comes out of relationships which are based primarily on body-type attraction, and its rewards.

Tangentially, we will mention that most cultures promote admiration for certain body types, and those who possess the body types in the "current style" are more likely to be admired than those who do not. From our point of view, of course, no body type is more or less attractive than any other, and each has its merits, as well as its disadvantages. We do think that it is unfortunate that many Fragments come to regard themselves in terms of body type alone and devote energy and care to attempting to achieve whatever body type is the most adulated one. This is not Good Work, for it denies the lesson that the Fragment chose to learn when the body type was chosen. Incidentally, we remind you that the in utero behavior of the unborn child is a function of body type, not of Essence, since in almost all cases, Essence does not enter the body until birth has been completed and the first breath taken successfully. There are a few Baby Souls who enter the body as much as eight weeks before the actual birth, to experience gestation once the fetus has developed sufficiently to be capable of sustaining life outside of the body of the mother without additional support.

Relationships founded on shared Essence are quite common and can be seen from first life until the last. Fragments tend to seek those with similar views of the world as their own, which in turn brings about a sense of companionability that can be shared without being puzzled as to where the other Fragment is "coming from". This basis of relationship fares better, of course, when both Fragments have successfully completed the Fourth Internal Monad and have manifested the Essence and Overleaves in their lives. Relationships predicated on shared Essence often give tremendous opportunities for understanding the diversity of the Overleaves, so that each Fragment develops a greater sense of how Fragments function in the world. Let us add that since Fragments of the same Essence are often drawn to similar life work and/or professions, there is always a good chance that they will be able to spend time in the company of those sharing Essence Role, which can be beneficial on many levels. Relationships that are allowed to develop beyond standard social limits often remain "solid" throughout much of life.

[*June, 2000:* In regard to the proposed venture to the twenty-fifth year high school class reunion, we would have to say that, should you choose to attend, this may provide many opportunities for insight and for recognition and validation. The Fragments in question were seen last before the arrival of the Third Internal Monad, and by now, most of them have had an opportunity to undertake, or even complete and validate the Fourth Internal Monad. For those transitions alone, there is much to be discerned from reviewing old relationships from the current perspective. There are likely to be those who may be far more changed than some, and a few who abdicated Third Internal Monad and have hardly changed at all. Renewal of relationships under such circumstances may tend to be brief and "superficial" but that is not to say that there are no connections to be made. It is also possible that those you disliked in your youth you will find much more interesting and "acceptable" now, just as there may be those who will be inclined to show you more interest and amity than was ever the case in high school.]

Another interesting development in relationships emerges when Essence and soul Level are different, but the Overleaves are shared. For example, one Fragment is a first Level Old Scholar in the Observation Mode with a Goal of Growth, a Skeptic in the Emotional part of Intellectual Center with a Chief Feature of Stubbornness, and the other is a sixth Level Young Sage in the Observation Mode with a Goal of Growth, a Skeptic in the Emotional part of Intellectual Center with a Chief Feature of Stubbornness. Fragments with these similarities will see things very differently but will go at living very much the same way. This is not as unusual as you might think at first in the relationships where partnership is the Goal, either as business associates, as lovers, as collaborators, and other similar contacts. These relationships are generally considered "enlightening" by those experiencing them, for the focus of the Overleaves being identical enables the Fragments not only to identify with one another, but permits each of them to look inward, to perceive the focus of Essence, which is a valuable lesson that can add much to the transitions in the life. We would wish to say that these relationships also bring about what you would think of as tolerance, because of the shared methods of life which compensate for the diverse basic orientation.

Relationships between members of the same Cadre—that is, the group of seven Entities cast from the Tao at the same time—are not uncommon, but not necessarily very compelling, for the relationship might be regarded as in-laws or step-relatives, meaning that there is a tie, but it is somewhat removed from the stronger ones of Entity, Essence, Cadence and the two immutable "links" of Essence Twins and Task Companions, or the flexible association of Configuration members. It is not uncommon for members of the same Cadre to gravitate to one another on a fairly regular basis, and to sense a familiarity from the Cadre that makes up for many other obvious differences, such as difference of national origin, sex, age, occupation, social position, and all the other examples of the rule of maya that is the nemesis of life on the Physical Plane. Cadre ties may occur in all manner of ways, and last however long they last, and to whatever purpose. The negative side of this is that roughly seventy percent of all karmic ribbons occur between members of the same Cadre. It should be apparent that those within the same Cadre with the same Role in Essence and/or the same Overleaves would have a stronger sense of fellowship than those who simply share the same Cadre casting. Certainly those Fragments have the opportunity to achieve recognition on many levels, and to validate their impressions. The more Fragments share, the more they are capable of freeing themselves from the rule of maya and the negative poles of their Overleaves. That is not to say such actions are required, for even such matters as recognition are chosen, and can be denied if the Fragment does not wish to have such contacts impinge upon it. Certainly there are Overleaves which tend to make this more likely than others, although we must point out that no Overleaves, no matter how negative they may appear, are designed to stop recognition altogether. Recognition is a crucial function of Essence, and Essence works through the positive poles of the Overleaves. We emphasize this, for it is basic to what we would wish to convey to you.

Members of the same Entity have a stronger relationship, not unlike cousins. Just as in families, Entity members do not always and automatically "like" each other, and in some cases where past experience or abrading Overleaves are present, there can be an active dislike present, even though the Entity bond is present. Often Entity members will spend much time "in the same class," in bringing their lessons to bear. There can be much worthwhile growth when members of the same Entity set out to accomplish their Life Tasks together, for that brings the weight of their tie to increase the impetus.

As we have said before, Task Companions are six times out of seven part of the same Entity, and that in large part reflects the nature of the Entity, which is a similarity of underlying purpose that transcends the demands of the Physical Plane. In the Baby and Young Cycles, members of the same Entity are often deliberately avoided so that nothing will interfere in the work in the world, which is part of the lesson of the Young Cycle, and to a lesser degree, the Baby Cycle.

Young Souls are eager to expand and enlarge their area of influence, and this requires that they move outside the influence of their Entity into the operation of the Cadre, or other Cadres, in order to gain the experience that is needed. When this expansion is done in the company of those of the same Entity, it is for specific reasons, and there are lessons to be learned for all involved. It is in the late Baby and early Young Cycles that Fragments make the Agreements that result in their Configurations, which do not always consist of members of the same Entity or Essence, but in almost all cases, members of the same Cadre. Members of the same Configuration are joined by mutual consent to work in the world, that is, within the limits of the Physical Plane. While it does not often occur that all members are present on the Physical Plane in all the continuing lives after the Configuration has been formed, there is still a tie to the Astral Fragments of the Configuration and that carries over, adding to the effectiveness of the Configuration, should the members of it on the Physical Plane choose to focus on the work of the Configuration.

It is not too rare to have either Essence Twins or Task Companions functioning in the same Configuration, but we would have to say that it is hardly the rule, and being in a Configuration does not assure you that you have found either the Task Companion or the Essence Twin. The tie of the Configuration is a compelling one, but without the impact of karma, or the compactness of a Monad to "drive" it. This is not to say that members of the same Configuration do not have karmic ribbons with one another, or that they never experience Monads together. Certainly it would be unusual to have so close an association and not have to take on such lessons brought to bear at one time or another. We do not mean to imply that members of the same Configuration must of necessity work together in the same place on the same thing for recognition and progress to be made.

We are aware of one triad where two of the members of the triad have the same occupation, but live thousands of miles apart and have never met. The third member of the triad is involved with both the others in a business capacity, and it is through this Mature Scholar that the lessons are brought to bear, although there is little recognition on the conscious level of any of these three Fragments. All are aware that their work has been going "better" since the point where all three became linked, but only one has a deep sense of the reason. One of the others, when it was suggested that there might be "arcane" reasons for this, was skeptical in the extreme and has since refused to discuss it. This has in no way kept the work from being done, and the lessons brought to bear.

Often the work of the Configuration is different than the Life Task of the individual Fragments making up the Configuration, but it is most often complimentary to the Life Task. Those whose Life Tasks or karmic or Monadal demands incline them toward other choices often prefer to distance themselves from the Configuration. There is nothing "wrong" in this, for the work will be done in its own time. By distancing we mean putting some form of distance between Fragments, such as geographical, political, sexual, religious, or age gaps that are not easily bridged. It may be that while on the Physical Plane some aspect of the distanced Fragment's Life Plan goes awry and completion of the karmic debt or Monad is not possible. At such a time it is not uncommon for the distanced Fragment to set out to close the gap in some manner. Of course, the individual Fragment is free to choose to work with its configuration or not to work with it, and abdication, while it can create difficulties in the life, is not "wrong," it is a matter of choice.

Members of the same Configuration are not necessarily of the same Essence, and the general rule is that there are at least two Essences in a Configuration, although there are a few that are limited to Fragments of a shared Essence. This can, upon occasion, make the tasks of the Configuration more arduous rather than less so, for the Fragments, by their very nature, will see the world from the same point of view, and therefore will have very similar strengths and weaknesses. Diversity in Essence creates more flexibility and provides a greater range of activity. Of course, we are not saying that any arrangement of Essences in a Configuration is "better" or "worse" but that each, by its nature and makeup will have a range of experience available to it, and that some will provide certain varieties of activities to its members, while others will tend toward other varieties of experience.

Members of the same Configuration, because the Configuration is an on-going Agreement, have the "pull" of an Agreement behind the action they undertake as well as the bond of shared past experience that will tend to strengthen as lives go on. However, it would be incorrect to say that therefore the relationship of the Configuration becomes more and more desirable, because this is not always the case. The nature of shared past experience can make a significant difference in the way the individual Fragments relate to one another. For example, if the members of a Configuration spent the life before last being hounded through the trenches of what you call the First World War, they might perceive that the experience, while compelling and valid, would not tend to awaken happy recollections, and for that reason, the members of the Configuration might choose to do their work at a distance for some time to come.

Again, there are no set formulae for how a Configuration must behave, or tasks it must do. There is no "must," for Configurations or for anything else. Even the relationship can be set aside and ignored for as long as the individual Fragment chooses to do so. Of course, it is likely that the

Fragment will eventually choose Overleaves that would make cooperation easier and more likely, but whether or not such a choice is made, be assured that the lessons are brought to bear, with or without the Configuration to lend a hand, and that the members of the Configuration, no matter what the personalities of each individual Fragment may think of the other members, do strive to progress along the same path, or very similar paths. The relationship between those with Agreement can be anything from the most trivial to profound lifelong contact. There are many reasons for this, not the least of which comes from whatever the nature of the Agreement is. Certain Agreements are fulfilled in a matter of minutes with almost no obvious involvement, liking, or even interest.

Other Agreements are completed in various "till death do us part" contexts. These Agreements can be handled on a friendly and/or intimate basis, [*October, 1996*: Duration is not the test for any experience in the Physical or any other Plane, it is the quality of the contact and the recognition and validation which follows. That is one of the many reasons why those Fragments who assume even the most fleeting connection is a sign of past-lives replete with intensely passionate relationships are inclined not to perceive, let alone recognize and validate, actual past-lives' connections.] and there are others that are no more significant than giving a stranger directions to the nearest post office. One Scholar in our little group, in fact, fulfilled a facilitating Agreement by just such an encounter, and thought so little about it that it was never asked about in a session. There are Agreements that involve undertaking ventures of some sort together, but this can be as insignificant as arranging to sponsor a girl scout troop for a year, or it can be as major as running an international corporation. The Mature Scholar who was William Shakespeare had such an Agreement with the Young Sage who was Richard Burbage. Often those in politics use such Agreements to further their ambitions and/ or their causes and/or their parties. Other Agreements can have to do with mutual or one-way support, and can be expressed in such ways as marriage, providing necessary physical or emotional therapy, or being available for lunch on short notice, among many, many variations. The duration of the Agreement is not as crucial from our point of view as the quality and understanding of the sequence the Agreement supports. The greater the contact during the Agreement sequence, the more progress is made. Again, it is a matter of choice. Not all Fragments desire to have such complex and demanding ways of completing an Agreement as others require. Abdication of an Agreement is not the major occurrence that abdication of a Monad or karma can be, but that does not mean that it is not disappointing or traumatic to the personality experiencing the abdication, or to the one who abdicates. Quite often irritation and hostility mark abdications of Agreements, and when the relationship has been a close one, it is not unusual for the Fragments to distance themselves for a time until the disappointment has faded.

In Monadal relationships, there is always a greater sense of "investment," and it is not unusual for a Monad to take a considerable portion of a life to complete. Where Monads are in force, the sense of being drawn together is very strong, and, we hasten to add, not always pleasant, although there is no reason for it not to be, even if the means of accomplishing the Monad is difficult or demanding, or simply exhausting.

Monads, if they are to be successfully completed, usually require a higher level of concentration than less compelling relationships, and the Fragments caught up in the Monad, especially the more common reciprocal variety, are inclined to set aside other aspects in the life in order to complete the Monad without interference. That is not to say that Monads are of necessity obsessive, and in fact, it is more effective for all concerned if the Fragments can avoid obsessive feelings while transiting the Monad. There are times when obsession would appear to be the only way to accomplish the Monad, but that is more the influence of fear and the rule of maya than of Essence. Fragments caught up in a Monad often show great preoccupation with one another, which is not surprising, and if there are other factors contributing to the bond, such as the same Essence, Cadre or Entity ties or shared Overleaves, to say nothing of body-type attraction, then the Monad can become more imperative because of the contributing factors that enhance the Monad.

Tandem Monads, while rarer, are often less engrossing to the Fragments going through them, although it is not unusual for such Fragments to spend significant periods of time together to gain understanding and perspective on what they are experiencing. This is not always easily understood by others, and it can lead to difficulties for such Fragments as the friends and living partners of the Monadal Fragments, because much of what is seen by others appears to be more "involved" than it generally is. That is not to say that Fragments undergoing tandem Monads do not become more complexly involved with each other, for often that provides ease in communication as well as a "united front," which is socially convenient. Nevertheless, the thrust of such tandem Monads can be likened to horses in harness, who do not necessarily share the same stall when the journey is over. Tandem Monads tend to require emotional generosity and where this is not present, there are apt to be impediments to the successful transiting of the Monad. If Monads of this sort are carried out with Fragments of strong links such as Essence Twins or Task Companions or, for that matter, members of the same Cadence, then a friendship for life will tend to be the result if the Monad is completed, and the Fragments are likely to rely upon each other and to trust each other on levels that are not often experienced on the Physical Plane.

Karmic relationships are often noted for their difficulties. Consider how the relationship is formed in the first place: one Fragment removes the choice of another, often in very unpleasant ways. Each then realizes on some levels that what has drawn them together is not pleasant, and that leaves its mark on all dealings that the Fragments have while the ribbon is being burned. Often Fragments burning karma feel "driven" or "helpless" about the relationship which has built up with another Fragment whom the other regards with ambivalence. Often these relationships are baffling not only to those involved in them, but to others on the outside, as it were, looking at the predicament that the karmic Fragments are in. Because karma never results from minor intrusions, it is not possible to dismiss it in a minor way.

We will give you some examples, both of karmic ribbons successfully burned and of attempts at burning karma that "compounded the felony," or added to the debt. Yes, it is quite possible for a Fragment, in the attempt to be rid of karma, to create more. This is where the Chief Feature and fear are apt to be their most seductive and thereby manage to distort the lessons of the karmic tie. We do not mean this as a dire warning, but to encourage you to keep your vision as clear as you are able to when dealing with these compelling phases of growth.

For our first example, we will begin with a Mature Priest who was what you would call insane, and because of that became a murderer, trying to eradicate heretics from his district. Of course, he owed killing karma to all of his victims, which meant that he had over sixty Fragments to pay over the next several lives. In one especially successful life, which ended less than a decade ago, he became a surgeon and specialized in critically ill infants, especially those born with birth defects of considerable severity. Four of the victims of this crazed Priest were able to burn the ribbons with him through his skill which guaranteed them a physically healthy and "normal" life which would not have been possible otherwise. It is interesting to note that all four karmic ribbons were burned with infants who were treated without pay, as part of the surgeon's "pro bono" work. We would have to say that this particular life did much to advance the Priest and rid the four Fragments he saved of the burden of their ribbons with him.

This next attempt to burn karma was partially successful, but did not cancel the debt entirely. A Young Slave, hampered by poverty and pressured by her relatives, sold her ten-year-old daughter to a brothel in southern China in the eighteenth century. The daughter did not have a long life and most of it was spent in misery. This, of course, created a ribbon between them. Two lifetimes later, the Fragments met again, this time as master and apprentice. The master did not demand the usual apprentice's fee for training the young man, but when the training was complete, the master insisted that the apprentice stay on in his business rather than going to establish his own, as compensation for the free training. The apprentice spent almost fifteen years working for very little money and not free of the master who trained him. Some of the karma was discharged, but for the most part, the attempt to burn the ribbon failed because the one who owed the debt put conditions on the repayment.

The third example we offer has to do with an attempt to repay karma that ended in adding to the debt. A Fragment who was in that life a first Level Mature King stood accused of treason, which he had not, in fact, committed. He had the opportunity to put the blame on another and equally innocent Fragment, a Young Scholar. As a result, the young Scholar was tortured and executed in the place of the Mature King, who, while innocent of treason, was certainly creating a karmic debt for himself. Three lives later, these two Fragments met again, this time as Brothers in the same Order. It was the intention of the Mature King to aid the Scholar in advancing in the order and rise to the position of abbot, to which end he began to educate the Scholar in several areas of Church lore. When the Scholar began to extend his reading into what were considered heretical texts, the King grew frightened and denounced his student, with the result that the Scholar spent the next eight years of his life immured in a very small cell in the walls of the monastery and eventually died of a combination of malnutrition and hypothermia. We should wish to add that the two ribbons have not yet been burned.

Karmic relationships are both demanding and engrossing, which is part of the nature of karma. The relationship of philanthropic karma ribbons, while equally engrossing, is rarely unpleasant, and often leads to the most pleasurable of friendships. We will discuss one such exchange. A Mature Sage who was the major domo in a large noble household in Prussia in the eighteenth century discovered that one of the footmen had an unusual gift for languages. He encouraged this Mature Warrior to study, and then took most of his life's savings to pay for a university education for this Mature Warrior, with the result that the Mature Warrior eventually rose as high in the government as his common birth would allow. The Mature Sage had no pre-arranged reason to do this for the Mature Warrior—not karma, not Monadal, not Agreement, not Cadence, or Entity ties, not Essence Twin or Task Companion bonds, just the "goodness of his heart." The education the Mature Warrior received, and the resultant broadening of life choices, would not have been possible without the wholehearted generosity of the Mature Sage, who had no reason but, as we have said, the "goodness of his heart" to provide the gift. Two lives later, it was possible for the

Mature Warrior to return the favor to the now Old Sage by hiring the halls, musicians and dancers needed to perform the ballets the now Old Sage had composed but had no means to bring to the attention of the public, for he came from a very poor household and had studied music with his uncle who was a prompter at the local opera house. The motivation of the Mature Warrior was disinterested, in that he had nothing but satisfaction to gain from his investment, while the Sage had a career he would not have been able to get for himself. In both instances, the two Fragments regarded each other with untrammeled affection. This is one of the most obvious differences between the relationship when the karma is philanthropic—the Fragments involved enjoy it.

The Cadence bond is a very close one, as it is the closest bond that exists outside of Essence Twin and Task Companion. Unlike the Essence Twin and Task Companion links, however, the Cadence bond often continues through a very high percentage of lives. There are members of the same Cadence who have known each other in every life, although it is not common to be that close so often. Members of the same Cadence are like brothers and sisters, and the sense of "family" is very strong with them. In the Mature and Old Cycles, Cadence members are often the best of friends or lovers, and the long familiarity lends a tolerance to the relationship that is not possible in any other link.

Cadence members often have the same or very similar Overleaves. One Cadence of Old Warriors known to our little group illustrates this very well. Of the seven, four are currently on the Physical Plane: one, three, six, and seven. The youngest Fragment is second Level Old, there is one third Level Old and two fourth Level Old. Three are in the Observation Mode, one is in Passion. Two have Goals of Dominance, two have Goals of Growth, all four are Idealists, two are in the Emotional part of Intellectual Center, two are Moving part of Intellectual Center and all four have Chief Features of Arrogance, two have secondary Chief Features of Martyrdom—"natural" to Warriors—one has Stubbornness, and one has "muted" Impatience. The Physical Plane age-spread is twenty-five years, although Fragments six and seven are two months apart in age. The friendship of the two Fragments who have actually met is Warrior-intense and extremely comfortable.

Members of the same Cadence often behave as if they were raised in the same family, although this is very rarely the case. We would not be overstating the case to say that Cadence members offer one another the ultimate "port in a storm". As we have said, Task Companions are six times out of seven in the same Entity and are never—and we emphasize this—never the same Role in Essence. Task Companions, we remind you, do the complement of each other's work, with or without ever meeting each other on the Physical Plane. Generally Task Companions choose Overleaves to complement one another.

The relationship of Task Companions, when they are able to "meet up" on the Physical Plane is, generally speaking, friendly and energetic. It is not unusual for the work of both to improve significantly once Task Companion contact has been made, and for the focus of the work to sharpen. One Fragment is always cardinal, one always ordinal, but often it is the ordinal Fragment who achieves success and/or recognition in the world, for the ordinal Fragments tend to have the more "grounded" approach and Attitude to what is being done. Several of you here gathered will recall the two gentlemen who met here five years ago. Neither wished to attend the session, and both came only because his companion wished to attend. Both stayed in the dining room. One was a Mature Sage, the other a Mature Artisan, with the Sage in the ordinal position. The Artisan is a geneticist, the Sage, an architect. Both Fragments spent most of the time in deep conversation about environments, speaking in what you might call a shorthand, and exchanging much information with a high level of understanding. Although it would be too much to say that they then became fast friends, it would not be incorrect to point out that each talks with the other when questions of work arise, and there is an inherent trust that cannot be "reasonably accounted for" by those who know each of them.

When we describe the matter of cardinal and ordinal, it is more to indicate the influence and receptivity of Fragments than anything else. The cardinal Fragments spur the ordinal Fragments to action or thought or change. That does not in any way invalidate the choices and action taken by any Fragment at any time, for it is always the choice of a cardinal Fragment to exercise its cardinality as it is the choice of an ordinal Fragment to respond to the cardinality.

Please note that we do not say that any of the interaction of Task Companions requires either Fragment to be subservient to the other, although it is possible that they may at some time choose to demonstrate the relationship in such a way. We would wish to establish in your minds that the close associations of Entity Mates is for most Young and Mature Fragments the most effective means to Essence growth accessible on the Physical Plane because this relationship brings about the most intimacy with fewer fears and complications than any other. This is one of the reasons for occasionally prolonged Astral intervals, which permit time to establish contacts firmly enough to sustain the Fragments through a lengthy life on the Physical Plane. Where this close association is possible for significant portions of a specific life on the Physical Plane, there can be lessons learned that are usually only possible on the Astral level. This means that where growth of the Essence is desired the Task Companion is of greater use to the individual Fragment than the Essence Twin. [*August, 1995:* Task Companions, when there is recognition and validation, are capable of expanding the individual Life Tasks beyond the anticipated limits of the Life Plan. We have said before but we will reiterate: Task Companions most often focus their attention outward, which brings about a broader ranger of expression of every aspect of the Life Task. When Essence Twins are brought together, the relationship is intensely inward and inclined to create its "own little world" which can interfere with the Life Task, unless, of course, being in the company of the Essence Twin is part of the Life Plan.] Of equal importance for insight is the relationship of members of the same Cadence, and examples of this are close at hand. The nature of the Essence Twin relationship will not often contribute to Essence growth but does provide the unity that is the closest on the Physical Plane that Fragments may become—so close, that it is often denied because of its force.

Rarely are all desired contacts achieved in any one life, no matter how long, for that, too, is a lesson of the Physical Plane and part of what can only be learned in your Cycle of lives. [June, 2000: No matter how long a Fragment's life on the Physical Plane may be, whether it is completed or interrupted, a significant portion of its validity is the "reality" of time, and the experience of moving "one way" through the life. Physicality makes "do-overs" in the chronological sense impossible. This is a valuable insight for those willing to perceive the experience of aging in an evolutionary sense. Contacts at any stage of life may be expressed and acknowledged in a wide variety of ways, and all are valid. The obstacle to the recognition and validation of contacts among those of disparate ages, unless it is within an extended family, is often regarded in your society as "suspicious" and assumed to be in some way perversely sexual. There are such instances, of course, but there is no valid intimacy in such manipulative and exploitative behavior, which tends to negate any hint of intimacy rather than to provide access to it in many ways that do not include compulsory sexual contact. Almost all Fragments are capable of having friends of all ages, and it assists in evolution to have such relationships.]

Which brings us to the relationships of Essence Twins. The link is inward directed and wholly compelling when it is recognized and not rejected. We do not wish to discourage you, but we do wish to point out that Essence Twins can "rub each other the wrong way" because they are so completely equal, and because there is no "mystery" and not much "romance" in Essence Twin relationships. We cannot overemphasize that there is an equality between Essence Twins that is the source of the twinning, and because of that the relationship is unlike any other possible to the individual Fragments. Where Task Companions direct their relationship "outward," Essence Twins direct their relationship "inward": there is a profound intimacy, but little involvement with the world at large, which is why you do not often choose to spend time with your Essence Twin.

If Fragments were to pass each life reveling with the Essence Twin, there would be very little growth, and it is the desire of the Essence to evolve. Let us say that once the contact has been recognized and validated by both of the Fragments, there is almost nothing that will separate the Twins short of the death of one or both. Essence Twins who accept their link are as close as what you call Siamese twins, and in a very real sense they are held by a bond stronger than flesh and bone. This is, of course, terrifying to many Fragments, and those whose Chief Feature blocks the recognition, distorts the perception of the Essence Twin in the most negative manner possible, often drawing on the fears and repugnance of the Fragment who is rejecting, since the similarity cannot be discounted. In other words, the Chief Feature paints the very thing the Fragment likes least about itself as the predominant features of the Essence Twin, making the rejection seem not only palatable, but absolutely necessary. Think, if you will, of the story of "Dorian Gray," and you will have some notion of what the Chief Feature does to distort the perception of the Essence Twin.

We would wish to say that we do not intend to show a bleak picture, but to reveal the hazards of Essence Twin contact. Those who have attempted it are aware of the risks and some of the difficulties that can arise from pursuing the contact. The link of Essence Twins is the culmination of all intimacy, and it is the reuniting of Essence Twins that is accomplished when the Cadre reunites. As compelling as this union is for a single Fragment, for the Entities of the Cadre the desire is immeasurably greater, for once the Physical Plane is left behind, there is very little fear experienced by the Fragments, and that permits the Fragments to perceive Essence without trappings. It is possible for Fragments on the Physical Plane to perceive Essence, their own and others, but few are willing to undertake the task, and tend to cloak such experiences in externalized explanations, such as the conviction that the Fragment has "seen God" rather than its own Essence or the Essence of others. Generally certain spiritual exercises are required, but those on certain drugs as well as those under extreme stress occasionally will have the experience. When the Fragment has not been prepared for it, the vastness of Essence can be "daunting," as well as confusing. Those who have prepared for the experience often find it difficult to accept that something as "enormous" as Essence could be contained within them, forgetting that the Essence does not occupy space in the same way that beings on the Physical Plane do.

Many of those in our little group have commented on the problems they have with others, especially understanding Fragments of Entities different than their own, and in answer to these inquiries, we will do what we can to simplify the matter. First, be aware that Scholars, being in the neutral or Synthesis position, are able to deal with and understand all Essence with less bias than the others. The Overleaves may modify this understanding, but they do not change the potential. Scholars are more "removed" from the interactions of others because of their position, and the perspective this provides opens many doors, although that "remoteness" often makes it difficult for the Scholar to walk through the doors that are open.

Members of the same polarity have a basic sense of the behavior of the entire polarity. Thus, Sages have a good understanding of Artisans, and the reverse is also true. By the same token, Priests and Slaves have an inherent understanding of one another, and the common good and/or higher ideal that they all serve. Warriors and Kings are both willing to act, and they both share a stern sense of loyalty that is often bewildering to others. We would have to say that members of the Expression Polarity, by their very natures, are often vexing to Priests and Slaves, for by their Inspirational lights, the Expression Polarity lacks "integrity" while the Expression Polarity senses that the Inspiration Polarity is not "flexible" or "sympathetic". The Action Polarity often sees the adaptability and diplomacy of the Expression Polarity as "disloyal" or "untrustworthy," while the Action Polarity appears to be "impetuous" and "touchy" to the Expression Polarity. For the Inspiration Polarity, the Action Polarity can appear "unprincipled" and "head-strong" or even "dangerous". This notion that the other Polarity is "dangerous" is sometimes shared by the way in which the Action Polarity sees the Inspiration Polarity, for the devotion the Inspiration shows to whatever is the "cause" is grounds for suspicion for the Action Polarity.

Again, we do not intend to discourage any Fragment here present in any way. If we have any desire, it is that the fear-ridden hold of maya be broken enough that the Fragments might experience the life with more love and less fear to guide them. That does not mean that we in any sense require this or even "hope" for it, but that there is a certain reciprocity in your growth that influences our own. That does not mean that we do evolve or do not evolve based on what you do or do not choose to do in this or any other life, but that the positive aspect of the life is of benefit to the happening of the Tao, and when the lessons are brought to bear on the Physical Plane, there are other lessons brought to bear on this and on all other Planes. These lessons do not have "grades" or "failures" in any sense whatever. We do not wish you to feel in any way indebted to us, or obligated to us. If you wish to thank us for information, we do not need thanks. We do not disdain thanks, either. But it is not part of the relationship that exists between us and our students. This is true of all Mid-Causal teachers throughout the Mid-Causal Plane. We offer our information freely and unconditionally, making no requirements whatever of the use to which it is or is not to be put. Such matters are, of course, part of choice and as such cannot have conditions.

Let us reiterate that no relationships are "right" or "wrong". Relationships, or the lack of them, are the result of choice, and their conditions and durations are the result of choices as well as being continuing choices in themselves. Those who choose to create relationships based entirely on body-type attraction are no more "right" or "wrong" than a Fragment searching single-mindedly for its Essence Twin. In such a case, we would only caution the searching Fragment to ask itself if the search for the Essence Twin was not, perhaps, blinding it to rewarding relationships on a different kind of footing, although what the Fragment did in response to this would be a matter of choice. Without choice, there is no insight. Insight is the outgrowth of choice.

Relationships of all diverse sorts make it possible for a wide variety of insights to be achieved. Intimacy, expressed in any number of ways, brings about the evolution of Essence and therefore is sought by Essence, but not at the expense of the choice of the individual Fragment. When a relationship is physically harmful or profoundly disappointing, there can be much insight, no matter how painful, that will aid the Fragment to pass through the crisis. And do not suppose that we underestimate the pain. We are aware that the suffering of the Physical Plane is intense and real, that the despair is as genuine as it is heartrending. For those Fragments who are willing to attempt intimacy and recognition in the face of such anguish, there are more choices than for those who cannot permit themselves to extend themselves for a valid relationship. If you are prepared to take the risks, even a very small one and for a very little time, the breaking of the prison of isolation and achievement of intimacy is one of the great triumphs of the Physical Plane. While all relationships are valid, those where there is recognition, though it may be nothing more than the vague sense of some connection that goes beyond a pleasant face or interesting conversation, can permit more perceptions than those where recognition is entirely lacking, even if that entirely lacking relationship is with the Essence Twin.

Much recognition is not on the levels of what you call consciousness, but that does not rule out the merit of such recognitions. We do not mean to suggest that therefore the only "worthwhile" relationships are those that are pursued because of the recognitions but we do wish to say that when relationships are chosen with a sense of "awareness," more can be gathered in the course of the relationship than where no such "awareness" is permitted to exist. Listening to "Requiem Mass" of any of a number of composers will be enhanced if the listener has a knowledge of Latin and/or the form of the Mass itself, but that does not mean that it cannot be enjoyed by those with no knowledge of Latin or the form of the Mass. The music heard will carry its own message, but that message will be reinforced if the listener brings some level of understanding to the work. The conduct of relationships can work very much the same way, and bring about similar benefits if the Fragment chooses to permit it. Many perceptions are distorted by societal institutions, which is the source for many misunderstandings. By societal institutions, we mean such things as politics, education, employment, marriage, religion, aging, the family, and status. Relationships hampered by these institutional fetters appear to need constant "work," which can do much to cloud the perceptions with external issues not truly germane to the relationship. Recognizing these societal institutions is one of the most persistent lessons of the Physical Plane. Many very sincere Young Souls perceive these societal institutions as being as valid as universal truths, which is, of course, not the case. Where relationships are caught up in these institutions, problems arise that have little bearing on the relationship itself, and many times the relationship fails, not because of problems in the relationship, but because of all the distortions brought about by the societal institutions that impinge upon it.

In general, the older a soul becomes the less stringent the hold of societal institutions on the Fragment. Very Old Souls, those in the last two or three lives on the Physical Plane, are often inclined to turn away from the pressures, either living very quiet lives, and occasionally living in circumstances that distress family and friends, or by finding the means to remove themselves from the most avoidable pressures.

To the very advanced soul, societal institutions make little sense, and the demands of such institutions are seen as intrusive and "unfortunate". Certainly there are relationships inherently more difficult than others, but societal intrusions often turn even the most benign of relationships into disappointments for the Fragments trying to maintain them. We do not limit these observations to sexual or "romantic" relationships: relationships occur at every level and crossroad of life and can have a wide variety of ways to be expressed.

Let us give you the following example: a Mature Warrior had a facilitating Agreement with a Mature King, and when the two met there was recognition of many levels. But there was more than forty years' difference in their ages, their background was diverse, one being from Portland, Oregon, the other being originally from Kazan. Family and friends were afraid that the relationship was "peculiar" and actively discouraged the relationship, and the result was that there was mutual abdication of the Agreement, leaving the two Fragments with an ill-defined sense of "missing something" in a way that has little to do with a Chief Feature of Impatience.

It is not completely misleading to think of the evolution of the Essence as being the task of the Physical Plane for all Fragments. As such, the relationships, in any and all aspects, are the tools which the Fragment uses to evolve. The greater the experience and understanding of the Fragments involved, the more effective the use of the tool is apt to be. That is intended entirely unmanipulatively, for manipulation is the most common way that intimacy is avoided.

It is our intention only to show that evolution and relationships are, along with choices, aspects of the same things and as such are of great value to the Essence, particularly when understanding is present. While we do not endorse the theology of the Fragment who was John Donne, we are in agreement with him that no one "is an island," unless personal insularity is the Fragment's choice. On the Physical Plane, relationships bring this lesson to bear.

CHAPTER FIVE
Conclusion of the Session

"Is there any other way Michael sees relationships, I wonder?" Lizzy asks as she looks over Katherine's shoulder. "What has he left out?"

"Are you asking a question or being sarcastic?" Camille wants to know.

"A little of both, probably," Lizzy answers. "But I think I'd rather use this round on questions I already have prepared." She goes back to her seat and picks up her notebook. "I'm involved in a project with a friend, one that I've already asked about before in other sessions, so I know that we're doing an Agreement. The project is a research project—well, what else to you expect from two Scholars?—and we've got most of the department to back us up, but for one guy who's convinced that we're just trying to get extra money for us to fool around with for a couple of years. Let me tell you, grant money isn't that plentiful, and the idea that I'd do that makes me boil. What I'd like Michael to discuss—"

"Getting back to the subject," John murmurs.

"—is how to deal with this guy. I don't want to go in there and get into a fight, I want to get the funds freed up so we can go to work."

"All right," Jessica says, picking up her planchette once again. "Everybody write, please."

The Fragment causing the problems is a fifth Level Young Priest in the Power Mode with a Goal of Acceptance, a Stoic in the Moving part of Intellectual Center with a Chief Feature of Impatience. As you can perceive, this Fragment has inwardly abrading Overleaves which cause him to be uncomfortable through most of his life. Let us suggest that since this Fragment is determined that the higher ideal should be served, that it would be useful to convince him that you, too, serve the same higher ideal. Otherwise you might find yourself accused of "heresy" and caught up in a fight you do not wish to endure. Let us point out that this Fragment sincerely believes that education, in order to be valid, must be a struggle, often painful, and often demanding sacrifices.

"Shit!" Lizzy interjects.

Therefore, if you wish to let this Fragment know all that you will have to give up in order to do the project and emphasize how long it has taken you to arrive at a position to pursue the subject, he might be inclined to view the venture more favorably. Be aware he is suspicious of anything that smacks of "fun".

"He sounds lovely," Camille says when Lizzy reads the answer back. "Just the kind of man to bring out the best in people."

Kim Ingvesson looks up. "There's something I don't understand. Can someone explain it to me?"

"What is it?" Jessica asks.

"Well, this Acceptance—does it mean that the person wants to accept things, or to be accepted? "

"Both," Jessica and Camille answer together, and Camille goes on. "You see, it can work either way, and sometimes both aspects will be present. Being in the Power Mode only makes it more so, but anyone in Acceptance will tend to have things to handle as well as wanting everyone else to go along with what the person is handling. In the positive pole, it can give agape, but that's hard to do, and harder to sustain."

Kim nods. "Thanks. A Stoic in Acceptance might go looking for things to endure, then?"

"Probably," Jessica says. "And with Impatience, he'd probably want to do it all now, as well."

"Now?" Lizzy challenges. "He wants to have done it yesterday." She flips through the pages of her notebook.

"Remember the flute concerto I performed last month? Well, I'd like Michael to rate the performance."

"What?" Henry demands. "Rate the performance?"

We would think that seven-point-five would be about the best for the performance, and that especially for the second movement. For the most part, seven would be closer to the truth, because you did not have as high a level of concentration in the performing, and therefore did not have as clear an inner concept of the piece. Your playing faltered because the vision was not as precise. We remind you that the ratings we provide are based upon the "vision" you have of the work and how close you come to fulfilling the "vision". It is not uncommon for the Fragment performing to forget that the performance has something to show to the performer as well as the performer does for the audience. The Fragment that can keep focus on its "vision" learns as much as the audience—sometimes more. When the performance becomes rote, it loses its import to the performer and for the more advanced and astute members of the audience, the performance is perceived as "lacking something" which is, of course, the "vision" and focus of the performer.

"So I had it more together for the second movement? Funny, that was the one that was the easiest for me." Lizzy looks at Jessica. "Can I get a comment, or have I used up my turn?"

"There's something more," Jessica concedes.

When Essence is brought to bear in the work, the personality finds the work "easier," which is to say that the energy invested has less to overcome in order to bring forth whatever it is that the performer desires to bring forth. The less that personality and Essence are in conflict, the "easier" the thing is, whether it is playing Bach sonatas, sailing a boat, or choosing an outfit for dinner out.

"It's going to take me a little time to figure that one out," Lizzy says. "I get it, but I know that what I'm getting is really quite superficial, and that if I want to understand what it is that Michael is saying, I'm going to have to think this over for a while. Thanks, Jessica."

"You're welcome," Jessica says, looking to Tracy. "What do you want this time, Tracy?"

She frowns. "What I'd like to do is follow up some of what Alex asked, but I know that's too much for you to do in one day, so I'll table those for the time being. What I'd like to know about instead, at least for the moment, is if Michael will give me any insight into what's happening with a friend of mine, who appears to be channeling another Mid-Causal teacher."

Jessica straightens up in her chair and exchanges uneasy looks with Camille. "You know that there's a lot of—" she begins cautiously, only to have Tracy interrupt.

"I know; I know. And I wouldn't bother to ask if she's been getting stuff that sounded like the usual silliness we hear about so often. The style that her teacher has is different, not as hard-edged as Michael, but he's—they're—saying the same thing, and in similar terms. Here." She opens her purse and brings out a sheet of paper. "Let me read this to her. Her contact calls himself Robert, by the way."

"Messages from Robert?" Henry suggests. "It doesn't scan, does it?"

"Listen to this, and see what you think," Tracy says, and then starts to read.

"'You refer to these as Roles, but we would suggest that the Essence may manifest in these forms: there are seven of them, as follows: one, the Keeper of Children; one whose task involves the care of others. This may take many forms but will always manifest in service. Two, Watchers of the Spirit; beings who carry information through external means, for example, historians who record events or those active in preserving; an aloof sort. Three, Defenders of the Flame; this is usually a Warrior type yet less aggressive; these souls are often true fighters and are usually intensely loyal. Four, Speakers of Knowledge; those souls who carry much knowledge within; these are gentle souls who support the growth of others; high intelligence is a usual trait and a high value. Five, High Teachers; as we have indicated, these souls carry compassion within; a High Teacher is able to reach many souls and usually does this in an emotional and often flamboyant manner. Six, Seekers of the Spirit; those souls who carry a sense of exploration within; their discoveries, whether minute or vast, are generally an inspiration to others. Seven, Healers of the Spirit; these as you know, carry love within and although they manifest it in many ways, most of all will influence the planet in a healing mode; this is perhaps what you on your Plane might describe as a true lover of mankind.

"'These are the seven forms from which the Essence chooses. None has any more value than the other. Each choice is equal to the other. We are seeking oneness always. Growth is not measured by what one accomplishes but by inner truths. The Physical Plane places much value on progress and neglects the soul. We feel for you because of the pain you experience over what you call progress. As always, we remain a resource. Inner truth, however, is always available from within. There is no greater help than what you carry within yourself. Hear your own song so that you may learn to sing.'"

The group members, who have been openly skeptical at first, now are paying close attention. Camille nods when Tracy folds up the paper she holds.

"That sounds a little more like the genuine article than most of what we keep hearing about from the outside," she admits. "You want to check Robert out for your friend, is that it?" Jessica asks.

"If you don't mind," Tracy says. "I know you don't like to get caught in the middle, but this struck me as more what Michael has been talking about. Does that make any sense to you?"

"Well, the seven Essences certainly is familiar," Jessica remarks, not quite certain yet if she wishes to deal with the question.

"I know my friend would be grateful if you'd do this," Tracy persists, not too forcefully.

"All right," Jessica says after pausing a little to think. "I have to agree that this Robert sounds pretty convincing."

Yes, this Robert is another Mid-Causal teacher, one comprised of Sages, Priests and a contingent of Warriors. We, as you recall, are composed of Warriors and Kings. The categories of Essence that Robert describes do not differ from what we have told you. What they call the Keepers of Children we call Slaves. What they call Watchers of the Spirit we call Artisans. What they call Defenders of the Flame we call Warriors.

"I like being a Warrior better than I'd like being a Defender of the Flame," Brad remarks to no one in particular.

What they call Speakers of Knowledge we call Scholars. What they call High Teachers we call Sages. What they call Seekers of the Spirit we call Priests. What they call Healers of the Spirit we call Kings. The principles are the same. The lessons are the same. You will all note that Robert reminds you that what you do is a matter of choice, that nothing is done that is not a matter of choice unless karma is the result. We would have to say that this reunited Entity that is called Robert is more aware than some other Mid-Causal teachers of the function of language. There are Mid-Causal teachers that do not communicate verbally at all, but through what you would probably describe as inspiration or revelation. Such teachers have students, but they do not often gather together as this little group does, but rather express what they are being taught through discoveries or performances. There is a very high Mid-Causal teacher that is made up of Artisans, Sages, Slaves and a few Scholars that teaches through movement and has as students athletes, dancers and sculptors, for the most part, along with a few wine-makers.

"Then I can tell my friend that she is getting worthwhile information?" Tracy asks.

Yes, we would think that this is so. It would not be amiss to remind your friend that the answers asked that do not pertain to herself will be apt to be the most accurate. Where personal information is desired, it is most beneficial to permit a Fragment to channel it other than herself. This is a reasonable precaution to all mediums: where personal questions are involved it is most efficacious to use another medium who is not as likely to "edit" the information.

"That's a strange comment," Jessica says when the message has been read back. "I don't answer any of my own questions, you know."

"Neither do I," Camille agrees. "I know that I tend to block information when I have something to do with it."

"Yes, I have the same problem," Jessica says. "But if Michael wants to comment on that again, who am I to quibble?"

"My turn?" asks Larry, who has been strangely silent for awhile.

"Unless there's anything else that Tracy wants to ask," Jessica says. "You haven't asked much for yourself, Tracy."

She shrugs. "Exercising Warrior protectiveness, I guess. I've been worried about my friends. But I do have a question about the Chief Feature. I can't put this very succinctly, but I'll give it a try. Michael has said that Chief Feature operates out of fear and influences all the negative poles of the Overleaves. He's also said that Essence has access to the personality through the positive poles of the Overleaves. Is there any way to get around this? Is there some way to hold the Chief Feature at bay long enough to give Essence a fighting chance, or is this something that can't be dealt with on that kind of a level? I warned you this was a bit incoherent."

The question is of course an entree into a rather complex mechanism which we shall nevertheless attempt to unravel somewhat and clarify for you, Tracy, and all here gathered. Unfortunately, the ultimate starting place lies where you have suggested, which is to stay within the mechanism in operation in the Chief Feature. In other words, the underlying fear can distort all the perceptions for the purpose of reinforcing its hold on the Fragment, for this is in fact the source of what you refer to as fear and as we have said before, it is fear which stands in the way of the experience of Essence. However, when the Chief Feature can be relaxed somewhat, it is possible to catch glimmers of the experience of love—or, to say it another way, it is through those moments that the positive poles of the Overleaves and attributes of the positive poles can be experienced, for when the Chief Feature is not wholly in control, much of its power is lost. This in turn allows the barrier of the Chief Feature to be dropped somewhat and again allows love to be experienced a bit more and again affects the perception of the positive poles of the personality, even when false personality is very strong. It is interrelated and interwoven on levels beyond the comprehension of most of you on the Physical Plane, but let us assure you that chinks anywhere in the vast armor of your existence do open up possibilities for chinks in other areas and no positive experience of any kind, no matter how brief it may be or how dimly comprehended is ever lost or wasted. For many souls, as we have recommended, the art of "photographing" both the positive poles and negative poles is an excellent beginning point and one which should not be overlooked for its power and efficacy in this matter. By photographing, we mean the conscious and deliberate observation of self when the experience of the Chief Feature— or other Overleaves, for that matter—is at its height. We would hasten to add that most on the Physical Plane are prone to point out negative poles in themselves and others. While this is not all "bad," it would serve you all well to make note of those instances where positive poles are active also, and observe the function in the life at those moments. It is definitely a case of practice helping to make perfect. [*February, 2001*: Chief Feature subversions are tied to all manner of experiences, and for that reason, they are dangerously ubiquitous, shaping themselves "anew" to all manner of situations, and presenting themselves as the Fragment's staunchest ally in the arsenal of the personality, which is why it is so difficult to step away from their machinations. A minor incident at a small gathering, in the hands of Chief Feature, can mutate into a disaster all out of proportion to the actual event. This is when it can be useful, should the Fragment decide to tackle the problem "straight on," to ask someone else who attended the event if he or she happened to notice your "disaster," and weigh your response based upon what you learn, then choose which perspective is more "in balance" with the event in question.]

"That's quite an answer," Katherine says as she studies the page. "Was it my imagination, Jessica, or was Michael going faster than usual?"

There are sympathetic groans from the others. "Yes, they sure were," Jessica says with a sigh. "It's hard enough when Michael is going at the regular brisk clip, but when he takes off like that, well, it's a job keeping up with him, even for me. It's probably worse for the rest of you. I know how hard it is to get all the letters down when Michael is going that fast."

"You should see this page," Lizzy complains. "I've got one word in three, I think."

Kim nods. "You're lucky. Aside from a few thes and one or two poles, this is gibberish."

"That's why I always want everyone to write," Jessica reminds the rest. "We might have lost this if you didn't all work on it, and I don't want to have to get any of it again."

"You mean you can?" Katherine asks, getting up and pouring herself a cup of coffee. "That surprises me."

"Well, I can sometimes," she says with less sureness. "It's not as easy, and I'm much more likely to block on something. I don't entirely know why I can't do it."

"Well, I can't do it, either," Camille points out. "And I know that our other medium has the same trouble."

"What happens if Jessica gets it first, and then you try to get the message the second time around, Milly?"

"Same thing," Camille says. "I block on it. And I know that our third medium has the same trouble, because we've talked about it. She called me once quite late and asked if I'd ever got information on a specific subject. I hadn't, but Jessica had. She was relieved, because she knew then why she couldn't get the information. She didn't know until after she tried that the information had been given already. The reason she asked was because she was blocking and couldn't think of a reason for it."

"Yeah," Jessica says slowly. "So, everyone, make sure you've got copies, or get copies, because I can't guarantee that I'll be able to do this a second time around."

"My turn now?" Larry asks. "After that, I feel kind of silly asking the next question, but not silly enough to keep from asking it."

Jessica chuckles. "She must be very attractive."

Larry flushes slightly, his fair skin turning rosy. "She is."

"Okay, what's the question?"

"Well, I want to know about this woman I've been seeing; you're right about that. And I want Michael's comments on past lives, Agreements, Monads and all that stuff in regard to the relationship."

This is a mid-Cycle Mature Artisan in the Passion Mode—

"I'll say," Larry whispers.

—with a Goal of Growth, a Skeptic in the Moving part of Intellectual Center with a Chief Feature of Greed fixated on experience. There are no past associations of note here, and no more involved relationship than body-type attraction, as you are doubtless aware.

"Oh," Larry sighs. "I guess it isn't worth doing much about her, then."

That is a matter of your choice. But let us point out that the focus on work is enhanced when the needs of the body are truly satisfied, and certain sexual gratification is as valid a need as hunger. When the body starves, either in reality or in the metaphoric sense, then there is a greater drain on Essence and it is harder to feel the pull of Essence ties, just as it is not easy to think clearly when suffering from advanced thirst. We wish to add that the experience of compatible body types can be most illuminating. And for that reason we wish to remind you that there is much to be gained from such a relationship. To abandon a relationship that is satisfying to Essence and is also pleasurable to personality is not Good Work. It is strange to us to see how little those Fragments on the Physical Plane trust those things that are pleasurable and rely only on experiences that give pain.

Larry reads this back self-consciously, then says, "The trouble is, I feel so much in the dark most of the time, that I don't know what to trust."

Most Fragments on the Physical Plane are so much in the control of fear and resultant maya that they are not even aware of the darkness you mention. The Fragment that has genuine insights can see the darkness. That means that the Fragment searches, which, of course, is the first step on the path. Those truly on the path can learn to perceive the light which is Essence. The foe behind the Chief Feature for all of you is maya, and the "soul" of maya is fear. The only means to combat fear is love. We have said this many times before and we remind you all yet again to recognize the stranglehold that fear can have on personality. Once this has been done it is possible to accept the strength of love. That love, we remind you, must be unconditional and without expectation. That does not mean without hope. We agree that the darkness, at its worst, can be pervasive and the resultant confusion can lead to symptoms that are linked with one of the conditions you call insanity. There is a statement in some of your religious writings that has some bearing on the predicament, but not with the "moral" the preachers chose to take from it. It refers to the creatures that walked in darkness who have seen a great light. This does not mean that God or anything else external has favored them, only that those who recognize that there is darkness have taken the first step toward leaving it, toward perceiving Essence, which is often described metaphorically as a great light. It would not be amiss to read further in various competent occult writings—and we must emphasize competent here because so much of what is written about arcane subjects is incompetent and misleading—to delve further into various techniques that would aid you in dispelling your personal darkness. You, Larry, have chosen occult awakening as part of your task in this life, and so it is to your advantage to learn what you can on the subject. Most of the others here gathered have had such experiences in the past, and most of them are renewing old skills as an adjunct to their Life Tasks. You, on the other hand, have chosen to devote much time and attention to improving your abilities in this area.

"Would Michael be willing to elaborate on this a little? I don't want to take up too much time, but I feel as if I have half an answer." Larry ducks his head in apology, then looks directly at Jessica. "I'm sorry to do this, but not sorry enough not to ask."

"It's okay with me, but if you don't mind, I need to take a break. If Milly will get it for you, I can go to the john." She puts her board aside and gets out of her rocking chair. "Milly?"

"Fine with me," she says, waving Jessica away. "Get out of here. And everyone, quiet, please."

While we do not speak of morality, nonetheless there is a cosmic "ethic" of sorts, and those with the task of arcane studies often serve to bring a sense of the ethos to the "world at large". The task defies common expression, for when the cosmic ethic or the Universal Truths are brought to bear on a world that has reached the fifth Level of the Young Cycle , which yours is fast approaching, [*September, 1989:* The average soul age for the ensouled extant upon your world, including Cetaceans, is now fifth Level Young, where it is likely to remain for roughly 2,000 to 3,000 years, barring major catastrophes] it must be communicated intact. When that level is achieved, watered-down truths are no longer appropriate, and therefore new concepts of learning are needed to reveal these truths. Most of the communication of World Truths where your species is concerned is likely to be through what you on the Physical Plane call the arts, such as theater and dance, literature and music, and many of the plastic and graphic arts.

We do not disdain film, even the most popular, as a means of conveying the truth. There is no set rule that truth is a bitter and unpalatable medicine to be taken as reluctantly as possible. There is no reason that growth must be painful or difficult, that change must be threatening, that progress must be marked with pain. All this, Larry, is by way of introduction to the second part of your query. You have reached that point where you are prepared to undertake the studies that you "signed-up" to do, and you hesitate now because you have glimpsed the scope of the project, and it appears to be overwhelming, something that you are not up to. We would reiterate at this point that no one ever comes to this "junction" prematurely. Some venture into uncharted waters and then quickly swim for the nearest shore. This is a juncture reached only by those who have agreed to hear the words and therefore are receptive to the concepts expressed. You, Larry, are no exception to this rule. You have it within you to discern that which lies behind these communications as well as other occult writings, and relate them not to metaphysical notions, but to the actions in the "real" world. Of course, you need not undertake anything you wish not to do. You are not "required" to pursue this if you choose not to. No one is ever coerced by Essence. Coercion is the tool of the Chief Feature and maya.

"Holy shit," Larry says when Camille reads back what she has written. "Does that mean that I'm just getting started? I thought that I'd been doing a lot of things that were just winding up."

"You probably are," Camille says as she hands two sheets of paper to him. "You're probably getting rid of old business so you can get to work on the new business."

"Sounds like the onset of the Infamous Fourth Monad to me," says Camille.

"Sounds like you've got quite a row to hoe," Henry remarks. "I thought I had my hands full with dealing with students and faculty, but you're taking on a hell of a lot more than departmental politics."

Kim clears her throat and stares down at the page in front of her. "So long as we're dealing with difficult questions—do you mind doing this, Milly?"

"Not at all," Camille says, on the verge of laughing. "I feel a little as if I'm here on false credentials if all I do is get an occasional answer for Jessica."

"Well, okay," Kim says, then goes on more seriously. "You see, I've wondered for a while how we got into this group. I know you're very careful about letting in new people, and you turn many away, or simply avoid the question completely. I've seen how Jessica operates in public, and you'd never guess that she does this kind of thing. I know when we mentioned to a friend that we'd been to a Michael session with Jessica, not one of the others that have sprung up and . . . well, there was quite a reaction. What I'm getting at is: I wonder why we did this, when there are so many, many others who keep trying and never get here. Is there some reason for it?"

"That's a good one," Camille says as she begins to write.

Kim takes the sheets of paper from Camille and reads them aloud. "Thank goodness you have such legible handwriting," she adds at the end of it.

"That sounds impressive," Jessica remarks; she has come back into the living room and takes one of the cookies. "These are very good," she says to Kim.

"Thanks."

"I hope this answers your question," Camille says. "That answer was a real palm-tingler."

"It sounds very impressive," Kim says a bit uncertainly. "I didn't think that a question like mine would get such an answer."

"You can't always tell which questions will open the floodgates," Jessica says. She runs a hand through her hair. "I remember the time that Dave Swan asked about . . . Oh, it was a minor thing, a matter of an aversion he had to the whole process of taxation, and he thought that his attitude was overreacting. That brought out this incredible lecture from Michael about past lives and avoidances in this life."

"I have it," Lizzy says, as she pulls out another notebook. "If there's a particularly good or apt answer, I copy it down in this, so I don't have to go hunting for material every time I want to check on an answer. Would you like me to read it?"

"Yes," Camille says at once, and all but Alex agree.

"The question was 'Every time I have to deal with taxation and related tariffs, I get deeply upset. Is there some reason for this other than Chief Feature, and if there is, will you explain the source to me'? And this is the answer."

This is what we would describe as a hidden insight, in that you in your personality are aware of a past association with this occupation and problems that you understand now make you uncomfortable without any apparent "reason". This reaction is not as uncommon as you might think: there are literally millions of Fragments dealing with questions of this sort every confusing day of their lives and with less knowledge than you have access to. We would wish to say that when a pivotal life has bearing on the current life, many recollections from that pivotal life are "echoed" in the current life in the manner that you describe. In your case, David, you were a customs officer in the fifteenth century in the Venetian part of Greece, where you made a small personal fortune in the pay of the Turks. You, in that life, deliberately set out to cheat both the merchants and the Venetian government as a way to ensure your favor from the Turks in the possible event of their conquests extending to the island of your employment. Your conduct in that life was far from honorable, for you made it a point to charge maximum tariffs and other duties, then accepted additional bribes from all parties so that you could line your own pockets and still appear to be the picture of vigilance and honesty. The fact that your predations went almost entirely undetected until very late in your career is evidence that you were very good at your little game. You retired from office under slight pressure and admitted to being corrupted by Turkish agents, which gained you a great deal of sympathy from the Venetians and the merchants you had cheated. In fact, you were regarded as a victim of Turkish treachery instead of an apt manipulator of all concerned. You were a small, self-effacing man with an unctuous manner and a deceptively humble attitude that many were fooled by. Essence, of course, is never fooled, and in this life, you are aware of resonances to that life and you can see parallels to your current work, and are aware of the potentials for misuse of power by those in the customs and tariff careers around you. When you import a piece of art, you are reminded on many levels of the official you were on that Venetian-Greek island and your own malfeasance. It keeps you alert to the potentials for abuse of station and power, although you are not very happy to be reminded of that experience. While the actions you took did not lead to karma, they did incline you to want to make amends, so that your on-going evolution would be more balanced than it would be without that concession. We would think that work on recalling that life in detail would be of use to you so that you may better comprehend what it is that troubles you about the memories of that life and its bearing on the current one.

"Then there's real worth in following up on past lives?" Larry asks, looking around the room for the reaction of the others. "Is there some reason that finding out about the past can be helpful?"

"All sorts of reasons," Jessica replies. "It isn't just the ego thing of finding out you did something worthwhile or were famous, or any of the rest of it. Knowing what you have done makes it easier to figure out what you're doing now, and why."

Kim speaks up at this. "If we know the lessons whether we remember them or not, isn't it . . . a waste of time to bother with the past? Unless there are past associations working in a relationship, I can't see why it would matter to know so much about it."

"It can be an answer to curiosity," Camille says choosing her words carefully. "I remember doing a private reading for a woman who was having some rather serious inner conflicts because she found herself wanting to take a more aggressive business stance. It wasn't appropriate to her work and she had a hard time understanding where this impulse came from. It turned out that she had been a privateer in a past life and some of the situations she found herself in now resonated to that privateer life. In a sense, some of her reactions belonged to the privateer and not to the fabric seller."

"And a friend of mine," Lizzy says, "was one of the Romantic writers the life before last. She's hardly the type today, but there is a lot of the man left in her, sometimes at variance to her, sometimes as an addition to her. She makes jokes about it, especially now that she knows what's happening with her. We all do. She gets into a certain frame of mind and we call her Charles, because she's picking up on that resonance so strongly."

"That sounds very odd," Henry says with a trace of criticism in his voice.

"Oh, it's not bad," Lizzy says, not allowing herself to be drawn into any dispute. "She's precisely the sort of woman who takes all this in stride. In fact, every now and then, when she's being her most sensible, she gets nostalgic for Charles and says that she knows he'd handle her situation with a lot more dash than she does."

Alex adds to this: "When I first encountered this resonance thing, I thought that it was not going on, and I assumed that those who were talking about it were doing some very fancy projecting and displacing. But that was three or four years ago, and I've seen enough of the resonances that I realize what Michael is saying is nothing less than the truth. There are resonances and they do have bearing on what you do in a life. I noticed that for the first time, really saw it, with my wife, who is not at all involved in this teaching, and tends to regard it as something between trivia and voodoo. According to Michael, she was an engineer in her last life, and specialized in designing bridges. This life, she's an attorney and knows almost nothing about engineering. We were traveling and happened to cross over a new bridge. She suggested we stop, and when we did, she took a half a dozen photographs of the bridge. I was a little puzzled about this, and mentioned that she didn't often show so much interest in bridges, and she replied that she hadn't seen the arch construction used that way before and she wanted a chance to look at it more carefully. This from an attorney specializing in domestic law. I pointed out to her that this wasn't her usual area of interest, and she said that of course it was. When I asked her how long she'd been interested in bridges, she became confused and insisted that bridges were an old hobby of hers. Well, that showed me how strong the whole thing of resonance could be. I'm certain there are examples of it going on all the time."

I remember when you asked about that," Jessica says. "You were not really upset, but you wanted some kind explanation for what had happened."

"And what Michael told me made a lot more sense than Amy's sudden insistence that bridges were a hobby with her." He folds his arms. "I mentioned this to Amy, and she said there was nothing to it, but she still put the pictures of the bridge up on the bulletin board and kept them there for almost a year."

"Did she have any idea why the bridge appealed to her? I mean, did she ever reach a point where she wanted to examine her reaction in Michael's terms?" Larry asks.

"No. That bothered me at first, but recently I've felt differently about it. This choice business is finally getting through to me. I've come to realize that it really doesn't matter whether or not she sees it the way I do. She's doing what she chooses to do, and that's what it's really all about."

He stretches out his legs and sighs a little. "That's not an easy perception to come to," he says more quietly. "It's one thing to hear Michael go on and on and on about it, and you don't know why he does until you come up against a situation like the one I have with Amy, and then you start to see that Michael has every reason to keep emphasizing choice over and over again, because otherwise it would be very tempting to put pressure on others where it seems to be important. And that isn't what this teaching is all about—in fact, it's just the opposite."

Katherine cocks her head to the side. "You know what brought that home to me? I was working on a film—not very big budget, a silly plot, but it was fun working the effects—and there was a guy who was really into one of the Oriental religions. He wanted to get the rest of us interested, too. He was out to convert the world to his brand of Buddhism, which is kind of strange when you think about it. That's when the whole thing about choice really struck me. This man said that we had to choose for ourselves, but he made it very clear that he expected us to choose the thing he wanted us to choose. I found it fascinating in a grotesque sort of way."

"Did you ask Michael about the guy?" Henry asks Katherine.

"Oh, you bet. I wanted to know what I was up against. Michael gave me some very good suggestions that worked quite well." Katherine flips through several sheets of paper in the file folders she carries. "Here it is. Have a look for yourself."

This Fragment is a second Level Mature Priest in the Passion Mode with a Goal of Growth, a Realist in the Intellectual part of Emotional Center with a very strong Chief Feature of Arrogance. He is not at all aware of the Chief

Feature, and thinks that because of his spiritual advancement he is above all the hurt and hassles of the Physical Plane. This, we need not remind you, is hardly the case as his zealous behavior should make quite clear to you, Katherine. In the past this Fragment has nine times been allied with various extremist groups, and this recent affiliation is part of the same pattern, but not as intolerant as many of his past alliances. This Priest has a great need to save the world from itself as well as to find ways to bring others into the fold for their own protection. He is not aware of the antagonism that his zeal inspires in many and it is extremely unlikely that you or anyone else would be able to enlighten him on this matter. What might be the best procedure from here is to bring various books on oriental philosophical and religious thought with you when you work with this difficult Fragment and tell him that he has piqued your interest in oriental religions, so you are exploring the possibilities, should you choose to do so. It might ease the strain of your dealings with him. It might be more beneficial to avoid the works of those associated with his particular school of thought. Let us suggest that carrying a copy of the I Ching and perhaps the translations of the work of Lao-Tzu, or Mo-Tzu would be your most tactful approach. It might be wise to avoid long discussions with this Fragment, and say only that you have not yet studied enough to understand the material well enough to discuss it. That sort of humility will have a direct appeal to the Priest in him as well as to his Arrogance, which desperately needs to believe that he understands this teaching more completely than anyone else around him. Difficult as it is, patience will serve you with this Fragment more than any other "virtue". Incidentally, this is not deliberate mendacity on your part, but a technique to keep the work being mutually undertaken on the point of the work, not wandering off into disputes unassociated with the tasks at hand.

"So did you do what Michael suggested?" Henry asks when he has read the transcript. "Most of it. I never did get a copy of the I Ching, but I found the Tao Te Ching as well as a book of the writings of Mo-Tzu—talk about something obscure!—and that calmed him down. He still calls once in a while to see if I'm ready to come to one of the services his guru holds, but so far I've had excellent reasons why it isn't possible."

Henry nods and Jessica speaks up. "That's happened here a few times, too. Someone will come not to find out what Michael is teaching, but to try to persuade us to join their movement or sect. Most of the time it isn't that difficult to deal with, but every now and then it's awkward and embarrassing."

"I did a private reading once for a woman who is a strict and very proper Jew, and she was determined to have Michael tell her that everything that her rabbi said was from the mouth of God, and everything else was pernicious lies." Camille shrugs. "I tried to explain that Michael doesn't work that way. In the end, I returned her fee and said that there was no point in continuing the reading."

"Was she angry?" Kim asks.

"Very. She kept saying that it was typical of Christians to look down on Jews. There was nothing I could say that she wanted to hear. I even tried to explain that I' m not a Christian. I was raised to be a lukewarm Christian, and there are members of my family who are really gung ho, but it didn't take with me. No religion has, and believe me, I've shopped around."

"Zoroastrianism, anyone?" Lizzy suggests impishly.

"Lizzy!" John admonishes her, not able to conceal his smile.

"My niece flirted with being a Moonie for a while," Larry says, concern in his eyes.

"That's the kind of organization that Michael has been asked about a number of times," Camille says. "Remember, Michael isn't very keen on organized religion in general and cults—all kinds: Christian, Hindu, Muslim, political, it doesn't matter—in particular. He's—they've—said that extremist movements always promote fear and block recognition."

Jessica agrees. "I've channeled several comments Michael has made about the ways in which extremism, especially religious and political extremism, have worked to create negativity. I have to say that Michael and I don't agree about some of these matters, but—" She makes a philosophical gesture with her hand. "Michael doesn't give a damn if I agree with them. They say what they have to say."

Camille shifts in her chair and twitches her skirt so that it falls well. "I know; Sages and costumes," she says, as if chiding herself. "I used to think that everyone had the same sense, but I know now that they don't, and that's a great advantage. Michael has been very good at making me aware of how marvelous diversity is."

"Kim, do you want to ask anything else?" Jessica inquires as she picks up the planchette again.

"Well, I would like Michael to give me some ideas about how to get more energy while I'm on this diet. I do want to lose about ten pounds, but I always get tired, and then I blow it. If that doesn't seem too trivial."

We do not see any question as trivial, Kim. As to the diet, in your case, the addition of chicken and/or fish to your diet, while it would slightly increase your calorie intake would more than compensate by providing the protein you are lacking at this time. Let us recommend that the protein be consumed at the mid-day meal rather than in the evening or morning because you will make a more efficient use of the protein. We would also recommend that rather than increase the amount of running you do, that you substitute swimming as your major exercise, for that will give you the same degree of exercise without the strain you are currently experiencing. Please note that our recommendation applies only to you and should not be regarded as general advice for the others here gathered. You, of course, may choose to follow our recommendations in whole or in part, or not at all.

"Buying cars and diets. What next?" Henry asks the air, shaking his head.

"Since the next turn is yours, I suppose we'll all find out what next," Jessica tells him. "It sounds as if Michael isn't very keen on red meat for you, Kim. If I were you, I'd give the chicken and fish routine a good trial and I wouldn't eat too much hamburger."

"Don't worry. I keep my meat consumption down most of the time." She shakes her head.

There is no error in eating meat or not eating meat. There is the manner in which individual bodies process what is eaten. Those with significant ancestral backgrounds in the far north or far south of the globe tend to require more protein in the diet than those from milder "climes". Those whose ancestors come from hot tropical climates tend to fare better with more fruits and legumes in the diet.

"I really think Michael's pretty amazing."

The rest of the group agrees with this.

"Okay, Henry," Jessica says. "What's on your mind?"

"I want to know in what life I earned the most karma, and what I did to earn it."

Jessica stares at him in dismay. "Are you sure you want the answer to that? I can get it for you, but I warn you, it isn't going to be pleasant if you insist on hearing about it."

"Listen to her," Katherine warns. "I asked about that once, and I was very upset about what I was told."

"I want to know," Henry insists. "I have an idea about it, and I want to find out if I'm right or if I've got it all wrong. I'm prepared to be upset."

Camille shakes her head. "Are you certain you don't mind the rest of us hearing the answer? I know how disruptive this can be."

"Go ahead," Henry says with conviction.

In what you call the tenth century, the Fragment who is now Henry was then a second Level Young Scholar, very ambitious and eager to please the men around him in authority. He was a Cypriot, and had three ships of his own to command. He was what you would describe as a pirate, and he suffered from an emotional condition that might today be thought of as sadism. He not only seized ships and all the cargo, but the crews and passengers as well. Although it was fairly traditional to ransom crewmen and passengers, this Fragment did not choose to do so, but sold the Fragments he captured into slavery or maimed them and made them into beggars who were compelled to work for him. He also subjected his captives to very brutal treatment and often for no reason other than that he was bored. He often gave the females he captured as gifts to local men in authority, or to his crew to reward them for their ferocity. In all, he sold more than four hundred Fragments into slavery and maimed, tortured and killed another two hundred or so. He had Agreements to injure less than one hundred of them, and the rest became karmic ribbons. Two of the deaths he personally "orchestrated" were burnings of earlier ribbons. This Fragment died in a battle at sea. While we would have to say that this Fragment was ruthless, for his time he was not especially remarkable except in his sexual satisfaction derived from the physical suffering of others. Many Fragments who had similar occupations at that time were no "better" or "worse" than he. His men regarded him with respect and he was counted a brave man. His death was sincerely mourned by many and his crew took a bloody vengeance upon the Genoese ships that had sunk the ship of the Fragment who is now Henry. Incidentally, there are still two karmic ribbons remaining from that life.

This answer is heard in silence, and Henry finds that he has not been able to write most of the dictated letters. The others in the room give him the information.

"It sounds worse than I thought," Henry says softly.

We would like to remind you, Henry, that when many ribbons have been burned, a Fragment tends to view the acts that created the ribbons in the first place as especially reprehensible, in part because in burning the karma, genuine understanding is achieved on many levels, and once this occurs, it cannot be lost to the Fragment. While we do not offer this as a "salve," we do believe that the chagrin that you feel, while understandable, is not necessary. All but two ribbons from that life have been burned, and it may give you some satisfaction to learn that you have not tried to avoid burning the ribbons in the past. You have undertaken arduous tasks for the simple purpose of burning karma from that life, and for the most part you have not abdicated your Agreements to burn ribbons.

"Thanks, I think," Henry says, still in a chastened tone.

"Do you have any other questions?" Jessica asks gently. Henry shakes his head. "Not this time. Next session, probably, but not now."

Emily looks up. "Is it my turn, then?"

"Go ahead," Jessica says, obviously relieved not to have to deal any more with Henry's pirate past. "And let me warn you, when we finish this go-around, I'll have to stop. I'm getting pretty tired."

"Would you rather I skipped my questions?" Emily volunteers.

"No. I can manage a few more. And Milly can take up the slack for me." She stretches before getting ready to get the next answer.

"Well, I have been having a recurring dream for . . . oh, years now, and I've begun to think that it isn't a dream at all, but some sort of Astral contact. I always see myself walking in a spring meadow, full of flowers and sweet grasses, and there is always a person there, a man, somewhat older than I am—"

"What does Craig think about this?" Lizzy asks.

"He thinks it's something Astral, too," Emily says, completely unperturbed.

"Go on," Jessica prompts.

"Anyway, we walk along, and for some reason, we always end up talking about work. He tells me about the newspaper business and I tell him about teaching. What's going on, if anything?"

As you are well aware, Emily, the mind creates metaphors for the occurrences it cannot explain in other ways. This meeting you describe is indeed Astral and the metaphor of a spring meadow shows the comfort and satisfaction you feel in the contact. The Fragment you meet there is your Task Companion, who is employed as a journalist for a European periodical, and has been for almost twenty years. He is a first Level Old Scholar in the passion Mode with a Goal of Growth, a Pragmatist in the Moving part of Emotional Center with a Chief Feature of Arrogance. You must be aware that these Overleaves are quite compatible with yours and his work complements what you do.

"If this is my metaphor, is it his too?" Emily goes on.

No. This Fragment sees himself in a library with an unknown young woman who is always trying to take the same books off the shelves that he is interested in. This consistent metaphor for such contacts is not unusual in older Souls, and it is not as rare as you might think for both Fragments to have a very real and "conscious" sense of the other Fragment as a "real person" instead of a "figment of the imagination". This does not mean that those who dream of "face famous" Fragments are having Astral contact with them: in more than ninety-eight percent of such dreams, that is wishful thinking, not, in fact, Astral contacts. The other one point six percent are legitimate Astral contact, and tend to be without aspects of "glamor" that attend most such "dreams".

"So there," Jessica says when Emily has been able to read back the answer. "That's not all that bad. I was afraid you were going to ask about your sister again, and I'm not up for that today."

"No. I think Michael's told me all that they can about what's going on with her, and I think I'll simply have to come to terms with the choices she's made. Never mind that. Thanks for getting this about my TC. He's a pretty good guy, I think."

"You're biased," Larry points out.

"I should hope so," Emily counters with more spirit than she often betrays at sessions.

"Any more phone-ins?" Jessica wonders.

"Not phone-ins, but Craig wanted me to ask—if there's time— about a patient of his who has been refusing to follow the regimen Craig has recommended, and he flatly refuses to consult the specialist that Craig believes the fellow ought to see. Craig would like a comment on the patient and any recommendations that Michael would care to make in regard to treating the man. He's about fifty and his first name is Ellery."

The Fragment who is now Ellery is a fifth Level Baby Warrior in the Repression Mode with a Goal of Acceptance, a Stoic in the Intellectual part of Emotional Center with a Chief Feature of Stubbornness. The Overleaves should provide insight in themselves, but let us add that this Fragment has for many years practiced poor nutrition and as a result has left his body depleted of strength reserves. Like most Warriors this Fragment does not like to admit he does not feel well and therefore only seeks medical help when it is absolutely unavoidable. Let us recommend that, should he choose to do so, the Fragment who is Craig have a very thorough analysis made of this Warrior's body chemistry and then set about a nutritional regimen more in keeping with good health.

The specific problem at the moment could be described as a "stiffening" of the bronchial tubes, which in turn has caused certain respiratory problems and mild, unidentifiable angina, which is not specifically coronary in origin. It would be useful if the Fragment who is now Craig could keep in mind that this Warrior will tend to resist any and all treatment.

"Sounds delightful," Alex says when he has read the answer back. "I hope Craig can make some headway with him."

Emily shakes her head. "By the sound of it, it would make more sense to send him to you than to Craig."

"Thanks; I'll pass," Alex says. "I like my clients to be just a bit motivated to improve and this guy doesn't sound like that's part of the plan."

"Do you have another question, Emily?" Jessica asks.

"Yes, but I'd rather Milly get it for me, if you don't mind."

"Be my guest," Jessica says, her voice starting to sound fatigued.

"What's the question?" Camille asks. "I have trouble getting medical terms."

"You won't have to; this isn't medical. It's about my older daughter."

Emily stares down at her hands. "The trouble is, Jessica's known her a long time, and I think she might block some of the information."

"That's a reasonable assumption," Jessica says, reaching out to pour herself one last cup of coffee.

"And the trouble is that she's been involved with kids at school who are . . . well, there have been drug problems with some or all of them in the past year. I've tried to talk to her, and so has Craig, and she listens but it's apparent that nothing is getting through, not about the risks or the legalities or anything. I was hoping that Michael might have some suggestions as to how we can handle this problem."

"Okay, I'll give it a try," Camille says. "And everyone, please, quiet."

This Mature Sage is drawn to the theatricality of the others and the thrill of the experience. Yes, she has been using cocaine, and we would agree that there are great dangers in this. However, it is probably not going to be much use to speak to her as you have been doing, for your warnings do not address what the issue is for the Fragment who is now Janet. It is not enough to offer her terrifying pictures of what might happen to her, either physically or legally for her actions. The real issue is that this Sage feels that there is no applause, no connection, no "magic" in her life except what the drugs provide directly or tangentially.

Directly there is the chemical stimulation as well as the delicious thrill of doing something that others frown upon. The resultant familial upheavals have given her a spotlight she has longed to have. The Fragment who is now Janet considers herself very "avant-garde" and scorns anything that smacks of tradition or "the establishment". The tangential thrill is derived from your worry and disapproval. She not only gets the pleasure of taking the drugs, she gets to be the center of your attention at the same time, and with no effort at all. This is more notice than she has had since she was a very young child, and it pleases her. If you wish her to discontinue these practices, you would do well to change your tactics.

First, it would not be amiss to seek out a professional near her own age who has experience handling youngsters of her age. No matter how difficult, you and the Fragment who is now Craig would have to take suggestions from this professional. Whether or not you followed them would be, of course, your choice.

It would also be worthwhile to find a good, semi-professional theatrical instructor who would be willing to provide theatrical training for the Fragment who is now Janet. Remember, you cannot turn a Sage away from glamor, you can only offer something more glamorous. At the moment, this Fragment is leading the most glamorous life she can imagine. If she is to do something else, it must be because she has decided that another way is more glamorous. Most Sages respond well to this method of behavior control. In fact, it is of use to remember that all Sages like and need applause just as all Kings like and need willing obedience and all Scholars like and need sources of information. It is not inappropriate to exercise this variety of control if you do not deceive yourselves about your actions and discontinue them when the behavior has been altered. In general we do not see Good Work in the deliberate control of others in such situations, but since this very young Mature Sage has already fallen into far more manipulative hands than yours, there is a certain logic in "fighting fire with fire".

"How old is Janet now?" Camille asks as she hands her sheets of paper to Emily.

"Fifteen. She'll be sixteen on January twenty-fourth. I'm very worried about her, to say nothing of our other two kids. If we have to go through this with them as well . . ." She makes a helpless gesture.

"Well, I hope this does some good," Camille says with genuine concern.

"So do I. And anything is better than nothing."

"Brad? Katherine? Would you like to have a turn before we all clear up?" Jessica looks at the clock hanging over the piano. "It's almost five and we should finish by five-thirty."

"I've got a couple questions," Katherine says promptly. "That's one of the reasons I drove up a day early."

"Somehow I didn't think it was a total whim," Jessica tells her with a smile. "Let's take one from you first, then one from Brad, and then if there's time, we'll get in another for each of you, okay?"

"Fine with me," Katherine says; Brad just nods.

"I'd like some information on locating my TC. Michael has told me that she's an artist living in the San Diego area, and that she is about to have a one-woman show. Would Michael indicate where this show is to take place and something about it? I'd like to see what she's doing, and I'd like the chance to meet her, if possible."

The task companion will have this show in the city of—

"I have trouble getting names—bear with me. I'll do my best," Jessica says as the planchette passes over the board in aimless sweeps. "And Michael, don't show me pictures. I can't work with pictures."

—city of the southwest famous for its galleries. The work is mixed media, photography and oils, most of the photography using filters and other sources of distortion such as special lenses. The addition of paint creates very surreal impressions. The work is often called stark by those who are not used to the concept of iconographic art. This Fragment would find great solace in the company of her Task Companion Katherine, and of course such contact is always Good Work. But the very social setting of the gallery might not be the best place for validation. Let us suggest that contact through those known to both of you might produce better results.

"But we don't know anyone in common; I already asked," Katherine protests.

There are those in the area of the gallery who are friends with the owners of the gallery. It would not be difficult to be invited to the small, private reception being held the day before the opening. That could produce the desired results. Of course, there is the matter of time and transportation to consider, and do not think that we necessarily make light of these hazards of the Physical Plane. However, in many ways these are the least of your worries, and with a little advance planning, you could be in a position to make the journey without undue squandering of money or time.

"Sounds good. I've got friends in Santa Fe. I think I'll give them a call tonight, if you don't mind, Tracy."

"My pleasure," Tracy says. "Just let me know how it all turns out."

"Brad?"

"Well, this isn't really a question, but I'd like Michael to comment on something very strange that happened to me last week. I've tried to figure it out, and it still doesn't make any sense at all." He gives a slight, apologetic smile. "I was playing a private gig with some friends, and this woman came up to me while we were taking a break."

"Nothing strange in that," Lizzy says.

Brad doesn't quite glare at her, but his jaw becomes a little harder. "Anyway, she just wanted to say she'd liked the way we did the Haydn "Serenade," but ... she stared at me very hard and said in an odd tone of voice that she'd thought I'd be older, that I was older last time. I asked her what she meant, and she couldn't or wouldn't explain it. She went away and I didn't see her for the rest of the evening."

As you, Brad, are well aware, this Fragment was remembering your contact in your immediately previous life. At that time, you were of Austro-Hungarian origin, high social rank and very old family. At the time of the collapse of the empire, you turned your back on the shambles in disgust and went to France and Italy for the rest of your life. You became a distinguished collector of rare manuscripts and maintained your rather lavish way of life by serving as a consultant to various other collectors and museums. You knew the Fragment who addressed you last week in that life when she was a professor, male, working primarily in France and Britain, specializing in very rare manuscripts, such as those found in Egyptian tombs. At that time, you were colleagues, of course, and friends of a sort. You became estranged because of a debate over the authenticity of some Romanesque manuscripts. You believed they were genuine, she, then he, did not. Incidentally, they were not genuine, but the fraud was from the early fifteenth century, so your belief in their veracity was not unreasonable. The renewal of contacts is not as rare as most of you think, and this instance is unusual only for its openness.

"That sounds like fun," Jessica remarks when she had heard the answer. "I wish I had such good contacts."

"Can I do another one?" Katherine asks. "If you'd rather not, I can always phone the question in later."

"I think I can manage a couple more, unless they turn out to be those endless lectures that Michael gives sometimes."

"I don't think this is one of those questions, but if it is, say so and I'll postpone it."

"Let's give it a try and see what we get," Jessica suggests, watching Katherine. "If I don't think I can get it, Milly can."

"Or, since Jessica and I are doing a catch-up session together during the week, we could get it then and pass it on." Camille reaches for the heel of her shoe, then squares it on her foot.

"Whichever seems best," Katherine says. "I've been wondering why Michael places so much emphasis on past lives. I understand the connections of various sorts of experiences, but they also say that since those lessons have been learned, they're over and there are new lessons to be learned. This seems contradictory to me, and I was hoping that Michael would be willing to clarify it for me."

"That's complicated, but I'll do what I can." Jessica braces her board on the arms of her bentwood rocker. "Everybody get ready to write. This one feels like it's going to come very fast."

"Faster than it's been going?" Lizzy asks with disbelief.

"Probably," Jessica says, resigned to it.

We have indicated before that it is easier to know where you are going if you know where you have been, and easier to concentrate on the path you have chosen for this life if you know what paths you have trod before. The lessons of the life are more easily identified and learned when the lessons of the past are recognized and perceived as valid. For instance, to put it into a simple metaphor, you are more likely to learn calculus if you have already got a working knowledge of mathematics and geometry. It is easier to learn surgery if you have already studied anatomy. It is easier to understand architecture if you know a little about engineering and climatology. To have some notion of the past you have lived aids you in the life you are currently living, for each life is not only a venturing onto new ground, it is a culmination of previous experiences. We cannot emphasize enough that each of you chooses the life you live for each and every life. Even those lives where nothing appears to be accomplished bring lessons to bear. The more you can validate the past experiences, the more you are able to decide from Essence in this life, and the lives you have yet to live. There are those who suffer from amnesia. They have not forgot how to read, or how to spell, but they have forgot their names and much of their personal history. To us, most of you suffer from a similar form of amnesia. Of course, whether you "remember" or not, you will live for your lives and progress, that progress being the function of Essence in the life, that is, evolution. The more that you can recall the totality of your past, the more complete will be your "identity" for this life and the choices you make. It would be too much to say that such recall is required for growth—this is obviously not the case, or most of you would not have advanced beyond the Infant Cycle. Let us remind you that just as your childhood has helped to shape your adulthood, so have your past lives shaped your present life and the lives yet to come. These elements are not separate, Katherine, but part of the same tapestry, as you are part of the tapestry. [*March, 1997*: The process of evolution proceeds along certain patterns, just as the climate of this planet shifts along certain patterns, and gravity pulses across the Physical Plane in certain established patterns. One of our little group has said that she perceives the progression of lives as being part of a continuum. While this is not the full answer, it is certainly a component of the manner in which past lives have influence on the current one, and on those to come, on which this present life will also have influence.]

"I don't think I really understand this," Katherine says as she reads back the message, "but I'll go over it a few more times before I ask more about it. Thanks, Jessica. I didn't think it was going to be such a heavy issue."

"That's okay. Brad?" Jessica says. "Any other questions, or would you rather wait until next time?"

"I do have a question," he admits, "but you look exhausted and it's ten after five. I'll ask next time, and since I won't have a rehearsal, I'll be here at the beginning." He stands up. "Do you want me to carry anything to the kitchen?"

There is a general scramble to clear up mugs and empty plates, and then to gather coats and jackets.

"I miss daylight saving time," Henry says wistfully as he looks toward the picture window at the last, fading glow of sunset over the distant water. "In the summer, when a session is over, it still feels as if there's a whole afternoon left for doing things."

Kim, who is reaching into her purse for car keys, turns to Larry. "We were thinking of stopping for supper before going home. Would you like to join us, or do you have to get back? We're in your car, so you choose."

"Where were you planning to go to dinner?" Larry asks.

"A fish place," Kim answers. "Henry's got a favorite spot about fifteen minutes from here."

"Sounds good." He looks toward Camille. "Milly, can you come with us? I was hoping to get a chance to talk some more."

"Sage and Sage?" she asks as she tucks her notebook into her voluminous soft-leather purse. "Sure, why not. Provided I get home at a decent hour. I have to be at work tomorrow bright and early."

Jessica looks around the room. "Thanks, everyone. Walter'll be home soon, and this way he won't feel he has to do housework." She smiles a little wanly. "I wish he hadn't decided to take a dislike to Michael, but . . . well, things turn out that way, sometimes."

"I'll call you tomorrow evening, and we'll firm up the catch-up session," Camille says as she prepares to follow Larry and the Ingvessons out the door.

"Good. I do think Thursday evening's the best bet." She turns toward Katherine. "How long are you going to be in town?"

"Oh, three or four days at the least. I hope I can get a week, but that depends on how the work's going. They don't need me right now. Eric'll let me know when I have to be back."

"If you can, come down to the office tomorrow and we can have lunch together. Tracy, you'll be at work then, won't you?"

"Yeah. And I don't think I can take time off just yet. I'll call you later in the week, if Katherine's still around, and we can plan on having a drink one evening, if that's convenient."

"Thanks, Jessica. Good-bye!" Henry and Kim call from the front door before closing it. Trudi starts to bark as if it is expected of her.

"Hush, Trudi," Jessica says quietly and the old dog toddles off toward the kitchen. "Brad, would you like to leave your question with me for the catch-up session?"

He pauses in picking up his cello case. "How full is your schedule for the session?"

"Pretty full," Jessica says.

"It'll keep for next time. Thanks, anyway." He motions to Lizzy. "You need a lift?"

"No, thanks. I came with Tracy and Alex." The three of them live within two miles of each other and often carpool up to sessions.

"Then I'll see you next time."

Emily taps Jessica on the shoulder. "Do you mind if I bring that Old Slave I mentioned to you next session?"

Jessica hesitates. "Let me think it over, Emily, okay? I don't mean to be off-putting, but you know what can happen if we aren't careful.

Milly and I will discuss it on Thursday and I'll give you a call on Friday." She is sincerely troubled that she has to be so careful, and it shows in her manner. "Try to explain to your friend, will you, please?"

"I will," Emily promises. "Craig wants to come if he can get someone to cover for him. He doesn't like missing sessions."

"That's fine. I'd love to see him again," Jessica says, sounding more at ease.

Lizzy waves and sets off with Alex and Tracy. "See you!"

"Drive safely," Jessica calls after them, adding to Emily: "I always say that, and sometimes it drives Walter crazy."

"I know," Emily says.

"Thanks, Jessica," Brad calls out before he leaves.

"I'll talk with you later," Katherine tells Jessica as she goes down the three steps to the front door.

Then just Emily and Jessica are alone in the high-ceilinged living room. Jessica turns out the lights and drops onto the sofa, putting her feet up. "I like channeling, but sometimes I think it's more exhausting than lifting weights."

Emily remains silent, and after a little while, Jessica looks over at her.

"Penny for your thoughts." Emily gives a faint smile. "I was just thinking about everything Michael said today. Especially about the past."

"Um." Jessica puts a hand to her brow. "I blew it last time. I wonder if that's why I'm a medium this time around—to make up for lost time. Michael would probably say that nothing is lost, but I wonder . . . I know it contributes." She pauses. "But then, according to Michael, it all contributes."

CHAPTER SIX
Michael On the Past and Past Lives

Every life has resonances to the past; even first cast Infant Souls feel the pull, in that case back to the Tao from which they were cast, even as newborn infants are not yet aware that they are separate from their mothers. While recall of such lives does not often occur on all levels, there are still "feelings" and "affinities" that appear to have no explainable reason for their existence. While some of these resonances are not valid, many are, and for that reason it is useful to explore the past and the Essence's participation in it. The greater understanding thus obtained can aid the Fragment in accomplishing more of the tasks in a life.

We will give you a thorough overview of the immediate past life of a Fragment who is now a graphic artist and poet, a female in her mid-thirties. This immediate past life has had strong bearings on this life, which we will discuss at the end of the overview.

The Fragment who is now Sylvia was the second daughter of a family of three surviving girls born to a Hydriot father and an Austrian mother. Her birth occurred four years after their marriage and was a relief to both parents, for her mother had miscarried twice. The parents met in Trieste while attending a diplomatic reception. The mother's father was of "good" family and a noted professor who had brought his five children to Trieste to enjoy the summer. The father, a marine engineer, was representing certain ship-building concerns and took full advantage of any chance to meet those who could aid him in his commercial ventures. The reception was at a very elegant villa, and the young Greek engineer was captivated by the well-mannered, monied and cultivated Austrians. The father of the Fragment's mother was not immune to flattery and he was pleased to have such an escort for his family when he himself was occupied with research and academic meetings.

The Fragment's father was not a "proper" suitor in the eyes of her family and they did not encourage his interest in their seventeen-year-old daughter. When they left Trieste, it was quietly suggested that the

Hydriot not cause any trouble. The father went back to Hydra, thought about it for six months, then went to Salzburg to see the Austrian family again. They did not greet him with enthusiasm and we would have to say that there were many attempts to discourage his interest. But by then, the daughter was interested in the Hydriot marine engineer and did not like the men her parents had been introducing to her, and was worried that she would be forced into a match that she did not want. She started to meet her suitor clandestinely and eventually became pregnant. Her family, being strict Catholics, were horrified at her "loss of honor" as well as the threat of their daughter being lost to the Church through her folly. They had little choice, however, and reluctantly consented to the marriage, with certain strict provisions about the bringing up of the children, who were to spend a certain part of their school years in Austria, so that they could have what was considered a proper education as well as Catholic religious instruction. The Hydriot father gladly accepted these restrictions and further suggested that the family should visit them in Greece at their earliest opportunity.

After a hasty and not very impressive wedding in the parish church, the Austrian bride left for Athens with her new husband, confident that she would be breaking the stifling bonds of family which had caused her so much distress over her dashing suitor. Of course, the conduct of Greek family life was as strict, if not more strict, than the life of Austrian academic Catholics, and since the Austrian was not used to the language or customs of Greece, she became "neurotically" dependent on her husband, which at first flattered and then irritated him. His own family consisted of two brothers, both older, and three sisters, one older and two younger. They were diverse in their interests but very engrossed in the affairs of the family. Most of them did not like the Austrian bride, whom they regarded as an interloper. Only when the Austrian began to learn the Greek language did some of this dislike begin to fade.

The Austrian bride also brought forth two girls, which was not acceptable to the Greeks, who all desired sons to continue the family name and honor. This was not an unfamiliar attitude to the Austrian bride, but it became very disheartening and after a time she made less and less of an effort to accommodate the expectations of her in-laws, preferring to withdraw into vague artistic studies and the occasional and defiant practice of her religion. Her husband, at first sympathetic, became more and more indifferent, content to leave his wife to her own life and to pursue her professional interests and sexual needs elsewhere.

He had a series of mistresses over the years, and ended up with five illegitimate children. Since three of these were boys, he was eager to bring them into the family, but on that issue, the Austrian mother was adamant and completely refused such recognition. She felt, with justification, that her own daughters were being neglected for the sake of the bastard sons, and she would not accommodate the demands of her husband.

Although the two daughters spent several years in Salzburg with their grandparents and their aunts and uncles and cousins, they were certainly aware of their mother's difficulties at home, which caused them great distress. It made for more awkwardness than already existed in the family and when the grandparents insisted on learning what was taking place between their daughter and her husband, both daughters were subject to terrible feelings of betrayal and guilt. It is also important to note that in spite of the doting behavior of various family members at specific times, the general sense that both girls had was a feeling of neglect. They learned to adapt to it in different ways. The older girl, a second Level Mature Slave in Observation Mode with a Goal of Acceptance, a Pragmatist in the Intellectual part of Emotional Center and an eventual Chief Feature of Self-Deprecation, became more and more acquiescent to the demands of those around her in roles and positions of authority. She saw herself as unworthy of consideration and when it was suggested that she marry a Swiss physician on her last visit to Austria before she was intended to go back to Greece, she accepted, although she hardly knew the man and had no reason to think that it would be a good or bad match. She did not like the acrimonious company of her parents and she found her tempestuous younger sister hard to deal with. She informed her parents that she was going to marry a Swiss physician, and let the grandparents handle the rest. The engagement was to be a long one, allowing the Fragment who is now Sylvia to finish her schooling and to be able to decide where she would want to live.

The younger, middle daughter, the Fragment who is now Sylvia, was a seventh Level Mature Warrior in the Passion Mode with a Goal of Dominance, a Skeptic in the Moving part of Emotional Center with an eventual Chief Feature of Impatience, developed early on an emphatic nature that distressed her teachers and vexed her family. Until she was well into her twenties, she was considered volatile and capricious, traits that were improper for young women of her station and generation to have. She flaunted rules and kept on the edge of scandal all through her school years and accepted any punishment with defiant enjoyment. In her Austrian school she was both a leader and something of a bully to her classmates, whose behavior brought many complaints from her teachers, although with the concession that she was intelligent and capable when she wished to be. It was acknowledged that she was very bright and academically gifted, but no one knew what to do to calm her down enough for her to concentrate on her studies. When she was home in Greece, she often castigated her mother for her docility and her father for his lack of concern.

When the Fragment who is now Sylvia was fifteen, her mother once again became pregnant, which caused a furor on both sides of the family. To everyone's distress the child was yet another daughter and that brought nothing but disdain from both sides of the family. The father was convinced that his marriage had been a mistake and he informed his wife that they should not live together any longer, since plainly they had offended God and the proper order of things by marrying as they had done. His wife, who had become increasingly depressed and indifferent to herself and others, did not protest, but agreed to take up residence in Athens with her younger daughters where she could raise the offending children in peace. An annual sum was settled upon her for living expenses, and the two parents were in effect divorced. The mother lived as a semi-recluse and the father spent most of his time attending to his ship-building. He had become very successful and was rich enough to afford to keep a mistress openly, which he did. This arrangement continued for nine years.

When the Fragment who is now Sylvia returned to Athens from her schooling in Geneva, she was eighteen years old, an attractive young woman, fairly tall, athletic and pleasantly built with dark chestnut hair and a pleasing speaking voice. She alternated her time living with her father, which also entailed living with his mistress, which she did not like at all, and spending as much time as she could bear with her mother and youngest sister, whose withdrawn way of living nearly drove the Fragment who is now Sylvia to distraction. At the end of a year she accepted the invitation of her father's sister to live with her and moved into her house in Athens at the age of twenty-one.

She admired her aunt's independence, but could not share her religious zeal. Her aunt had first entered a convent as a girl, and discovered that she had no true vocation. Upon leaving the convent, she was married while still quite young, and her husband had died within six weeks of the wedding. The aunt had decided that it was not God's will that she be married and so was content to remain a widow, actively involved in community Good Works, especially relief and education of the poor. Occasionally the Fragment who is now Sylvia assisted her aunt, but most of the time she spent her hours in the company of what might be called the "fast set," where she caused a number of near scandals, and often came into open conflict with her parents over her behavior. Finally, nearing age twenty-three, she agreed to go on a trip to Europe with her aunt and was there during the beginning rumblings of the First World War, as you call it. This Fragment remained with her aunt in Europe for just under two years.

By the time she returned to Greece, she was twenty-four and the war was about ready to begin, although actual hostilities and battle were still more than a year away. She was introduced to a wealthy man-about-town, twelve years her senior, who set about a determined wooing of her. While it is true he was sincerely attracted to her, he was also aware of the fortune her father possessed and he knew that he would do well for himself in such a family. He subjected her to all the usual courtesies of courtship as well as a few more daring tributes, which she found intriguing and novel, both of which were important factors in her life. She expressed her fascination with her usual caprice at first, then became more passionately involved. Although neither parent was particularly pleased with the suitor, they were both relieved that someone had at last captured their daughter's interest and was presentable enough to permit into the family.

The two were married with a fair amount of pomp. When the war began, the Fragment who is now Sylvia's Austrian mother became concerned about her parents, still living in Salzburg and determined to remain there. She told her husband that she wanted to return to Austria and visit her family before travel became so dangerous that it was impossible. Her husband was willing that she go, and in fact, was relieved to put an end to the more awkward of his domestic arrangements: while his wife was away, it would be less incorrect for him to live openly with his mistress, and there was always the chance that he might be able to make some arrangement for the recognition and legitimization of his sons. The Austrian mother took her youngest daughter and left for Austria where she died of influenza in one thousand nine hundred nineteen, common reckoning.

The eldest daughter, from her vantage point in Switzerland, kept the Fragment who is now Sylvia apprized of the conduct of the war throughout the hostilities, and asked about news from the Balkan regions as well as the Sudan, in exchange for her information. For the first time in many years, the two sisters benefitted from their relationship and developed a degree of understanding that had been lacking earlier in their lives.

The war provided a good opportunity to turn a profit for the Hydriot father, who was willing to take advantage of the situation to develop better ships. He went into partnership with one of the more prestigious Greek ship-builders and moved his family, by which we mean his mistress and his bastard children, to Pireas to be closer to the ship-building center there. He was injured by a bomb set by political dissidents, which sent him into semi-retirement, suffering from brain damage.

In spite of the good beginning to the marriage, it did not thrive, and when their first child was stillborn, the husband was worried that he had chosen badly and that the Fragment who is now Sylvia was a poor bargain. A second child was born, but died as the result of accidental drowning at age four. An estrangement developed between the Fragment who is now Sylvia and her husband, which never resulted in actual severing of the marriage, as had happened to her parents, but was never truly healed or whole.

The Fragment who is now Sylvia spent more time with her aunt and became more active in teaching children, especially poor children, which was not always the most applauded thing she could do. Her father, especially, was infuriated that she should do this, as he considered her to be supporting the very people who had made him a semi-invalid. She permitted herself to argue with him, but would not change her mind, and refused to be persuaded to his point of view.

At the end of the First World War, there was a burst of prosperity that benefitted the Hydriot father, and he took advantage of it. Now that he was a widower, he married his mistress and legitimized his bastard sons and one daughter. He also invested his money carefully and established trust funds for his three legitimate daughters. This was considered most generous of him by all his family except his legitimate daughters, who were irate.

His youngest daughter, in one thousand nine hundred twenty-one, common reckoning, announced that she was going to enter Catholic holy Orders in spite of the horrified objections of her Greek relatives. The Fragment who is now Sylvia and her aunt went to see her in the hope that they would be able, if not to dissuade her, to make her understand how opposed the paternal side of the family was to such an action, which seemed a deliberate affront to them. The youngest sister heard them out and then went into the convent.

While in Europe, the Fragment who is now Sylvia and her aunt also visited the eldest daughter in Switzerland and found that she had accepted her placid existence without complaint. She had a nice enough husband and four intelligent and well-mannered children and wanted nothing so much as for things to return to the way they had been twenty years before. She even disliked riding in automobiles because she felt they were too fast and somehow improper.

The degree of change in Europe was amazing to the Fragment who is now Sylvia. She found it a sobering experience to see what the war had done to the various countries. The Austro-Hungarian empire was gone and Germany was in complete disarray. She was struck by the privations of the war and became more aware of the social inequities of the old system, and as a result, began reading extensively in the works of various political and economic philosophers in an attempt to understand what had happened and how it might be avoided in the future. She also became very worried about the size of the war and thought that if so much of Europe and the Near East could be caught up in it, another war would be much worse. She confided her thoughts to her aunt, who was more concerned about the spiritual consequences of the war and the psychic privations than she was the socioeconomic ones.

The aunt, who had occasional bouts of what was called melancholia, and today would be regarded as chronic depression, and had had them since her twenties, was starting to have them with increasing frequency and of longer duration. This was at first attributed to her age and dismissed as an unfortunate consequence of menopause. The Fragment who is now Sylvia was concerned that it might be more than that, and while they were still in Switzerland persuaded her aunt to undergo a thorough examination. The results were not explained to the aunt, but the Fragment who is now Sylvia was told that her aunt suffered from a degenerative mental condition and that there was nothing, at that time, that could be done for her. The physicians and alienists urged her to return home so that her aunt could be in more familiar surroundings and not to have more stress than she was prepared to handle. The Fragment who is now Sylvia agreed that this was necessary and immediately arranged passage back to Greece.

Upon their arrival back home, she learned that her father had become worse and when she visited him she was aware that he had got much weaker. He admitted that he was afraid to die, and confessed to his sister, who had accompanied the Fragment who is now Sylvia, to his home, that he knew he had neglected his soul while he tended to his flesh and family. He was not aware how precarious his sister's state of mind was, and did not know that she was near another period of withdrawal.

Seeing her brother suffering and feeling herself out of control, the aunt became semi-catatonic and had to be placed in a "special" hospital. This brought about a crisis in the larger family, the brunt of which was borne by the Fragment who is now Sylvia. For the first time in over four years, the Fragment who is now Sylvia attempted to reach her husband for emotional support, but found that he was not able or willing to provide it. She grew angry and demanding at this lack, insisting that he owed it to her as her husband, which only made him more obdurate. They parted with angry words, and after that time he made a point of avoiding her.

In desperation, and as a kind of tribute to her aunt, the Fragment who is now Sylvia went back to the school she had helped start and began to be a teacher in earnest. She had never thought of herself as having a way with children, and it is true that not all of them responded well to the force of her personality, but many of them, caught in poverty and having little hope, were grateful for that chance to break the patterns that had held down their families for so long. While in general the Fragment who is now Sylvia concentrated on basic information, what is now called the "three Rs," she eventually got involved in discussing sociopolitical and economic issues with her students as they grew older and more sophisticated.

The effects of the terrible inflation in Europe during what is called "The Twenties" had some influence in Greece, and as a result, the Fragment who is now Sylvia started to become more outspoken in her observations and criticisms. She continued to teach basic education, but she began to urge her students to expand their studies and prepare themselves for dealing with the sophistication of the real political machines working in Greece and in Europe. She insisted that understanding the socioeconomic systems would be necessary to anyone attempting to do business in the larger market place of international trade.

She spent some of her money providing an expanded library for her students, and she arranged for translations of several texts not readily available in Greece, doing some of the work herself when the language was German. She found this very stimulating, and the opposition of her dying father only goaded her on. To increase the Fragment who is now Sylvia's convictions on her philosophy of education, for a while her aunt was well enough to come home from the "special" hospital, and she was genuinely pleased at what the Fragment who is now Sylvia had accomplished with the students.

But as soon as the Hydriot father died, the aunt once again withdrew, this time more completely. She was placed in an asylum with reasonable care for the time and country, but for the rest of her life, she was increasingly unresponsive, often standing in the same position for several hours, staring at a place on the wall or ceiling without true focus of her eyes. Her brother's will provided for her care, so that was never an issue, but the Fragment who is now Sylvia found herself very upset by this, since she had come to rely for emotional support and companionship from her aunt, and had not been aware of it until that support was withdrawn. Her inheritance was not large but it was sufficient to allow her to keep the school going.

While the aunt's condition deteriorated, the Fragment who is now Sylvia made many attempts to "reach" her aunt and establish communication and response once again, but the aunt appeared to be unwilling or unable to respond, and as a result, the Fragment who is now Sylvia sensed failure in what she did, instead of an appreciation for what she had tried to accomplish.

As the school she had helped to found prospered in its way, the Fragment who is now Sylvia came under severe criticism for what she was teaching her students. There were those, particularly in certain parts of the government, who made various attempts to stop or at least contain her, without any genuine success. The Fragment who is now Sylvia refused to stop teaching without actual legal steps being taken against her. She often spoke before various groups, particularly the poorer groups, to outline to them the problems facing them as she saw them, and to propose means to deal with them. She was particularly worried about what had happened in Germany, for although she agreed with many principles of the National Socialist German Workers' Party, she also disliked the means they employed to gain their ends. Since the "Nazi" ideals were attractive to a good number of the poor, she found herself for the first time since she became a teacher, attacked by the very people she wished to champion. This troubled her very much and she had no one to whom she could turn for comfort and advice.

In this state of mind, she was especially vulnerable to the interest and sympathy of others, and when she was approached by a young Italian academic, she was grateful for his assistance as well as his flattering attention. He was six years her junior and a very attractive man. She enjoyed going places with him, being seen with him and developing the companionship he appeared to offer her. She became intensely involved with him, telling far more than was wise and permitting him to advise her in matters she would not in general let others comment on at all. The affair was a difficult one, fueled as it was by karma as well as strong body-type attraction. The Fragment who is now Sylvia was willing to indulge her suitor in ways that she never had permitted her suitors in the past, and she made no attempt to sort out her feelings. After those years of emotional deprivation, she clung to what she wanted to have.

Essence, of course, was aware that there was a ribbon here, a debt of abandonment from the past, when the Fragment who is now Sylvia had been a Kievan nobleman who deliberately abandoned his most able captain to the vengeance of the tsar, giving the captain blame for a treason that the Fragment who is now Sylvia had, in fact, committed. Now the captain returned to her life with a debt to be paid. Between that powerful link from the past and the strong body-type attraction, the relationship was a powerful one in every respect.

While it is true that much of what the Fragment who is now Sylvia taught to her Greek students was considered at that time to be subversive, she herself was not particularly, either in attitude or intent. On the other hand, the Italian was—in fact, he had been sent to Greece to act as an agent provocateur, which he did with great success. When the government began to take issue with the teaching being provided and to suspect that the instruction extended into more serious political activities, the Italian was willing to set the Fragment who is now Sylvia up for the blame and the punishment.

She was arrested on charges of subversive activities and the possibility of treason and was held in prison for more than six months. During that time she had one visit from her lover, and then he begged her to do what she could to protect him, meaning he demanded that she lie for him, implicating herself for things he had done. Out of her love and the demands of their karmic debt, she agreed and refused to admit he had been part of the crime of which she stood accused. She exonerated him when she was questioned by the authorities. Her husband denounced her to those officials who would listen, and her step-siblings refused to be drawn into the matter at all, claiming that she was "foreign" and therefore not part of their family.

At last, having no one else to blame, she was determined to be guilty of treason and anarchistic activities and was hanged with piano wire, her body interred in a nameless grave with the bodies of other subversives. The ribbon was burned, which was Good Work, and there was growth and recognition on many levels. The Italian returned home in time to die in a riot in Modena shortly before the entrance of the United States of America into what you call the Second World War.

The eldest daughter lived until one thousand nine hundred fifty-one, common reckoning, and died a very old lady in her home near Lausanne. The youngest daughter died in her convent during a bombing raid in one thousand nine hundred forty-three, common reckoning. Two of the bastard brothers are still alive, both very elderly, one senile, the other with cancer. One still lives in Greece: the other lives in Romania. [*June 1994*: Both these Fragments have since died, the one in Greece six years ago, the one in Romania three years ago.]

The Fragment who is now Sylvia had one karmic ribbon, fifteen primary and twenty-three secondary Agreements for that life, and, of course, her own Internal Monads to accomplish. Her decision to choose a life where she would come to work with those who are oppressed although born to privilege came from the experience of the life before when the Fragment who is now Sylvia was working in India, part of the military, and died during what is called the Sepoy Mutiny. The experience of that life led the Fragment to desire to develop the lessons more, and in the immediate past life, it was possible for the Fragment to accomplish this end.

Let us point out that the choice was always there. It was possible for Sylvia to ignore the lesson she set for herself and enter into a life of international travel, or to remain in Germany or Austria, or to travel abroad and remain in a foreign country. It was never required that she do anything she had chosen to do with her life, for as the lessons of the life are chosen, so are the experiences of the life. [*May, 2001*: Many Fragments choose travel as a way to avoid the struggle of Monadal transits, while others immerse themselves in religious or physical disciplines that serve to keep the Fragment "too occupied" for the hazards of Monads and Agreements and Life Plans. Occasionally this serves to bring the Fragment in question to a place where Monads, Agreements, and/or karma is waiting, but generally this "escape" succeeds in postponing the experiences and perceptions that Essence seeks for evolution. There is nothing "wrong" in this, but it tends to leave the Fragment with ill-defined frustrations in the life. Where the Fragment is inclined to compulsive activity, avoidance can take the form of compulsions to "get lost" in recreational chemicals of all sorts. We assure you this is not a matter of addiction for almost all Fragments so encumbered, but one of compulsion. Such compulsions have many components associated with them, but most of those who embrace compulsivity do so as a means of avoiding fears originating, of course, with Chief Feature activity and fueled by disappointments, scripts, and Family Icons.]

It is well to realize that the Mature Priest Fragment who was her aunt was in fact abdicating two major "lessons" the Priest had chosen for that life, which was in part the source of her insanity. The Priest in this life is an actor, very gifted and temperamental, but we would have to say that this time he has found an oblique way to gain the necessary experiences that he had been avoiding for three lives in the past.

The karmic ribbon of the Fragment who is now Sylvia was successfully burned, as we have indicated. Of the Agreements, eleven of the primary Agreements were fulfilled; the Fragment who is now Sylvia abdicated two—one with one of her students with whom she quarreled, the other with a Mature King whom she never actually met—and had two abdicated by the other participant: the relationship with her husband was one such abdicated Agreement, the other was with her younger sister; and we would have to say that, given the circumstances surrounding the family at that time, it would have been next to impossible for either Fragment to accomplish their Agreement as they had planned to.

The secondary Agreements—that is, Agreements that "kick in" when something goes "wrong" with an Agreement; a backup Agreement—fared less well, which is not uncommon with secondary Agreements, which is in part why there are apt to be more secondary Agreements in a life than primary ones. Of the twenty-three secondary Agreements, thirteen were successfully completed, which is a fairly good level of accomplishment. Agreements, of course, are most often binding for one life only, and are renewed or discontinued by common consent between lives. These secondary Agreements ranged from giving instruction to certain Fragments to providing shelter for a certain family. The latter was never accomplished, but that is because the circumstances of social unrest made it unwise for the Fragments involved to ask for such shelter, which, of course, was an abdication.

In this immediate past life the Fragment who is now Sylvia was able to bring her lessons to bear and to do work on the task at hand, as well as on the Life Task. Such work advances the Fragment and leads to the evolution of the Essence. The Fragment who is now Sylvia lives in Canada in this life, away from the scenes that might cause her distress or confusion, and for that reason, she often feels that she is "starting fresh". There is validity in that insight. Many Fragments decide to be born where they have not lived before in order to be free of the memories that seeing old haunts might bring. We remind you that such memories are not always pleasant, and that in some cases, it can be very disorienting for a Fragment to be in a place that is a constant reminder of what has gone before.

Of course when previous lives have been successful and pleasant, there is an urge to return to the place and to enjoy it again. Let us give you a few examples. A Fragment is born female in Austria in the year one thousand eight hundred two and, for reasons not in her life plan, she ends up working in the household of a minor nobleman who seduces her. Instead of abandoning her, he decides to set her up as his concubine, takes her in, and when he finally lets her go, she is in a position to establish herself in her own right as the mistress of a "salon" and establishment of prostitution, and as such lives a fairly long and relatively successful life.

The nobleman who treated her so honorably gained a karmic ribbon of philanthropy for his generosity, in that he provided her life opportunities and choices for her that would not have been possible for her without his intervention. The life, while not what the Fragment had planned for herself, was a distinct improvement on what she had been prepared to get, and so, when she was born again, this time as a male in Ireland, there was a lingering affection for things Austrian, an "unaccountable" facility with the German language—an unusual but useful gift for a cab driver to have—and a real sympathy for the prostitutes who lived and worked in his city. That life did not go as well, and the Fragment died while still fairly young—thirty-seven—in one thousand nine hundred one, common reckoning, and decided between lives that it had been more pleasant in Austria, so decided to return there as a female and to resume her former profession. The Fragment was reborn in what is now part of Poland, and quite young went to Vienna, assuming that it would be a repeat of former delights. But by then it was one thousand nine hundred thirty-seven, common reckoning, and the economic and political climate had changed a great deal. Instead of the satisfaction of previous experiences, this Fragment lived a very short and sadly brutal life that ended in her sadistic murder in the year one thousand nine hundred forty. This Fragment is extant on the Physical Plane again, male, living near Auckland, New Zealand, in an effort to break with past patterns.

Here is another example of location and action. A Fragment, at the time a fifth Level Young Scholar, was born in the Byzantine empire in the year five hundred twenty-two, common reckoning. In time he rose to the position of court censor, gaining great political and economic power, but at the same time blocking insights and development in such a way that not only did he incur several karmic ribbons for such actions as unjust imprisonment, but he ended his life in utter despair for the limitations that seemed endless and growing worse by the hour; he was forty-eight when he died. The Fragment was born again in Africa, some twenty-eight years later, the oldest son of the village shaman, and therefore regarded with respect and suspicion. The experience of the censor was still fresh, and as a result, the Scholar chose to take a more iconoclastic approach to life and ended up in serious conflict with his father over the nature of the role of the shaman in the lives of the villagers, which the Scholar son believed to be too great. Tried by the village, the Scholar was made an outcast and ordered to leave the village forever. He was not permitted to take his wives with him and he ended up near Egypt where he was made a slave and where he died of blood poisoning at the age of twenty-nine.

The Fragment was then reborn in southern Spain, a Moor, and in a merchant's family. During that life, the Fragment took two orphans into his household and raised them as his own children, then established them in their own business and backed the businesses, occasionally at the expense of his own business. As you might suspect, this Fragment was burning karmic ribbons from the life before last, and although he was not "happy" in that life, the lessons were brought to bear and there was much growth. The Fragment ended that life at what was a reasonably advanced age— fifty-eight—and with all seven Internal Monads completed.

The next life, begun almost thirty-four years after the last life, lasted for less than two years and brought certain lessons to bear that had been started in a life prior to that of the censor.

As a sixth Level Young Scholar, the Fragment was born in seven hundred forty-one, common reckoning, this time as a female in Normandy, where she became fascinated by the Christian religion and eventually entered a convent where she took it upon herself to do the lowest and most menial tasks available in service to the nuns and those who came to them for help and aid in time of sickness and/or need. The Fragment gave service all of her life, which permitted another nine ribbons to be burned, but we would have to say that there was little recognition of this by the Fragment, who was often indulging a Chief Feature of Arrogance, which had become set on showing the greatest humility possible. That did not change the burning of the ribbons, although the Fragment did not benefit from the ribbon-burning in that life.

In the following life, the Fragment was born, again female, in a village in central India, and there lived a quiet, bucolic life, raising crops and tending to seven children for most of her years. This was a resting life, one that gained little ground but created no karma or other burden, either.

In the life after, the Fragment was born in what is now part of Turkey, the second son of a family of criminals. In that life, the Fragment spent a good ideal of time with his Task Companion, who was what you might call a fence, in your terms. The Scholar waylaid travelers, took their goods and often sold the unfortunates into slavery, or killed them. When the victim was rich, then a ransom was demanded. The Fragment created more ribbons to burn, but also burned two by defending their stronghold while others made their escapes, as it turned out, at the cost of his life.

The last life as a sixth Level young Scholar was spent as a trainer of horses for a Moroccan prince. Again, the life was not terribly eventful, and it was possible for several minor Agreements and a Monad to be done without interference from the activities of the life.

The first life as a first Level Mature Scholar was begun in Tunisia where the Fragment was sold into slavery, rebelled at the inhumane treatment being given her and the other slaves owned by this particular spice merchant, instigated a plan for escape and revenge, and was killed in the attempt, although most of the others escaped. This, of course, burned several ribbons and created a few that were owed to the Scholar.

In the next life, the Fragment was born in what you would call Ecuador, where the Fragment lived quietly as a fisherman, raising a family and tending to the problems of making better fishing nets.

In the life after that, the Fragment returned to more familiar ground, to Greece, where he became a monk at an early age and spent most of the life copying texts. In this he was aided by three of the members of his pentate, who were also at the particular monastery, striving to preserve certain Biblical translations in as pure a form as possible. Two Agreements were fulfilled and the Monad begun as a horse trainer was completed as a monk. The Fragment died of cholera at the age of thirty-one.

The life that followed was more active. The Fragment was a Tartar woman, and married into what passed for wealth in that time and place. She was intelligent and active, often "chafing at the bit" for more chances to study. In this she was aided by the elder of her group who was not only her champion but her Task Companion as well. Eventually the two were accused of adultery—which they had not, in fact, committed—and she was executed for her supposed transgressions.

In the life that followed, the Scholar was born in Scotland and spent the better part of his life as a carter. The life was short, the labor exhausting and the conditions grueling. In the process of tending to the carts and the horses that drew them for upper-class clients—lower-class clients had to be content with oxen or mules to draw the wagons—this Fragment developed serious joint disease quite young and was crippled before he reached the age of twenty-eight. He was forced to become a beggar when he could no longer work in that capacity, and died of starvation at age thirty-one. This life was important because it brought many lessons to bear, and although there was a formidable misery throughout it, the Fragment managed to appear both cheerful and accepting of what he had to endure. His family—which consisted of three spinster sisters, one of whom was retarded—could not comprehend what the Fragment was so cheerful about and regarded him as "touched" in his mind. We would agree in a way, but for different reasons and with different intent in the work.

The life that followed was brief and ended when the Scholar drowned accidentally at age three. This life was obviously not complete, and so the Fragment decided to choose circumstances that would permit a greater degree of comfort and a chance at longevity, and for that reason, chose to be born in what you call China into a family of court musicians. The Fragment had poor eyesight from birth, and therefore was deemed unsuited to any life but the musical one. The Scholar passed almost all of that life at the imperial court where he played several instruments with virtuoso ease. He composed many works, married another Mature Scholar who was part of his Entity and who bore him six children, four of whom lived into adulthood and who were regarded as gifted musicians in their own right. Although the Scholar was never wealthy, he was financially comfortable for the seventy-three years of his life, honored by those around him and loved by his family. Incidentally, his eyesight, which made him technically blind at that time and place, would have been easily corrected by modern optical techniques.

As a second Level Mature Scholar, the Fragment chose to undertake the burning of more karmic ribbons, and so was born female in what was then Hungary. She became a camp-follower, and trekked over much of eastern Europe as well as part of what is sometimes called the Holy Land. She was as formidable a fighter as the men with whom she lived, and she met her end defending wounded soldiers, thus burning nine karmic ribbons and getting another owed to her from the two soldiers who raped and mutilated her before she died.

In the life after that, the Scholar became what was sometimes called a troubadour, going from town to town and from fort to fort singing songs and telling tales, many of which were drawn—without conscious recognition—from past experiences. This Fragment enjoyed something of a reputation for performance, both as an entertainer and a lover, and it was because of the latter skill that he met his end at age forty-one at the hands of an enraged husband.

In the next life, the Fragment became a scribe in the general vicinity of Moscow and earned an adequate living writing letters and reading them for illiterate adults, which described most of the population at that time.

What we have been attempting to show in these continuing lives are the varieties of ways that lessons can be learned, the various means of gaining and burning karmic ribbons, and the range of experience that is possible for any Essence, no matter what the perceptions of the Essence are. We would wish to make it clear that this Scholar did not always have the life that it planned to have—such lives happen rarely—but that choices kept the Fragment focused when the Scholar was willing to listen to the insights of Essence and when circumstances gave the Fragment some opportunity to broaden experience in a given life. Remember that we have said that Scholars dislike being female because of the restrictions usually put on females, particularly in the realms of learning. [*November, 2004:* We would wish to point out that evolution does not occur in a "straight line," but in a series of curves, expanding and contacting, so that the Fragment may experience a wide range of lives in order to increase the insights and perceptions available to the Fragment. The more varied the experience in the Young and Mature Cycles, the more insights are accessible to the Fragment in all lives chosen, all of which contributes to the evolution of the Fragment.]

This Scholar is now a second Level Old Scholar, male, an electrical engineer doing developmental work on sophisticated computers and recognized within the field, if not without, as something of an expert on the nature of programming in the terms of mathematical philosophy.

We would wish that those of you here present would regard the information given on past lives as a kind of guide post to your current activities, and to go over the information from time to time with the possibility of gaining insights that can add to the progress of the Essence. The past teaches many things to those on the Physical Plane, including the reminder that hazards of the Physical Plane are indeed genuine and capable of causing much interference with contact and the subsequent growth that all will seek, if not in this life, in another.

We will stress again that the lessons of the Physical Plane are concerned with choice. Regard the lives of the Scholar chronicled and consider what the Essence decided to do in order to bring the lessons to bear. It is not accidental that the lives that were chosen required that the Fragment live in certain circumstances and with certain limitations put upon it. Those limitations, although basically part of the rule of maya, are nonetheless the strongest and most persuasive part of the Physical Plane and therefore of great interest and importance to those Fragments currently incarnate.

Let us take another case, this time concerned with Monads, Internal and external. The Fragment in question was a third Level Mature Sage, one concerned with the machinations of the religion of the area in which it was born in the thirteenth century, common reckoning. At that time, the Sage was in the passion Mode with a Goal of Acceptance, and therefore sought out difficult circumstances in order to deal with them, or more accurately, to express them not only for those caught up in them, but for itself as well. In that life, the Fragment was an archbishop in what is now part of southern France and as such, became actively involved in searching out heretics that were thought to be dangerous to the Church. This Fragment at the time strove to define and interpret the definition of heresy so that all would understand its meaning and no possible doubt could bring those not guilty of the crime to the stake. This, while laudable in a sense, was not the intent of the Young Priests in charge of the religious purge in that region, and the superior of the Sage, and after a time, the Sage came under scrutiny himself, and was at last brought to trial. The trial process was conducted by one who was not only part of the Sage's Entity, but one with whom the Sage was Monadally bound, and therefore eager to interact with the Sage. The Monad had to do with the Accuser and the Accused. Under the prosecution of the Young Slave who was the head of the religious tribunal, the Sage was found to be guilty of heresy, although that crime was still not defined to the Sage's satisfaction. Within a short period of time, the Sage was brought first to be broken on the wheel, and then, rather than be left hanging in an iron cage or in chains, he was burned for the edification of the public at large. The Young Priest who accused him went on to denounce many heretics and was eventually made a saint for his efforts. The Young Slave who tried and convicted the Sage went on to become a bishop.

The Sage was then born as a trainer of performing dogs in the imperial Chinese court, followed by a life as the town magistrate in Korea. This was in turn followed by a life spent in the southern Pacific as the chief teller of tales and singer of songs for an island people. All the while, the second part of the Monad hovered over the Sage and in time the pull became irresistible. The Fragment was born in what is now Estonia, a minor nobleman, the second son of a very aggressive warlord who allied himself with the most powerful nobles around him on terms that were to his advantage. The Sage, harking to the prompting of Essence, did not wish to wage war or be caught in any spying, urged his father to negotiate more openly, volunteering to do the negotiating himself, which is entirely in character for a Sage. For most of his younger years, his father refused, but upon the father's death, the Sage commenced the negotiations that he had assumed would lead to the ending of open hostilities. He therefore made contact with the chief officer of the opposition and the second phase of the Monad with the Young Priest was under way. In the process of these negotiations, the Sage discovered that the officer with whom he was dealing was guilty of treason, and since the bonds of loyalty are not as stringent for those on the Expression Polarity as they are to others, the Sage brought forth proof of the officer's activities and the Monad was completed when the officer was executed for the treason that the Sage had discovered. The choice made by the Sage was crucial to the completion of the Monad, and if the pull to completion had not been so strong or so clearly recognized, it is likely that the Sage might have resorted to simple political blackmail, which would not have completed the Monad. Obviously, there was no karma created by this exchange of accusations and the results of the accusations because the Monad and hence the results of the Monad had already been chosen, so the accusations, just or unjust, were not the removal of choice for either Fragment at either time.

Agreements and Monads that involve actions that might, under other circumstances be karmic, carry the strength of choice with them, and cannot be regarded in the same way that karmic associations are perceived. Let us illustrate this difference in a more cogent way: a Mature Artisan had a partnership Monad with a Young Priest and to that end they went to work in a dry goods business. One was to be the partner with the money, the other the partner with the product. This is a fairly common Monadal experience and many Fragments choose to have it. In the course of their partnership, the Priest encountered serious business reversals and began to take money out of their business in a covert and illegal fashion which resulted in an investigation of their business by governmental authorities. This took place in China during what is called the Tang Dynasty. In those days such frauds were treated harshly and as a result the Priest became terrified and did everything he could to throw suspicion on the Artisan, who was at a loss as to what had happened or how to defend himself against the accusations leveled at him. As a result, the Artisan was disgraced and unjustly imprisoned. He died in prison. The first half of the Monad had been somewhat accomplished, but the falsifying of records leading to the incarceration of the Artisan created a karmic ribbon as well as the Monadal bond, for the Monad did not include imprisonment for the Artisan. The ribbon was burned three lives later when the Priest permitted the crew of a pirate vessel to escape his ship without harm—a humanitarian gesture that baffled him and earned him severe punishment from his superiors—but the Monad was not completed until two lives after that when the Priest came to the Artisan, who was then the local overlord, with plans for an improved flour mill. In constructing and operating the mill the Monad was finally completed. The pull of the karmic ribbon being stronger than the Monadal link, the karma had to be burned before the Monad could be recognized. It is appropriate for Fragments to be self-aware—please note that we do not say self-conscious or self-centered—so that the lessons can be perceived as they are encountered. This self-awareness is part of the growth of the Fragment, although of course each Cycle has its own version of self-awareness.

It is through self-awareness that the past, both in the current life and in previous lives, is recognized. Self-awareness begins with validation of the individual Overleaves and a sense of what direction the life is taking. That is not as simple a task as it sounds, for there are many aspects to this recognition that do not come easily to Fragments on the Physical Plane. Much of the past is cloaked in misunderstandings and misinformation, and many Fragments are eager to learn of distinguished past lives but not the karma-bound ones, or those—and they are by far the most frequent— spent in simple or "disadvantaged" social positions.

We remind you of a Fragment who attended sessions for several months three years ago who had been the private secretary to a French minister of state. This Fragment was anxious to believe that she had been that minister, and not his secretary, and was convinced that she had never been less than educated and wealthy in her various incarnations. This is, of course, nonsense. There would be little growth or development in repeating such patterns endlessly, and Essence, we remind you, yet again, is eager to evolve. While we would agree that the life deserving of the greatest attention is the one currently being lived, we would like to point out that the choices made for this life have been predicated on what has gone before. There are many paths to the goal, in this immediate life and in the course of all the lives led by any and all Fragments. The process is the lesson of the Physical Plane. There are no paths that are "wrong" and none that are "right" but there are those that are chosen from the positive poles of the Overleaves and those chosen from the negative poles of the Overleaves. Evolution and contact are, of course, the products of the positive poles.

Most of those here present are by now familiar with the experience of meeting old friends for the first time in this life, and the degree of confusion this occasionally creates. When the nature of the past associations is understood and appreciated, and when the Overleaves are known, there can be much benefit to such associations. That is not to say that there is no merit in the company of old friends who are unrecognized, but the greater the recognition, the greater the opportunity for validation and advancement. For example, if a Fragment who is now working as a laboratory assistant comes into contact with an old friend who is now pursuing a career as an accountant, but their past associations were in religious Orders and as comrades before the mast, then it might be pleasant for such Fragments to spend time in church or rowing about on a lake together, to further experience the bonds created in the previous lives.

Two Fragments often attending these little groups, both Old Warriors, both women, have often been comrades at arms in the cavalry and now enjoy trail-riding together, "for old time's sake". Task Companions belonging to our little group several times toured the various cities of the past as trainers of animals, jugglers, and clowns. To this day, the Task Companions, who in this life are husband and wife, enjoy going to the circus and to fairs because such entertainments seem "comfortable". These Fragments who take advantage of the past to enhance the present do much to bring the lessons of this life to bear and to profit from lessons of the past already learned.

We do not wish to discourage any of you in pursuing your goals and tasks for this life, or in making choices, but we believe that you will perceive more clearly the reasons for many of your choices for a life with an enhanced understanding of the past. For this reason, we do encourage those who wish to do so to make a study of the past, not necessarily in any academic sense or in a formal setting. A curiosity about the history of fashion and costume is often an excellent way to build up recognitions, as is the study of architecture. This does not mean that we are suggesting that everyone here undertake to study these subjects; we merely point out that when a clearer resonance to the past is desired, these two ways are some of the most easily and casually pursued methods to develop a sense of the "reality" of what has gone before. No one is required to do this, of course, and it is up to you, how, when, and if you pursue this particular method of gaining resonances. Memory on the Physical Plane is at best an unreliable tool—how many of those here present can describe the color of their grandmother's eyes or what they had for lunch a week from last Tuesday?—but it can be a useful tool, not only for this life but for all the lives which have gone before. There are several reasons why the lessons are difficult to bring into focus, not the least of which is the working of the Chief Feature and the negative poles of the Overleaves, but where there is genuine self-awareness and interest, much can be learned, from this immediate life and all the lives that have led up to it.

There is one question that must be answered here: while Essence endures "forever" and is immutable in any sense that you can perceive it, personality and persona exist for one life only. There would be no real evolution if every life were simply a repeat, with "theme and variations" of what has gone before. The Old Sage that is Camille will return many times until all the lessons of the Physical Plane have been inculcated, but Camille, the woman known to this group and an accomplished medium, will not return. The brevity of what you call "self" and the mutability of personality are a part of the Physical Plane and the nature of this experience is concerned in large part with that brevity. While we are fully aware of the truth of reincarnation, we also, in the sense of "self" agree that "you pass this way but once," which is a major lesson of any specific life.

CHAPTER SEVEN
A Conversation With Jessica and Camille

Jessica and Camille have known each other for more than ten years. Their association goes back to the time both were working as substitute teachers in the same school system.

"We were both a little on the outside, being substitutes rather than regular teachers, and after a while, when we were working at the same school we made a point of keeping each other company at lunch and during faculty meetings when we weren't able to participate," Jessica explains. "I left teaching when I got my current job—well, actually, when I went to work for the company I now work for, since I'm doing a lot more now than when I started. But since it turned out that Camille and I lived fairly close to each other, we kept running into each other, and, well, after a while I found out that Camille was as interested in this kind of material as I am."

"I wish I'd known about it a lot sooner," Camille concurs. "But you know what it's like—most people look at you funny if you talk about esoteric teaching beyond the 'What's your sign' gambit."

"I'll admit I hesitated for a long time because I didn't want Milly running to the Board of Education saying that I was some kind of freak. I still hadn't married Walter then and my daughter was quite young, and after my first husband left and then died, I really needed a job. Anything that might blot the record worried me, and with good reason." She folds her hands in her lap. "And some of that was Arrogance, loud and clear."

"Well," Camille says with a shrug, "my Self-Dep wasn't in any hurry to make it seem I wasn't up to snuff, either." She runs her hand through her tousled brown hair. "At the time, it seemed very important to present a good, sensible appearance." She laughs. "So much for sensible."

"Actually, if I hadn't asked Michael for Milly's Overleaves, I probably wouldn't have invited her to a session, and she might not have decided to develop her mediumship." Jessica looks questioningly at Camille. "What do you think?"

"I don't know. At this point, it seems impossible that I would have decided to shelve the mediumship for this life, but you never know. I've been doing this long enough that it's natural. It's like trying to remember how afraid I was of water before I learned to swim. I know that I was afraid, but the fear hasn't any meaning to me because I love swimming." She motions around her living room where the two women are seated. "I'll admit it worried me when I first started out, and I've never got used to giving bad news, but I suppose all mediums go through that once they start to develop their abilities."

How did you know you had the ability in the first place?

Camille smiles and makes an airy gesture. "I did it the easy way: I asked Michael if I could channel."

"In fact," Jessica adds, "I let our other medium get the answer, because I was so eager to have another medium in the regular group that I didn't trust myself to get the answer."

Yes, we would agree that this Fragment is able to channel should she choose to do so. We would recommend that the process be learned slowly, for it is often difficult to develop what you might call your mediumistic muscles, as the Fragment who is now Jessica is well aware.

"I asked then if there are Overleaves or Essences that are more likely than others to have mediumistic talents," Camille goes on. "If there were others in the group, I thought it would be a good idea to know about them."

First we would wish to say that most here present who might have such abilities should they choose to act upon their various potentials are Old Souls. While many Mature Souls are capable of close contact with the Astral Fragments of their Entities, it is rare that mediumship of the nature you explore and that contacts reunited Entities such as we are occurs before the Old Cycle. [January, 1994: Sixth and seventh cast souls in their Cadences can occasionally develop mediumship abilities, if—and we stress if—they have made the choice to have such abilities during the sixth and seventh Levels of the Mature Cycle. Before that, mediumship, as such, is "beyond" the reach of Fragments. Just as Olympic diving is learned only after the Fragment has mastered swimming and basic diving, and even then, only a few have the talent and discipline to excel in the "sport," so mediumship comes after lives of exploring esoteric teachings and all manner of philosophy and "natural sciences".] Then we would wish to point out that the Goal is of primary importance in permitting the Fragment access to this talent. Those with Goals of Dominance and Growth are the most likely to be able to develop this ability. Those with the Attitude of Realist, Idealist and Pragmatist are often most able to keep the channeling clear. Spiritualists, while they are drawn to teachings of this sort, often encounter difficulties in bringing the information forth in such mundane form as words. Those with Moving Centers available to them are likely to find mediumship less of an energy drain than others, and of course, the Chief Feature must be considered. The Chief Feature of Arrogance and of Self-Deprecation are often the most useful for mediums. Impatience has difficulty getting a full message or will try to finish a thought on its own. Stubbornness is just the opposite and will tend to do nothing when the impulse is present. Greed can prove capable of channeling if the fixation of the Greed does not adversely influence the gaining of teaching; if it is fixated on such teaching, then mediumship becomes hazardous to the medium, for there is the constant drive to do MORE, and that leads to eventual exhaustion of the medium. Martyrdom will tend to block this or any other teacher. Self-Destruction, since it is based on fear of lack of control, cannot release the Fragment sufficiently to permit a teacher to channel via the Fragment.

"I have Arrogance, I'm in Dominance and I'm a Pragmatist," Jessica declares. "And an Old Scholar."

"I'm an Old Sage, I'm in Growth, I'm a Pragmatist," Camille says. "The other medium is Old, has a Goal of Growth and is an Idealist. The pattern seems to be pretty reliable."

Obviously it takes energy to channel, but how does it affect these two women?

"It's tiring," Jessica declares, "but not the way jogging or pulling weeds in the garden is tiring, and not really the way that studying or going over facts and figures is tiring. There is an energy drain, no doubt about it, and it's not always easy to ration the strength you need to do this for very long, but . . ." She makes a helpless motion with her hands as if she is trying to find words to describe her experience.

"When you first start channeling," Camille says, picking up the thread, "it is hard to do for any length of time. Because I do my channeling through automatic writing—sort of—I can't do it as long as Jessica can, partly because I have to work harder to keep me out of the way. That's one of the difficult aspects of channeling, getting the personality to sit back and shut up while you let Michael come through. That's part of what's tiring, but there's the energy as well, and it really does take a lot of energy to channel."

"Afterwards, sometimes I just sit around the living room, not doing much of anything. I don't even want to read much, and there's hardly a time when this Old Scholar doesn't want to read. It's not that I can't concentrate, but that I have trouble involving myself in things for a while after doing Michael."

"Involve is the Scholar word," Camille reminds her playfully.

"I agree. I feel kind of . . . spacey. Not the way you do when you're taking antihistamines, not that kind of feeling, but a little bit out of it. That's part of the fatigue. There are other things, too, that probably play a part. Anything I have a serious interest in is harder for me to get. There are questions about people I know that I'd rather Jessica or our other medium get because I don't trust myself to keep out of it." "That's one of the hazards of automatic writing," Jessica explains, "and one of the reasons I can't do it. There's a greater potential for the personality to edit the information. Michael has made remarks on the various sorts of mediumship that apply to this problem."

When it comes to accurate transmission of messages, we would say that trance mediumship is the most completely successful method because the personality, for all intents and purposes, is disengaged and we, or other Astral or Causal teachers, can speak unimpeded. Of course, there is less discipline as well, and it is not possible for the medium to "monitor" the source. Working with the board has the advantage that because of the speed at which the material is dictated, the medium is generally not able to interfere with what is being provided. This allows for more information and "monitoring," and has the advantage that when blocking of information occurs, the planchette tends to stop moving.

"It also stops when Michael can't find a word, or when they're trying to say something in a foreign language, like Chinese or Greek." Jessica shakes her head. "The board is in English—not even with the accents and tildes that we might need to use."

The speed is, of course, often difficult for those in attendance to follow, and while this is awkward, it also makes it possible for the ones taking the dictation to listen without jumping to conclusions, without attempting to guess the words. In time, as you all have observed, facility comes and it is possible both to write the dictated letters and recognize most of the words, but by the time this is done, the anticipation urge has faded. We would wish to inform you that one of the main hazards of being new to a teaching—this teaching or any other—is the understandable tendency to try to leap ahead of what is being taught. Even young children in classrooms make this attempt, and with similar results.

"Sometimes I can get a sense of the words," Jessica says, "and other times, I can't. Often, while we're reading back what's been dictated, I'll be able to recall words that I couldn't make out while I was channeling, but that doesn't last long. I might be able to recall a word for an hour or so, but if you asked me the next day, I doubt I could bring it back. I think that's because I'm still doing a . . . residual channeling. I think that it doesn't stop immediately just because I put the planchette down."

We would agree with that. A water faucet rarely cuts off abruptly but slows and stops. This analogy is a clumsy one and not terribly accurate, but it does capture some of the experience that our student Jessica has while she channels this teaching.

"I find that my experience is similar, but not quite the same," Camille remarks. "I've been busy for years trying to figure out what I call the P.S.es that Michael drops in after I finish doing the automatic writing. Sometimes it will keep on for hours after a long session, or after one of those very intense sessions when there is a lot of major information coming through."

The technique of automatic writing is more vulnerable to editing by the personality than is the direct use of the board, but our student Camille is generally capable of recognizing when such interference occurs. We have found that those mediums using automatic writing are inclined to avoid getting answers on issues and Fragments about which and whom they have strong feelings, especially if these feelings are negative. The Fragment who is now Camille is self-aware enough to recognize her own personality, which many, many Fragments cannot do because the rule of maya is so pervasive in their lives that all perceptions are distorted and misleading. This is often the source of not only major misunderstandings but much of what you describe as neurotic behavior. To return to the matter of automatic-writing mediumship, we would also wish to point out that it is most effective where there are well-focused Fragments present who know how to keep from distracting the medium, and that does not mean simply that the other Fragments avoid speech.

"There are a couple of people who've come to sessions from time to time that I can't get anything for, and sometimes I can't get anything for anyone while they're around. Some of it is abrading Overleaves, according to Michael, and I certainly believe that." Camille shrugs as she thinks about what she's said. "There are times I can't get my focus right, too. We were having a session on one very stormy evening, and all I could think about was that tree limb that was hanging over my deck from the neighbors' up the hill. It had been leaning all through the summer and I was certain it would come down and ruin the deck. There was no way I could channel that night. And incidentally, the branch did fall and it did put a hole in the deck and it was almost two months before I could use it again. That night, with the weather so terrible, everyone was a bit edgy."

"I've had times like that, though not when I was worrying about the neighbors' trees." Jessica adjusts the folds of her skirt. "I know that while Walter was in the hospital, there was no way I could channel. I wanted to, God knows, but I was too distracted, and I think that even the degree that I wanted to, made it more difficult and less likely that I'd be able to sustain the effort." She looks over at Camille. "Milly took a lot of phone calls from me for the three weeks Walter was in such dreadful condition. She was very patient."

"Well, you were patient with me during the family crisis I had to contend with," Camille says in her most reasonable tone of voice. "You know as well as I do that the times when you need to get information for yourself are the times that you're going to make those calls and ask for a few pick-up sessions."

"Still," Jessica sighs. "Arrogance doesn't like to admit that it needs help, since its underlying fear is the fear of vulnerability." She touches her hair nervously. "I've been trying to work on my Chief Feature, but it isn't easy, and when I think I've made some progress, it exacts revenge. And that's not too strong a word for it."

Camille nods vigorously. "You're right. I've had to come face to face with my Self-Dep in the last few years, and I'm not real pleased with what I see. And I know that the Self-Dep distorts the recognition, as well, and so I shouldn't depend on what I think is going on."

"Tell me what happens to you," Jessica requests. "I always end up thinking that I've made myself completely foolish and that everyone who had anything to do with it will hold me in contempt for what I've done. No one will believe anything I say, no one will want to associate with me—the whole works." "Mine convinces me that no matter what I tried to do, I failed and that I would be foolish and irresponsible to try anything again. Chief Feature really does its best to convince me that I can't handle things, even when I know—intellectually, objectively— that I can do it, that I do do it, that I have done it. The Self-Dep isn't willing to let me know that, because that would undermine its hold on me."

We remind those Fragments who have asked that the Chief Feature exercises its control through the Goal, primarily, and through the Attitude secondarily. This control imposes conditions and limitations on the actions and perceptions of the Fragment and does so in such a way that validation becomes difficult if not impossible. Let us point out again that the Chief Feature is the very base of all fears that operate on you, and that without it, there is little to block the perceptions of Essence in the life. While this is an excellent achievement, there is no reason to believe that those who fail to extinguish the Chief Feature have failed or "lost". Most Fragments go through each and every life contending with the Chief Feature, which is one of the lessons of the Physical Plane. In those very, very few Fragments who have extinguished the Chief Feature, there is often what is thought to be a lack of "dash" or "verve" and many consider such Fragments to be "uninteresting" or "dull" because they lack the edge that the Chief Feature provides. We remind you of the religious exercises that have seven steps to spiritual perfection, the last being to take no pride in achieving the other six. Those who extinguish the Chief Feature have actually done so when it does not matter to them that they have done it. That it matters is the last hold of the Chief Feature, and by far the strongest.

"I think that about thirty percent of our sessions over the years have been devoted to dealing with Chief Features and recommendations for finding ways to get around it, or at least minimize its influence," Jessica says. "It's clearly the biggest stumbling block any of us have, and it can be extremely subtle in how it exercises control."

It is not incorrect to see the Chief Feature as separate from the rest of the Overleaves and the personality, but disowning it will not release the Fragment from its hold. Just such perceptions led the Fragments extant in what you call the Medieval years to invent demons and other externalizations of their fears. If there is true desire to be rid of the Chief Feature, it is necessary to understand that you—that is, the individual Fragment—has the Chief Feature and it is part of your self. While it is true that the Chief Feature is a means of protection, it is also true that the protection is not valid, no matter what it may appear to be. Let us point out that, as long as the Chief Feature is relegated to a place outside of the personality, it will continue to "run the show". Only when it is understood that the Chief Feature controls the personality through fear can the Fragment learn to deal with it. [*June 1989*: It is not amiss if you choose to identify those situations that tend to "set Chief Feature off" and either prepare for having a distorted reaction or to avoid the triggering altogether. For many Fragments, keeping distance between themselves and the incidents that start Chief Feature activity is a primary means of lessening the most obvious hold of Chief Feature. That does not mean that Chief Feature will not find some other means of exercising control, but by identifying those kinds of events, situations, relationships, and the rest of the possibilities, can serve to buy the Fragment some time for self-examination and the chance to discover what techniques can lessen the degree of Chief Feature hold on the Fragment.]

"I've done my best to see what the Chief Feature does as clearly as I can, and I've learned to anticipate the circumstances when it's apt to be the most aroused," Jessica remarks. "I can't say that I have any real resistance to it, but I've come to recognize when it's running the show, which is a step in the right direction. Pardon," she adds, addressing the air, "there is no right direction. It's a step away from fear."

"That's one of the hardest concepts to grasp," Camille declares. "That there really isn't a wrong or a right. I've got so I can think in terms of constructive and destructive rather than right and wrong, but that's about all I can bring myself to do. Apparently it's almost impossible for those on the Physical Plane—unless they're on their last life and have extinguished the Chief Feature entirely—to get away from a certain degree of right and wrong labels for things."

"I may be second Level Old, but that's a long, long way from the last time around." Jessica stares out the window toward the rebuilt deck. "When I think of everything that can go wrong—and I do mean wrong—on the Physical Plane, it . . . frightens me. I'm active in the nuclear disarmament group around the university, which Michael seems to think it, for the most part, a waste of time, but I can't ignore the threat."

While we would agree there is a risk, we do not perceive it the way that those on the Physical Plane do. It is true that there could be a catastrophe that would render this planet uninhabitable, but that would not release Essence from the experiences of the Physical Plane. Another species on another world would be found and "inhabited" until the Cadres of this planet had completed their evolutions from the Physical Plane. It may be of interest to know that those responsible for the destruction of the planet, or its rendering uninhabitable, would be the ones who would choose to return to the ruins until it was no longer possible to do so. Those who create the chaos would be the ones to live with its results, and doubtless would never forget the lessons taught. What concerns us more than the possibility of annihilation is the flagrant disregard for the planet itself, through overpopulation, the use of poisonous substances in the atmosphere and land, and the lack of concern for the long-range effects of this callousness. You scoff at the old Romans for preparing their food in vessels of lead, describing them as foolish and stupid and irresponsible for this activity even though they had no means at hand to determine the long-range consequences of lead poisoning. Yet you have no such excuse in regard to such problems as chemical-waste dumps, toxic industrial fumes, insecticides, herbicides and other substances. You are aware of the danger, you have determined the possible outcome of such abuses, you have already documented the results of these abuses and still it continues, and, in fact, escalates. We would agree that there are those who turn this neglect to monetary advantage, but that is of little significance when weighed against the sort of world your grandchildren— and you in your future reincarnations—will inhabit. It is not inappropriate to remember that many of you will reincarnate in those grandchildren to experience what has been done. Not many of you have access to the Fragments who make and influence the decisions that control the use and abuse of the planet, and we do not suggest that you spend time on such matters unless you choose to do so. However, it is puzzling to us that those who are aware of the problems and their ramifications and who do have access to the Fragments making decisions are as reluctant to act as they have been. A few of this little group have suggested that it is a question of "which side the bread is buttered on" and certainly that is a factor, one much under the influence of the Chief Feature, but in many species, the threat to offspring is regarded as more significant than a threat to income or prestige. This behavior is not unusual for Young Souls, and this is a Young Soul country in a Young Soul world, but current actions have been consistently underestimated in their significance and we would doubt that this luxury can continue for much longer without serious consequences becoming apparent.

"I don't like what's happening to the environment, either," Jessica says. "I belong to three environmentalist groups and I read up on all the impact studies that affect the Bay Area. It isn't the most pleasant reading around, and it makes me very angry." She sets her jaw. "I'll be fifty soon, and my daughter is planning to have children. It troubles me to think that my old age might be spent on a garbage dump and that my grandchildren could end up living in a world more like the seventeenth century than the twentieth."

"Except that the seventeenth century had pretty clean air," Camille adds.

"Great," Jessica rejoins with heavy sarcasm. "Filth, disease, poverty and smog."

"I do know the feeling," Camille says. "I have one child, in college now, and two step-children, one in college and one in high school. They're all pretty good kids, and so far there's been no real trouble with any of them other than the crisis we've had, which did not involve any of them directly. I wonder how their lives are going to turn out. I read about those children born with brain damage or other serious birth defects, and I can't help but worry about the children my kids are going to have, one of these days." She clears her throat. "They've already come through some rough times. I'd hate to think that there was much worse ahead."

"All parents feel that way, I think," Jessica says, then amends her comment. "Maybe not all, but most of them, anyway, those that care about their children and want to take care of them."

"A lot of the people who let the abuses go on have children of their own, and grandchildren," Camille points out. Jessica nods. "As I said that, I remembered my mother, who was a Young Warrior in Rejection and Martyrdom. She would have done anything to further her favorite cause."

"Would you say she was a good parent?" Camille asks. "After all, my mother is a Young Warrior, too, but in Acceptance. She has Martyrdom as well, come to think of it."

"There's a big difference between Rejection and Acceptance," Jessica says, "though both of them are on the Expression Polarity."

"They have similar backgrounds: Midwestern rural," Camille reminds her.

"Even then, there's a world of difference," Jessica insists. "Would I say she was a good mother? In some ways, I suppose she was, but in others, she was a disaster."

"Don't you think that's true of most parents?" Camille asks. "I know it's true of my parents."

It is the misfortune of parents to lose sight of the fact that their children are not simply extensions of themselves, or limited to the Family Icon. One of the aspects of the rule of maya is the expectations that parents develop very early for their children. It is not unusual for a parent or both parents to decide long before the child is born or even conceived that the child must fulfill certain expectations and/or demands that the parents have for their children. This can range from being the most successful, brightest, accomplished child in the town or the country or the world, to the programming that will tend to create a pattern of failure in the child so that it will never eclipse the parent. There is a greater reward for the latter than the former, incidentally, and you have only to observe the attitudes and behavior of children in school to see the truth of this, for with certain few exceptions, the bright and capable children will tend to be regarded with jealousy and suspicion by other children, and that jealousy and suspicion is often present—and often denied—by the family of the very bright, capable child. There are reasons that many such children never develop what you would call social skills, and not the least of these is the problem of families where such a child is always seen as something of an "odd man out" even when praised and urged to greater achievements.

We would wish to digress for a moment on the matter of childhood. There are many misunderstandings about the nature and experiences of childhood and this in turn leads to difficulties for the adult Fragment. Childhood is neither a sunny time of no cares and total innocence nor is it an unrelenting time of horror. Certainly some children have less stressful childhoods than others—a child born to wealth and comfort is likely to experience less immediate environmental stress than a beggar's child in Bangladesh—but that does not mean that therefore the child of privilege has fewer difficulties than the child of the beggar.

Of course, the nature of the childhood is chosen by the Fragment before coming into the incarnation, but there are circumstances that can be altered, such as a child of a very well-to-do German merchant born in one thousand nine hundred twenty-one, common reckoning.

By one thousand nine hundred twenty-five, the wealth of the family would have melted away never to return and the Fragment anticipating dealing with the problems of success and privilege is faced instead with a life of poverty and social disgrace. It is also possible that a child born in destitute circumstances in Naples might be taken under the wing of a wealthy uncle or other patron as a repayment for services rendered by one or both of its parents, and instead of a life of want and hardship, the Fragment is then provided with the opportunity of privilege. All these experiences are indeed part of what shapes the adult, but of course, the Overleaves are the most crucial element, for if the child has a Goal of Rejection, the chances are that no matter what circumstances the Fragment is born to, it will decide to do something else with its life. If the child has a Goal of Acceptance, it will be likely to adapt to the changes it faces, no matter what. The Fragment who has sometimes been called "the elephant man" was noted for his kindness and lack of bitterness in what was certainly an appalling life experience. The Fragment was a sixth Level Mature King in the Perseverance Mode with a Goal of Acceptance, a Stoic in the Emotional part of the Intellectual Center with a very mild Chief Feature of Arrogance. With such Overleaves, it is not surprising that the Fragment could endure, and endure cheerfully, a life that would drive many others to despair, rage and bitterness. A child experiences the world as new in the personality it has chosen for the life being lived, but it brings with it all the experiences of previous lives and all the karmic ribbons, Monads, Agreements, and bonds that every Fragment carries through all incarnations. If all here present could be willing to consider childhood in this kaleidoscopic sense, it might be easier for you to accept the lessons and experiences of childhood—your own and others—as valid on many different levels, and not an isolated bit of heaven or hell.

"Raising children is hard enough without trying to figure out what went on before," Jessica says a bit wearily, "but looking back, I know that I might have done things a little differently if I'd known that my child is an Old Sage. I can see now that there were things that would have been less difficult for both of us if I'd been able to take that into consideration while she was growing up."

"Yes, I agree," Camille seconds Jessica. "I can see how my son was giving me signals that I couldn't understand at the time, and if I had been aware of what I was dealing with, we could have saved ourselves many problems. It's done now, and we don't have too bad a relationship, all things considered, but there are areas of our relationship that are not easy for either of us because of early blunders I made. The family problems we've had have made both of us reevaluate our understanding of each other, and in certain ways we've grown more tolerant and understanding, but it's sad that it required something so drastic as a series of crises to make it possible for us to talk."

"If I hadn't had the opportunity to use Michael's material, I think that there would have been some really difficult times for my daughter and me while she was a teenager. Knowing that I am dealing with an Old Sage really helped. I knew that she'd need more applause than I'd tend to give her by nature. That saved us several problems once she reached the age that I started to gain enough understanding of the differences of our natures that it was possible for us to take advantage of what we were told." She cocks her head to the side. "That's a very complicated couple of sentences, isn't it? And it's not as clear as I'd like it to be."

"That's okay, Jessica," Camille says with a laugh, "you can think about your footnotes on your own time." This evokes a smile from Jessica.

"She's right about Scholars—we love our footnotes. As much as Sages love their applause." Both women look at each other and start to laugh.

"One of the things I like most about Michael," Jessica says when she has stopped laughing, "is that we can be serious without having to be solemn. So many times these study groups take themselves so seriously, and that turns me off." She looks toward Camille. "You know what I mean, don't you, Milly?"

"God, yes," she concurs. "I was asked to an occult study group about ten years ago and I can't tell you how . . . dreary the people were, always caught in deep thought and morose reflections on the meaning of their lives. It drove me crazy, and after about three meetings, I stopped going. In fact, I almost refused to come to a session at Jessica's because of that experience, but my friend Corinne promised me that this group wasn't like that."

"Corinne was in the group for more than ten years, but she moved recently to the Seattle area, and only occasionally calls in questions. She was a real asset to the group because she had a very good background in all sorts of esoteric philosophies and that helped us to get good solid explanations from Michael when it seemed that they were becoming a bit too abstruse." Jessica grins. "You know, if Corinne hadn't told me that she thought Milly was serious, I might not have invited her to come to a session, simply because I wasn't sure how she'd take it, in spite of the conversations we'd had when substitute teaching." She shakes her head. "One of these days I've got to learn to trust my hunches."

"Corinne encouraged me as well," Camille goes on when Jessica falls silent. "And she was the one who introduced Leslie to the group, that's our relief medium."

"And we're glad to have Leslie around whenever she's free," Jessica adds. "It was pretty obvious, but we asked anyway, if Corinne had any reason to do this," Camille says.

As all here gathered are well aware, there is a facilitating Agreement between the Fragment who is now Corinne and the Fragment who is now Jessica. This is emphasized by the Fragment who is now Corinne's position in casting which tends to encourage her to bring other Fragments together. These Fragments are more likely to enter into facilitating Agreements to bring Fragments together simply because it enhances the work on the Life Task as well as fulfills Agreements. While that does not mean that every Agreement supports the Life Task, it does remind you all that when an Agreement supports the Life Task, it is more easily accomplished. Of course, during the course of lives, a Fragment will choose to work against the imperative of casting, since that imperative is part of the rule of Essence and therefore wholly without demand or coercion. Let us point out that the Fragment who is now Corinne is very willing to follow the prompting of Essence and therefore rarely resists the promptings of Essence.

"Whatever the reason, Corinne has done a lot for the group, and I'm glad she stayed with us as long as she did," Jessica says with real conviction.

"I don't feel she's really left the group, just moved away so that she isn't close enough to commute." Camille smiles. "Leslie didn't think she'd like a group of this sort, even though she's done a lot of occult studies over the years, but Corinne convinced her to give it a try, and she ended up being our relief medium."

"If she lived closer, we'd probably divide the job with her on a more equal basis, but she had to drive eighty miles to get here and that's a bit rough to do, twice a month, especially if she has to channel as well." Jessica points in a northeast direction. "She lives that way, more or less."

"She works for a company that insures livestock, including breeding stock. She has a partner who's a vet and they evaluate the stock to be insured, check the pedigrees and all that sort of thing. She's very down-to-earth. If you think the people Jessica and I work for would have fits if they knew about the channeling, believe me, Leslie's company would be aghast." Camille gestures for emphasis.

"Aghast. That's a very Sagey word," Jessica remarks.

"I like it." She shrugs, then returns to the subject. "For some reason, Leslie's very good at getting health questions answered, better than

Jessica and I are. She hasn't got a medical background and she doesn't come from a medical family and in her last life she wasn't a physician, but she really has a feel for it. She gets more information, more clearly than either of us can. I'm pretty good with matters of nutrition and exercise. Craig, when he's around, which isn't often, gets medical information, but he's a physician, so that's to be expected. Leslie isn't a doctor, but the way she gets medical material is amazing."

"That's one of the strange things about Michael," Jessica says. "So often what you think you'll be good at channeling, you aren't. I thought that I'd be able to do more on subjects related to my work, but I'm no better at it than Camille is, and the other way around." She stares down at her hands as she laces her fingers together. "I used to think it was because I'd already formed opinions about the material, and so I was editing it, and that might be part of it, but the rest of it comes from something else, something deeper, I think."

There are always resonances, and not all are with the past. The Fragment who is now Jessica has links with many others on the Physical Plane, and those links provide some of the resonances that enter into her ability to get greater or lesser amounts of information. While we would agree that in general the Fragment who is now Leslie shows a greater aptitude for medical channeling, let us point out that there are many in the healing arts and professions in her Entity, not all of them on the Physical Plane at this time, and many of them enhance her concentration—this is not a literal explanation, but a tangential one, for the actual experience is outside of the limits of your language to describe—as well as providing what you would call a grasp of the subject. The same is true for the Fragment who is now Jessica on matters of world problems, for many of her Entity, which is the third cast in the Cadre, are active in such areas and have been for some time, and by that we mean several centuries. Members of her Entity were among those pressing for changes in the working conditions of coal miners during the last century, as well as active in changing laws governing what children could be required to do. At the present time, roughly one third of the Fragments of her Entity currently extant on the Physical Plane are active to some degree or other, in various organizations whose aims are to improve the environment, either through improved sanitation, better medical facilities, environmental reforms, nuclear-freeze groups of several varieties, and similar sorts of projects and groups. Some of their work extends to such areas as child abuse, drug and alcohol abuse, and branches of the socio-legal organizations and professions. In the case of the Fragment who is now Camille, many in her Entity now extant on the Physical Plane are active in teaching, in various sorts of performing, and especially in teaching and therapies that address the troubled personality, be it as psychiatrists, physical therapists, ministers, and those who combine several techniques. As a result, the Fragment who is now Camille can more easily delve into matters having to do with personal growth and development. That is not to say that either of these mediums cannot work well in the area of the other—we did not say that, and we did not intend to imply it—for each is very capable and focused. What we wish to explain here is why one of them is able to bring more of the teaching into focus on certain subjects "and with more ease" than others. The same is true, of course, of the Fragment who is now Leslie.

"That caveat of more ease really struck me when we got that information," Jessica says. "There is a kind of very energetic ease that comes with channeling, and I can tell that some of it comes more easily than other parts of it. From the conversations that Milly and I have had over the years, I know that we find certain things easier, and they're not necessarily the same things."

"Yes," Camille agrees, nodding. "One of the things I've noticed is that when the material is really coming easily, that there is a very good feeling about it, not quite like a high or anything like that, but a very pleasant sensation, and a strong feeling of closeness with those around me."

"That's the part that can be fun, if you don't let it embarrass you," Jessica adds.

Let us remind you that Essence is never—emphasis never—coercive or intrusive. The experience of Essence is marked by great facility, ease, comfort, well- being, and "effortless" progress, usually followed by pleasant and contented exhaustion. When one Fragment is working very much in Essence, it is often "contagious" to those around them. Essence Contact between Fragments is often marked by expansive visions of the cosmos and a high level of intensity. Obviously, this is more easily accomplished with physical intimacy than during a board meeting, but this is not to say it is impossible in these unlikely moments. Essence does not require any special conditions or surroundings to work—in fact, it is often blocked when special requirements are made. It is the nature of Essence to require "nothing." It is the Overleaves and especially the Chief Feature that create the illusion of requirements. Let us point out that the Life Task is what can be most easily accomplished by the focused and realized action of Essence. In other words, when you are acting in Essence, any work accomplished under its influence, even if it is only transplanting petunias, leads to the development of work on the Life Task. In a very real sense, attaining that state "is" the Life Task.

"It sounds so easy when Michael says it," Camille laments. "And when you have to wrestle with it for yourself, that's another matter entirely. It's like everything he says about Chief Feature. When Michael describes what it does and how it does it, I find it's very clear, and I can see how negative its effect is. But when I get into a situation where Chief Feature is in charge, then it's another story and I find that I can't keep clear what's really Essence in action and what's Chief Feature seduction."

"That phrase that fear is seductive," Jessica goes on, "is really much more instructive than it sounds. You hear those words and it seems a trivial way to put it, but I've come to see that Michael uses the word seduction very accurately and very deliberately. Seduction, aside from being bullying at its heart, is so very convincing, and often quite flattering, at least in terms of its outward appearance. There are times when fear can masquerade as so many other things that the last thing in the world you or anyone else would suspect is that you're actually afraid. You might appear prudent or reserved or shy or aloof or any number of things, but what isn't clear is that you are acting out of fear, not out of love. That does not mean, by the way, that Michael wants us to go around embracing everyone."

While agape is the highest state that can be attained on the Physical or any other Plane, it is most difficult when caught in the rule of maya and the limitations of the Overleaves. Between lives, only the Essence and Cadence remain to be your "personality". The links continue but without distortions. While on the Physical Plane, it is not possible for most Fragments to transcend the limitations in order to perceive the greater truths that are present. Those who insist that they "love everyone" rarely have taken the time to examine the implications of that remark. What is generally intended is a careless good feeling about those they feel some degree of companionship with. When most Fragments speak of loving everyone, they do not include criminals or pimps or those terribly violent in actions, or those of cultures so diverse as to be incomprehensible to the Fragment speaking. In these sorts of cases, to be able to keep a sense of goodwill toward all Fragments is closer to agape than the assertion that you "love everyone," if that remark is uncritical, both of self and others. Let us suggest that learning to say to one other Fragment, with utter Personal Truth, that there is nothing that that Fragment can do or be or say that you will not love the Fragment is the first step toward genuine loving Acceptance of all Fragments. Such inner assertions are often the core of lifelong friendships. We do not mean to imply that in loving another Fragment there must also be approval of what that Fragment is and does at all times. You can hold profound love in your heart for a Fragment while disliking certain aspects of the personality of the Fragment. For example, you may have the most abiding love for a Fragment with whom you have many positive past associations as well as Entity and Cadence ties, but that does not necessarily mean you like the way the Fragment behaves at parties or that you enjoy and approve of the Fragment's fascination with gambling. We can not stress enough that genuine agape is unconditional and disinterested. Few but the very oldest Fragments are capable of this perception.

"I've found that comforting, in an odd way," Camille says, and turns to Jessica, who nods. "For a long time, I was convinced that I ought to love everyone, no matter what, even if I felt they were repulsive. Now I know that, because of Overleaves if nothing else, I will not like everyone I meet and not everyone who meets me will like me, and there's nothing wrong with that."

"You might find that comforting," Jessica says with a touch of sarcasm, "but I've got another Chief Feature, and I find it galling. That doesn't mean I want to change it. My Chief Feature doesn't like that idea, either. I think that for me, realizing that my Arrogance often blocks positive as well as negative dealings with others has been very helpful, though I have to admit that I don't often have a clear sense of how much it distorts what's going on around me."

"I've noticed that my Chief Feature is very good at getting me to stop before I've accomplished too much. When I got my promotion, Chief Feature did a whole number about why being promoted was bad for me, and getting a title—junior vice- president—was nothing short of disaster. My pocketbook convinced me otherwise, but that was the only way I could recognize that the Chief Feature was in full flower, as Michael says."

Camille leans back against the flowered cushions in her high-backed chair. "I thought at the time that I had it all figured out, and it must have taken me two or three months to understand that I hadn't got the point at all."

"Arrogance doesn't do that very much," Jessica observes. "But it has other ways of keeping control. In my case, the Arrogance works with my Dominance and convinces me that I have no power or authority in a given situation, or that in some mysterious way, I've exceeded my authority and therefore this is terribly poor logic, but the Chief Feature makes it work—everything that goes wrong is my fault and I will be expected to answer for it. I get defensive and then it takes me quite a while to open up again."

"That's always amazed me, Jessica," Camille says to her, "because you're so open with Michael. You're a capable executive, and then you can do this as well, and you're able to work longer than I can at channeling. And I know from what we've talked about over the years that you're often scared of disappointing people, or convinced that they hold you responsible for problems over which you have no control."

Jessica considers her answer before she speaks. "That's true, I guess. I am always worried about disappointing people. That's why I hate it when Michael gives negative information—you know, when they say that there are difficulties or karmic debts or some other unpleasantness. That's probably why I have trouble with the medical questions, too."

"I worry that I don't get enough information for the person asking, or that it doesn't address the issue. Good old Self-Dep doing its number again. It troubles me the most when Michael says things I simply don't agree with." Camille looks over at Jessica, who nods twice. "Those are the hardest answers; the ones that you don't agree with or that go against what you want to believe."

"And it happens more often than you might think," Jessica says. "I remember once when Leslie was getting an answer for me about a person in my Cadence, whom I had identified but not met yet. I asked where the person was and what he was doing simply because I was curious. As far as I knew, he was in Europe somewhere. When Leslie got the answer, none of us believed it."

This Scholar is presently enjoying a late supper in a European restaurant in New York City.

"Well," Jessica goes on with a trace of exasperation, "I thought that was a case of real wishful thinking. New York! Michael had to have his wires crossed. Leslie apologized, Milly said that she didn't trust herself to try to get anything and I was . . . disgusted. Then," she goes on, her voice less emphatic, "about six months later, to my complete astonishment, I had the opportunity to meet this member of my Cadence. The strange thing was I wanted to avoid him, because I was convinced by that time that all the information about him, including our Cadence link, was suspect or false. As it turns out, I'm the only person in my office who speaks fluent German, and his English is . . . interesting at best. So my boss asked me to accompany this man on his various appointments while he was here. And in the course of taking him places and translating, I asked if he'd been in New York recently. He answered that he'd spent about six weeks there half a year before. Well, that brought me up short. It's given me more respect for Michael's information, even when I don't agree with it."

"Jessica's active in politics, after all, and Michael has very little good to say about politics," Camille says.

We would agree that politics are part of the rule of maya and the Physical Plane. On higher Planes, there is, of course, no need for politics since there is understanding on all levels. We do not say that political action is not appropriate or productive. We do not make such judgments. What you choose to do is up to you, and that often includes politics. However, what we would wish to point out is that political involvements tend to create false comradeship, false recognitions, false victories and false defeats. Politics often substitutes activity for work on the task at hand. In other words, in politics, the perpetuation of the political process is often far more important to those involved than in making those changes and compromises that might advance the particular situation the institution and process is supposed to address. Politics are very exciting to Young Souls and political activities—that is, becoming involved in such aspects of society and government—are often a good way to bring the lessons of the Young Soul Cycle to bear. In the Mature Soul, where one of the most compelling cyclical Monads is that which causes the Mature Soul to honorably serve a corrupt master, politics many times provides the best arena for this interaction. It is of interest to some to know that some of the "honorable" men around the Young Warrior who was Adolf Hitler were Mature Souls honorably serving a corrupt master. It is of importance here, incidentally, to understand that corrupt masters rarely think of themselves as corrupt, although there are exceptions to that rule, as in the case of the persevering Young King known to history as Lady Wu.

In the matter of politics, there is always, by the nature of the political process, much fear. Politics thrives on fear, and as such, reinforces negatives poles and strengthens the Chief Feature in those actively caught up in the political "games" of your planet. All Young Soul worlds populated by independently mobile ensouled species exhibit similar patterns. In time, this gives way to a less fear-driven manner of redressing "wrongs" and the action taken is brought about more by the positive than the negative poles of the Overleaves. Those of you interested in politics would not be unwise to examine what it is that draws you to the political arena. Where much fear is present, it would not be inappropriate for each Fragment to be circumspect in what it chooses to do. Let us point out that donations to a preferred cause or candidate are as welcome as bodies attending a rally. If you believe that the political actions are causing fear to be enhanced in your life, it might spare you more distress if you consider changing how and to what degree you are active in that political cause or candidate's campaign. Political causes often mask other actions, and we do not mean anything as absurd as the "communist threat" or the "military-industrial complex" or "radicalisms" of any sort. What we mean by this mask is that Fragments who feel unimportant or powerless or dissatisfied with their lives often seek out the political world as a means of supplying what they fear they do not have. Many with precarious personal relationships, with spouse or family members, will take flight into politics as a means of avoiding the very real problems closer to home, and have the excellent excuse to neglect the mundane domestic problems because the political issues are "more important". That is not to say that we are not in sympathy with those seeking to save the environment or stop the hazards of nuclear wastes and nuclear war. We have said before that such concerns are "worthwhile" for a Young Soul country in a Young Soul world, and that the care of this planet is, of course, in your hands. However, when the political aspect of that defense supercedes the basic concern, then we would have to point out that it has become a case of "the tail wagging the dog" and that what is being accomplished is not necessarily related to the actual situation that instigated the actions.

"I don't care how many times Michael says that," Jessica protests. "I won't ever agree with them on it, and that's that."

"Michael didn't say not to be in politics," Camille says reasonably.

"Michael never says not to do anything," Jessica snaps. "Bad grammar, but good Michael."

"And he has said that casting order can make a difference, too. Sometimes the order in casting does more to change how a person brings about the completion of a Life Task than any political interest." Camille does this prompting kindly and with obvious concern for her friend. "You know that it can make a difference."

"Politics or casting?" Jessica responds with an ironic chuckle. "Yes, okay. Casting can make a difference. And Life Task can make a difference. And Overleaves can make a difference. And false personality can make a difference."

"But the casting and Overleaves and Life Task aren't the same thing as false personality or the Chief Feature, for that matter." Camille has had this discussion with Jessica before and neither of them is unfamiliar with their arguments.

"I don't argue that—" Jessica begins.

"You don't?" Camille counters, wide-eyed.

"All right, I do argue it, but not because I think Michael is wrong. I simply don't agree with them, and that's not the same thing. I like Mahler and you don't, but I don't think that makes you less of a person." She grins suddenly. "Okay, a truce. It's not an issue we're going to settle today, or next week or next year. Maybe next life."

"In between?" Camille suggests.

"Well, in theory it's easier between lives, but that's not a whole hell of a lot of help right now." Jessica pauses, staring up at the ceiling. "Sometimes I think that Astral interval, other than a debriefing, is just one long course in Michael-math."

"Oh, goodie," Camille drawls. "Michael-math."

CHAPTER EIGHT
Michael-Math

Introductory Note: Over the years since this book was first published, this chapter seems to have been the most difficult one for readers to grasp. To those struggling with the material, I have a suggestion to offer—don't try to get it the first time through. Skim the chapter and go on. Then skim it again, later. Spend a couple of weeks just browsing through the chapter. I've been told that this technique can be fairly painless in bringing about comprehension. If you'd rather wrestle it two falls out of three, go right ahead.—CQY

As we have said, the Cadres are composed of seven Entities, and the Entities composed of Fragments of various Essences which are cast in order at the same time. The functions within the Cadre and Entities are cardinal and ordinal. Those who are in the first half of the casting, be it of Essence in Entity, Entity and/or Cadre, are cardinal. Those in the second half are ordinal. As it is apparent, there is a great deal of flexibility in this, or it may be that a Fragment is in the cardinal part of his Essence-in-Entity but in an ordinal Entity within the casting of the Cadre. And the reverse is also true. As an example, in an Entity of Slaves, Scholars, Sages, and Priests, if the Slaves were cast first, although the Role of Slave is ordinal, the position of Slaves in the Entity is cardinal, doubly so for those in the first half of the Slaves.

Let us urge you not to assign a greater or lesser degree of approval or favor to any of these concepts. Within your society, it is held up that to be first is to be successful and envied, but in fact, that is also considered a suspicious place to be. Those in the highest places are never "one of the boys" in any sense that the Fragments can understand. The same might be true when thinking of cardinality and ordinality, but that would, in fact, block how these functions are manifest in the world. Between lives, all that remains of the "personality" is the Role in Essence—that is, Slave, Artisan, Warrior, Scholar, Sage, Priest and King—and the Fragments' order in casting. All the rest can and does change, but those two are immutable in any sense that you might perceive.

Cardinality applies no matter what the Role, for the Role may be ordinal–Slave, Artisan, Warrior—and the casting order very cardinal. For example, the first cast Fragment of the first cast Entity of this Cadre is now an Old Warrior, which is an ordinal Role in a very cardinal position. By the same token, the very last cast Fragment in this Cadre, that is, the last cast Fragment of the last cast Entity, is a Priest, which is a very cardinal Role, but in an ordinal position. Let us review the polarities of the numbers for you.

One has as its positive pole purpose and as its negative simplicity. Two has as its positive pole stability and as its negative balance. Three has as its positive pole enterprise and its negative versatility. Four has as its positive pole consolidation and its negative achievement. Five has as its positive pole expansion and its negative adventure. Six has as its positive pole harmony and its negative connection. Seven has as its positive pole inculcation and its negative eclecticism. These polarities apply to casting order as well as to levels and, in fact, resonate through all the Overleaves. That resonances are what you in our little group call "Michael-math" and it is central to understanding the evolution of all Fragments, on and off the Physical Plane.

You can perceive that while one is ordinal and seven is cardinal, that the first half is cardinal and the last half is ordinal—in other words, the pattern "doubles back on itself". This is what is implied by the "yin-yang" symbol, and it would probably be of use to keep the "yin-yang" in mind while considering what we tell you of the function of levels and numbers.

As the levels and numbers reveal functions, let us discuss this in terms of a Cadre. The first cast Entity is of course the cardinal-most while also of the most ordinal number. The seventh cast Entity is the most ordinal in casting yet is also the most cardinal—that is, number seven—in number. Within the Entities the individual Essences are cast, and they are cast in sequence.

Therefore, let us assume that the second cast Entity has Priests—cast first—Scholars—cast second—Artisans—cast third—and Sages—cast fourth. That casting order will influence function of the Essences within the Entity. The Priests would be the most cardinal and of most ordinal numerical position, the Scholars, in the second position, would still be cardinal but with reduced impact. Because there are four Essences in this Entity, the last two—Artisans and Sages—are the ordinals, with the greater ordinality going to the Sages, who are in a cardinal Role in Essence. As a second cast Entity, the Entity has cardinality, but not the cutting-edge cardinality of the first cast Entity. Yet, of course, there is a stronger position in terms of the number. As some of you have recognized, all the Overleaves can in fact be expressed as numbers. For example, the Scholar, in the neutral position of four—that is, neither cardinal nor ordinal—has much in common with the fourth Level and with all the neutral Overleaves. The ultimate Scholar might, perhaps be a fourth Level Mature Scholar in the Observation Mode with a Goal of Stagnation, and be a Pragmatist. All the positions are neutral, and the Mature Cycle, concerned with fourness, while not precisely neutral in the sense that the fourth Level is, still strives for understanding and displays a desire to withdraw from much of the activity of life in favor of a more contemplative existence. We will present the number and Overleaves patterns for you now.

One: Infant, Slave, Retardation, Stoic, Emotional Center, Self-Deprecation. That is not to say that all Slaves will behave like Infant Souls, or that they will want to hold everyone back. It does mean that a Slave can come into its own manifestation before any of the other Essences, and achieve full self-realization earlier than any other Essence. The cardinality of being in the numerical position of one gives the Slave an impetus to work in Essence that none of the other Essence Roles possess. It also means that the Slave does not require special circumstances to complete the Life Task, as do all other Essences, but can accommodate all circumstances to the Life Task, and "hit the ground running" on first incarnation. This is what we sometimes call "the Slave advantage".

Two: Baby, Artisan, Caution, Rejection, Skeptic, Intellectual Center, Self-Destruction. You will notice that the positive poles of all the Overleaves associated with two provide for achieving balance. The Artisan first comes into its own as a Baby Soul, often creating in the crafts and arts long before other Essences are able to do so.

Three: Young, Warrior, Perseverance, Submission, Cynic, Sexual Center, Martyrdom. Considering that this is a Young Soul world, it might not be amiss to consider these Overleaves and the nature of the three Level to gain greater understanding of what is taking place around you, no matter what your individual Overleaves may be. As you perceive, we have moved from the Inspiration Polarity to the Expression Polarity to the Action Polarity, and have completed the ordinal Roles that manifest in cardinal numbers.

Four: Mature, Scholar, Observation, Stagnation, Pragmatist, Instinctive Center, Stubbornness. As we have already stated, this neutral, or non-cardinal/non-ordinal position gives access to all other Roles, Essences, Levels, and Overleaves far more directly than any of the others. That is the significant advantage of the four/neutral function, and it is one of the reasons that most Fragments have at least one four-function Overleaf to provide some neutrality. The cardinal Roles are, of course, ordinal numbers.

Five: Old, Sage, Power, Acceptance, Idealist, Higher Intellectual Center, Greed. This five Level, being part of the Expression Polarity, requires that there be an emphasis on access, both to self and to others. This five function provides much energy, as the five is the expansive number, but it can bring problems of the sort that often plague Sages—the tendency to perform a life rather than to live it, which is why the Old Cycle is concerned with being. At this Level, the Sage is able to set aside performance unless it chooses to do otherwise, and to express not others but itself.

Six: Astral, Priest, Passion, Growth, Spirtualist, Higher Emotional Center, Arrogance. The two-channel input of Priests makes it possible for a constant awareness of the Astral, or "higher" aspects of life, and the Priest Role, which always serves the "higher ideal," whatever the Priest deems that to be in any given life. At the same time, it is helpful that the six number is an ordinal one, or there would be little to anchor the Priest to the Physical Plane, which is often a problem for that Role.

Seven: Causal, King, Aggression, Dominance, Realist, Moving Center, Impatience. It is on the Causal Plane that the Entities, now reunited, strive to join with the Entities of the Cadre, which is the purpose of the inculcation of the seven number, as well as the impetus to make all the knowledge at our disposal available to you. Recall that Entity Robert refers to Kings as Healers of the Spirit, and you will realize how much of this cardinal-ordinal reciprocity functions.

[*July 2002:* It is useful to keep in mind that Priests and Kings never do come into their own on the Physical Plane as the other five Essences do; their ties to the Astral and Causal Planes give them access to the perception of possibilities beyond the Physical Plane. This is often perplexing for these six and seven Fragments because others do not seem to share their understanding, which, of course, is a valid insight, but frustrating both for Priests and Kings and any of those striving to work with them who are not Priests and Kings.]

It is of course possible to describe all Overleaves in terms of Essence Role, although it is limiting in a way that is unfortunate and inflexible. For example, instead of saying that this Fragment is a fifth Level Young Artisan in the Observation Mode with a Goal of Acceptance, a Realist in the Moving part of Intellectual Center with a Chief Feature of Stubbornness, it could also be expressed: this is a Sage Level Warrior Cycle Artisan in the Scholar's Mode with a Sage's Goal, a King's Attitude in the Kingly part of Artisan Center with a Scholar Chief Feature. This, as we have already indicated, is limiting, but can give some insight into the various aspects of the Overleaves, especially when viewed in the positive poles of the Overleaves.

Of course, these can also be expressed entirely mathematically: the Overleaves given as a third Level Mature King in the Caution Mode with a Goal of Submission, a Skeptic in the Emotional part of Intellectual Center with a Chief Feature of Arrogance can instead be expressed in these terms: three/four/seven/two/three/two/one of two/six. Again, we would caution you that this limits the perceptions severely because it does not allow for the various ways in which the Overleaves manifest in the life, and it tends to distort the various experiences of the Overleaves by limiting the range in which they are demonstrated. It should be apparent that the conduct of a Mode is substantially different in the Overleaves than the conduct of a Goal. The Attitude colors all the perceptions as well as the behavior in relation to the Mode and Goal. In realizing the "natural" Overleaves of the Role—that is, those Overleaves that have the same number as the Role in Essence—much insight may be gained in terms of how the Overleaves are expressed, for there is always a "flavor" of the "natural" Overleaves present as part of the Role in Essence. This brings us to the very crux of the question, which is the matter of Cadence, the position of the Fragment in the casting of the Entity, which is always part of the manner in which the Fragment functions, not only on the Physical Plane but the Astral and the Causal Planes as well.

Each Fragment occupies a unique position in the casting of its Entity, and that position is reflected in each and every life that the Fragment leads. Whether the Fragment operates in Essence or simply opts for false personality, there is a constant undercurrent of energy that is the product of the Fragment's position in casting that is as powerful or, when it reiterates the current Level and/or Cycle of evolution, even more powerful than Role in Essence. The bond with the Essence Twin and with the Task Companion is the direct result of this position in casting, and, as we have already explained, the ties of those within the same Cadence are enduring, unaltering and profound. We will use the analogy of beating time in music to show what we mean by the Cadence position and casting.

The first Cadence is one, and all seven Fragments of the Cadence have one properties, which can give all the members of the Cadence great purpose in all that they do. As with a musical score, the count, in what is probably seven/eight time, is one/one two three four five six seven, two/ one two three four five six seven, three/one two three four five six seven, four/one two three four five six seven, five/one two three four five six seven, six/one two three four five six seven, seven/one two three four five six seven, two/one/one two three four five six seven, two/two/one two three four five six seven, two/three/one two three four five six seven and so forth for all of the same Essence Roles within any given Entity.

The first Cadence will have a very strong one-ness to it, the second Cadence an equally strong two-ness and so on through the first Greater Cadence, that is, the first seven Cadences, or, to put it another way, the first forty-nine Fragments of the Essence within the Entity. Then, the second

Greater Cadence, the Fragments of the first Cadence will have a generally powerful two-ness but with the purpose of the one-ness.

The double two-ness of the second Cadence will bring a stronger manifestation of two-ness, and so on through the second Greater Cadence. Obviously, in any case where there is a double emphasis, as in a three/three or a four/four, the Fragment in that number of the casting will tend to exemplify that number with special power and clarity. This carries through all incarnations, all Overleaves and all other choices, and many times the manner in which these choices are made reveals the position in the casting.

Let us give you some examples. One of the members of our little group is a sixth Level Mature Scholar—which you may also express as a six/four/four or as a Priest Level Scholar Cycle Scholar—is in the third Cadence of her Entity, in the fifth position. This means that her Cadence is one that will tend to strive, to be enterprising, which is the nature of the Cadence. This Scholar in particular will do so expansively, because of her fifth position in the Cadence. And as you are all aware, this Fragment has many diverse interests and is especially fond of travel. Add to that the sixth Level which has to do with connections for this lifetime—and the two previous lives, for that matter—and you will begin to sense the various pulls in her life. In her next life it is likely that she will be at the seventh Level, or the King Level, where inculcation occurs, and therefore the emphasis of her enterprising wanderlust is likely to find other outlets, such as the study of archeology or pioneering work in the biological sciences. The evolution of this experience should be apparent if you consider the nature of the Overleaves.

Certain sorts of journalism would also be a likely place for this Fragment to put its energies at the seventh Level of the Mature Cycle, and such work is appropriate to the nature of the Scholar, and the imperatives of casting.

We will provide another example, again from this group. The Fragment in question is a fourth Level Mature Artisan in the Caution Mode with a Goal of Growth, a Skeptic in the Moving part of Emotional Center with a Chief Feature of Stubbornness. To express it in numbers, a fourth Level fourth Cycle two Essence, Mode two, Goal five, a two Attitude, the seven part of one Center, Chief Feature of four. In terms of Roles a Scholar Level Scholar Cycle Artisan in the Artisan Mode with a Sage Goal, an Artisan Attitude in the King part of the Slave Center with a Scholar Chief Feature. In terms of casting, this Fragment is in the third ordinal Cadence of his Entity in the first position. He is therefore receptive rather than catalytic, and with the third or Warrior Cadence, and the first or Slave position, he is strongly motivated to act when he is presented with the circumstances which require it. Since Artisans in general are not as quick to respond as the Fragment is, Caution Mode or no Caution Mode, there are those who have expressed surprise at this. With understanding of the Cadence and casting, the reasons behind it become clear.

Here is another example, carried from a past life into the current life. In the past, during the time in the history of Italy that you call the Renaissance, this Fragment was the leader of a small duchy, noted for this fiscal responsibility and his ability to deal with his difficult neighbors and in-laws. At that time, he was a seventh Level Mature Warrior in the Caution Mode with a Goal of Dominance, a Pragmatist in the Intellectual part of Emotional Center with a Chief Feature of Stubbornness. Expressed in Role terms, he was a King Level Scholar Cycle Warrior in the Artisan Mode with a King Goal, a Scholar's Attitude, the Artisan part of Slave Center with a Scholar's Chief Feature.

Mathematically described, a seventh Level, fourth Cycle, three, Mode two, Goal seven, Attitude four, the second part of first Center with a four Chief Feature. Strong Overleaves to be sure, but rather surprising in a man who held much larger states at bay and kept his duchy running smoothly for as long as he did—although it gave him ulcers—and it is when you are aware of his casting that his full strengths and integrity become apparent, for this Warrior is not only the first cast Warrior of his Entity in which the Warriors were cast first, but in the Entity that is the first cast of the Cadre. In other words, he is the cardinal-most Fragment of the Cadre, giving him extreme cardinality and one-ness on an order that can be experienced by no other Fragment.

This Fragment in most of its lives has chosen lives of great purpose and served its task with awesome allegiance. In this life, this first cast Warrior is a fourth Level Old Warrior, in the Observation Mode, a Goal of Dominance, an Idealist in the Emotional part of Intellectual Center with a Chief Feature of Arrogance. In Role terms, a Scholar Level, Sage Cycle Warrior in the Scholar Mode, King Goal, a Sage's Attitude, in the Slave part of Artisan Center with a Priest's Chief Feature. Mathematically described, that is a fourth Level, fifth Cycle three, Mode four, Goal seven, five Attitude, one part of two Center, six Chief Feature. He is now a major figure in international music, in his fifties, deeply respected by his colleagues, which—as is not surprising in such a Warrior—means far more to him than his moderate fame.

Let us discuss yet another Fragment and its place in casting. This is a sixth Level Baby Sage in the Passion Mode with a Goal of Acceptance, a Cynic in the Intellectual part of Moving Center with a strong Chief Feature of Impatience. In Role terms, this is a Priest Level, Artisan Cycle Sage, Priest Mode, Sage Goal, Warrior Attitude, Artisan part of King Center, King Chief Feature. Expressed in numbers, this is a sixth Level, second Cycle five in the six Mode, five Goal, three Attitude, two part of seven Center, seven Chief Feature. This Fragment is a singer for a world-traveling evangelist. Because this Fragment is an ordinal Fragment, it often requires the presence of strong cardinality, which the evangelist has, being in the third Cadence of his Entity, and another Baby Sage. The singer has all the Sage enjoyment of performing, getting applause and the added pleasure of being convinced that he is doing something superior to what other singers do because he is doing it evangelically, following the Baby Cycle motto: Do it right or don't do it at all.

There are many Baby Souls who need the sense of god-approval in order to enjoy or indulge themselves. Let us digress for a moment on another Baby Soul who has been causing difficulties for those around him as well as for many others. This Fragment is a sixth Level Baby King in the Repression Mode with a Goal of Dominance, a Spiritualist in the Emotional part of Intellectual Center with a Chief Feature of Martyrdom. This Fragment is currently in charge of the country currently called Iran. To express the Overleaves in terms of Role, this is a Priest Level Artisan Cycle King in the Slave Mode, King Goal, Priest Attitude, Slave part of Artisan Center, Warrior Chief Feature. In terms of numbers, a sixth Level, second-Cycle seven, Mode one, Goal seven, six Attitude, one part of two Center, three Chief Feature. This is, of course, a cardinal Fragment and we would have to remark that his actions "abuse" his cardinality and in this life the King has gained and is gaining much karma. He is the fourth cast Fragment of the sixth Cadence of Kings in his Entity, an Entity which is made up of Priests, Kings, Artisans and Scholars. We perceive many extremes in this Fragment's Overleaves which are reflected in the current life of this Fragment, including a lack of neutrality in his Overleaves. It may be of interest to know that in the immediate past life, this Fragment was born of racially mixed parentage—his mother was the victim of rape—in what you call South Africa. Raised by his black mother, he was rejected by all around him, including his mother who resented the child, not only for how she became pregnant but because of the ostracism that resulted at his birth. He was beaten to insensibility by angry boys when he was ten and some brain damage resulted, causing a condition not unlike epilepsy, which only resulted in greater rejection from everyone around him. Eventually he went to a mission hospital run by Dutch nuns who took pity on him. When the hospital burned, the nuns were ordered to go to another hospital and were not permitted to take their unfortunate patient with them, who regarded this as nothing short of treason. He died of infections—the result of a very bad fall which occurred during one of his seizures. While this in no way lessens the karmic debts incurred in this life, it may in part explain the highly extremist attitude of this Baby King.

We would wish to provide two more examples for you to consider. To begin, a second Level Young Warrior in the Observation Mode with a Goal of Growth, a Pragmatist in the Intellectual part of Moving center with a Chief Feature of Stubbornness. In Essence terms, that would be expressed as an Artisan Level Warrior Cycle Warrior in the Scholar Mode, Priest Goal, Scholar Attitude, Artisan part of King Center, Scholar Chief Feature. Described in numbers, a second Level third Cycle three, Mode four, Goal six, four Attitude, two part of seven Center, four Chief Feature. This Fragment works around the world putting out fires in oil wells, is an ordinal Fragment in the seventh position of his Cadence, which is the King position. He is a man of good sense and great daring. This Fragment is doing the complimentary work to his Task Companion, of course, who is a fourth Level Young Scholar in the Power Mode with a Goal of Growth, a Pragmatist in the Moving part of Intellectual Center with a Chief Feature of Stubbornness. Let us express this in Roles: a Scholar Level Warrior Cycle Scholar in the Sage Mode, Priest Goal, Scholar Attitude, King part of Artisan Center, Scholar Chief Feature. This Fragment is a cardinal Fragment in the seventh or King position in his Cadence. This Fragment is a stunt man living and working primarily in Europe. Their shared work has to do with risk.

Our second example is a mid-Cycle Mature Priest in the Observation Mode with a Goal of Stagnation, a Realist in the Intellectual part of Emotional Center with a Chief Feature of Stubbornness. This Fragment's Overleaves may also be expressed this way: this is a Warrior/Scholar Level Scholar Cycle Priest in the Scholar Mode, Scholar Goal, King Attitude, Artisan part of Slave Center, Scholar Chief Feature. It can also be described mathematically: a three/four Level, four Cycle six, Mode and Goal four, Attitude seven, two part of One Center, four Chief Feature. This Fragment is, as should not surprise any of you, a teacher. She lives and works near the Black Sea. She shares her life with a man eight years younger than she who is an animals physician with the following Overleaves: a fifth Level Mature Priest in the Observation Mode with a Goal of Submission, a Skeptic in the Intellectual part of Moving Center with a Chief Feature of Greed fixated on service. This Fragment may be described through Roles as a Sage Level Scholar Cycle Priest in the Scholar Mode, Warrior Goal, Artisan Attitude, Artisan part of King Center with a Sage Chief Feature. In numbers, the Overleaves may be described thus: fifth Level, fourth Cycle six, Mode four, Goal three, Attitude two, two part of Seven Center, five Chief Feature.

Both of these Fragments are ordinal Fragments in casting and cardinal in Roles, and both occupy the same position in their respective Entities, which are in the same Cadre. Both are first cast, fourth ordinal Cadence priests, which, of course, describes Essence Twins. Essence Twins are each other's true equals. We have said this before, and we will now explain how this occurs. Each twin is in the same, precisely the same, position in its Entity as the other twin. Six out of seven of them have the same Essence, but that means little when compared to the position that is occupied by these special Fragments. Of course all Fragments have an Essence Twin, and the twins remains bonded to one another from first life to last.

The nature of the bond should be apparent, but we will enlarge upon it. Let us take a first cast Cadence, let us choose arbitrarily the first cast Cadence of Scholars in the third Entity of your Cadre; that is the Cadre from which almost all members of our little group come. The first six are twinned with other Scholars in the first cast Cadence of other Entities in the Cadre. The first cast Scholar of the first cast Cadence of Entity three is twinned with the first cast Scholar of the first cast Cadence of Entity five. The second cast Scholar of the first cast Cadence of Entity three is twinned with the second cast Scholar of the second cast Entity, the third cast Scholar is twinned with the third cast Scholar of Entity one, the fourth cast is twinned with the fourth cast Scholar of Entity four, the fifth cast goes back to the fifth cast Scholar of Entity five—we would have to say that these two have a very strong Sage flavor about them because of their order in casting and one of the twins being in a five or Sage Entity—the sixth cast Scholar is twinned with the sixth cast Scholar of the second Entity. The seventh cast Scholar is twinned not with a Scholar but with a Priest, in the seventh cast Entity of the Cadre. This Priest is the seventh cast Priest in the first cast Cadence of the seventh Entity.

In the second Cadence, it is the sixth cast Scholar that is twinned out of Essence. In the third Cadence, it is the fifth cast that twins out of Essence, and so on, until in the seventh cast Cadence, it is the first cast Scholar of that Cadence who is twinned with the first cast Warrior of the seventh cast Cadence of the first cast Entity. The bond, as we have indicated many times, endures for all time and continues until the Cadres have reunited beyond the Causal Plane.

We have indicated before that the tapestry weaves itself, and the casting is the beginning of the tapestry.

As to Task Companions, as we have already indicated, they are always cardinal and ordinal, and generally on the same polarity where possible. Scholars, lacking the polarity, can become Task Companions with any other Essence, but most often with Warriors. Six times out of seven, the Task Companions are in the same Entity, the seventh is out of Entity, but still in the cardinal/ordinal position. We have indicated before that often the cardinal Fragment is less outwardly successful or recognized than the ordinal one because much of what the cardinal Fragment does initiates action in the ordinal Fragment, and it is the ordinal Fragment that realizes the work and in the "worldly" sense, gets the credit. Often when the cardinal Fragment is the more visible of the two, it is because the ordinal Fragment is not currently on the Physical Plane. The bond continues whether or not both are extant on the Physical Plane at the same time. When both are on the Physical Plane at the same time, there is a strong tendency to have complimentary Overleaves, whether or not the two Fragments ever meet "face to face". It is interesting to note that Task Companions, even more than Essence Twins, are often thought to "look alike," or "talk alike". That is because the relationship, being an outwardly focused one, tends to be reflected in similar ideals, goals and attitudes.

Task Companions often choose the same body types, as Essence Twins choose complimentary body types. There is greater physical attraction between complimentary body types than there is between the same body types. Between those with the same body types, there is a greater degree of comfort. To give a similar example of Task Companion bonding, let us take the same group of Scholars, the first cast Cadence of Scholars in third Entity of your Cadre. The first cast Scholar of the first cast Cadence has as the Task Companion a first cast ordinal Warrior in the first cast Entity of the Cadre. The second cast first Cadence Scholar has as its Task Companion the second cast ordinal Priest of its Entity. The third cast Scholar has as its Task Companion the third cast ordinal Warrior in its Entity. The fourth cast Scholar has as its Task Companion the fourth cast ordinal Sage of the Entity. The fifth cast cardinal Scholar has as its Task Companion the fifth cast ordinal Priest of its Entity. The sixth cast cardinal Scholar has as its Task Companion the sixth cast ordinal Warrior of its Entity. The seventh cast cardinal Scholar has as its Task Companion the seventh cast ordinal Artisan of its Entity. In the second cardinal Cadence, it is the second cast Scholar who has the Task Companion in another Entity. This bond, as we have said before, carries over from life to life, from the beginning to the end. The sixth Cycle that can be experienced by individual Fragments occurs on the Astral Plane, where the Entities gather to reunite. This experience is the fulfillment of the Priest experience and has to do with the nature of the sixth Level, which in the positive pole is harmony. More than connection— the negative pole of six—this harmony is inherent in reunited Entities. The Entity would not and could not reunite if this were not the case. On the Physical Plane, the six experience occurs during manifestation of the Transcendental Soul. This soul is not a Fragment and not a reunited Entity, but a totality which generally brings about massive social and cultural rebirth and/or change.

We remind you that the Transcendental Soul has manifested in your species as Socrates, Zarathustra, Mohammed and as Mohandas K. Gandhi. All these manifestations were marked by profound social changes and by a new "harmony" in the followers of the manifestation. Because the Transcendental Soul perceives others as itself—this is ultimate compassion, which is the positive pole of the Priest Essence—it shares all the perceptions and tribulations of those it encounters. It should not surprise you to realize that all the Fragments who gave up their bodies to the manifestation of the Transcendental Soul have been sixth or seventh Level Old Priest Essences. While it is possible for the Transcendental and Infinite Soul to manifest through any Fragment extant anywhere on the Physical Plane, most often the Fragments who are most willing and who achieve the greatest growth from the experience are "in tune" with the manifestation, through Essence, casting position and/or Overleaves. [*August, 1998:* In general, the sixth and seventh Level Old Priests and Kings are able to sustain the manifestation for significantly longer periods than others. Those seventh Level Old Kings manifesting the Infinite Soul can support the manifestation for up to a month, the sixth and seventh Level Old Priests can support a manifestation of the Transcendental Soul for up to six months before the body "gives out" on them.]

The Infinite Soul, being of the seven nature, brings the Logos to bear during its manifestation. When the Infinite Soul is extant on the Physical Plane, it does not so much teach as exist in the state of culmination that is the way the Physical Plane experiences the presence of the Logos. What we offer is teaching, what the Infinite Soul provides is Universal Truth. The Infinite Soul has manifested in the physical forms known to you as Lao-Tzu, Sri Krishna, Siddhartha Gautama and Jesu bar Joseph, and from these manifestations, the Universal Truths have been brought to bear on your planet, as they have been brought to bear throughout the Physical Plane by manifestations in other forms. The experience of the manifestation of the Transcendental Soul on the Physical Plane does much to make Astral Fragments more accessible to those on the Physical Plane. The experience of the manifestation of the Infinite Soul on the Physical Plane brings more Mid-Causal teachers—reunited Entities such as we are—to the seeking students on the Physical Plane. While those on the Physical Plane are not yet into the sixth or seventh Cycles, which are experienced on the Astral and Causal Planes, validation of these Cycles is possible for even very Young Souls during manifestations of the Transcendental and Infinite Souls. We emphasize this particularly so that it is clear that six and seven states are possible to those on the Physical Plane. Of course, those with a six and/or seven influence in their casting order, Role, and/or position in the Cadence, find such validation through other experiences than the manifestations of the Transcendental and Infinite Souls.

That is not to say that others cannot or do not experience such validation many times during all lives, but it is often explained, or explained away in other terms, or assumed to be "unnatural" or "supernatural" or "incorrect" by the Fragments confronted with those aspects of themselves. Those with strong six and/or seven resonances are not usually inclined to reject such experiences. Which brings us to what you call psychic ability.

While we are aware that this word is used to describe all manner of abilities and shams, we would want to assure you that such abilities do indeed exist. The mediums who channel us would not be able to do so if there were no psychic abilities, and, in fact, there would be no group of students, either. Those with mediumistic abilities have strong six or seven positions in casting. The six-ness is present in Jessica, and seven-ness is present in Camille. The Fragment who is now Leslie has a very strong six position in casting, and one of our students who rarely attends sessions, while he is not a medium, has pronounced psychic abilities, being the sixth cast Fragment in a seventh cast Cadence. For this Scholar, there is much difficulty because of the high degree of sensitizing, which is enhanced by the nature of the Mature Cycle. That is not to say that only those with these positions in casting have abilities of this nature. However, if a Fragment chooses to experience psychic abilities during a specific life and is not in a sixth or seventh position in casting, then strong six and/or seven Overleaves are chosen to bring these resonances to bear in the life.

We do not wish to create the assumption that there are only certain Fragments who are "endowed" with psychic abilities and that the rest are doomed to grope along in confusion. What would be the point of depriving a Fragment of choice when the lessons of the Physical Plane from the outset have to do with choice and its consequences? Every Fragment has the option to choose such Overleaves that will make psychic abilities a part of a life. Many do so and use the talents they have chosen to manipulate others, which, of course, leads to karmic debts. It is also important to note that psychic abilities are not always pleasant, either in their application or their effects. [*May, 2006:* Those Fragments in the Young Cycle having chosen psychic abilities often find them difficult to handle, due to the "do it my way" motto of the Cycle, and many of those Fragments tend to become compulsive users of "mind-altering" substances as a way of lessening the barrage of psychic impressions constantly impinging upon them. That does not mean that all compulsive "drug users" are harried psychics. We did not say that nor did we mean to imply it, but for those choosing such abilities while in the Young Cycle without the "buffer" of casting to mitigate the perceptual onslaught, psychic talents can prove to be more of a burden than an advantage, particularly for those living in technologically advanced societies with the extreme emphasis on left-brain intelligence.]

In general, it is older souls who choose to employ their psychic Overleaves, but they are not the only ones to do so. What we would wish you to understand from this is that like all other abilities, the psychic abilities are chosen and the use of the abilities and the consequences of the use are important lessons of the Physical Plane, which every one of you will learn in your Cycles of lives. Those Fragments with strong six and/or seven influences are apt to choose psychic abilities more times than those who do not have such resonances, yet even that is not required, desired or mandated. When the Fragment who has the psychic ability is also a very cardinal Fragment in casting order, though not necessarily in Role, it is not unusual for others to seek the Fragment out for aid and comfort and support.

That does not mean that all Fragments so sought are by definition very cardinal psychically gifted Fragments, but that there is a tendency for this to be the case. The problem that can arise for the psychic and cardinal Fragment, as the Fragment who is now Camille is well aware, is that the casting and Overleaves, as well as the Essence, are inclined to provide what has been asked for with little regard for the drain on the self, which results in energy depletion much the way doing hard physical exercise can do. If there are no Fragments willing to return some of the energy to the cardinal and psychic Fragment, exhaustion can result and often the psychic activities must be suspended for a period of time until the energy levels are restored. What makes this difficult is that the cardinal Fragments do not easily accept such energy from those with whom there are strong links. This is where the Task Companion is most important, and it is through that relationship more than any other that such arcane energy levels can be most easily restored. We would wish to point out again that the Task Companions do not need actually to know each other for this to happen, but, of course, familiarity does make such things much easier, given the limitations of the Physical Plane. Where the Task Companion is not available, then members of the same Cadence, members of the same configuration, and those with whom there are many past associations, are likely to be able to provide energy. While it is possible for the Essence Twin to do this as well, it is often the case that the Essence Twin suffers from the identical or highly similar forms of fatigue, and no matter how willing and eager to supply the energy, cannot do so without greater loss for itself.

When the six/Astral Plane and the seven/Causal Plane have been transcended, the Fragmentation is at an end, and the "individuality," that is, the result of the Fragmentation comes to an end. In the Buddhic Plane, there are no Fragments as such, and no Entities or Cadres, for that matter. Beyond those high Planes, is the Tao itself, which is a culmination of all Levels and Cycles and Essences, as well as the source of all Levels and Cycles and Essences. The Akashic Plane provides the greatest access to "the meaning of life," and it is the balancing point between the experience of Fragmentation and the experience of totality. It is as difficult for us to grasp the concepts of the Tao as it is for you to grasp the concepts of the Mid-Causal Plane. Nevertheless, all concepts are valid and true, though, of course, you may choose to believe this or not to believe it, as you prefer. We would think that many of you have found the mathematical concepts here expressed somewhat difficult to follow, but there are a few more aspects to the mathematical resonances that are deserving of attention. When such links as Monads and karma are present between Fragments, it is not unusual for the Fragments to choose complimentary Overleaves that will not only aid in recognition and completion, but will address the nature of the karma or Monads: thus, when a Fragment has created a karmic ribbon through religious intolerance that resulted in, for example, burning another Fragment at the stake, it is likely that when the karma is to be burned, that the Fragments will enforce the experience with Overleaves that resonate to the Priest/six nature, so that the entire lesson may be brought to bear and positive validation result from the burning of the karma.

This is often seen more clearly when the fourth internal Monad has been successfully completed and the Overleaves are manifested rather than disguised under false personality. We have indicated before that often members of the same Cadence will choose very similar Overleaves for lives together on the Physical Plane so that they may more completely function as the unit they, in fact, are.

We are aware that many of you sense the connections in your lives but are reluctant to act upon them, or are unwilling to risk the possible rejection that might be the result of so "illogical" an act as pursuing a connection that is valid. Let us emphasize that the connection is not the product of wishful thinking but rather of Essence Level perception. Where this is truly present, the knowledge of the Overleaves of the Fragment with whom the connection exists can be most helpful, as well as knowing whether or not the Fragment is a cardinal or an ordinal one. While this does not guarantee success in contact, it can lessen the chance of outright rejection. It is obvious, of course, that Fragments with Goals of Dominance respond to different impulses than those with Submission or Rejection. It is also obvious that those in, for example, the Power Mode, are likely to be more forceful in their personality than a Fragment in the Repression Mode. If, for example, a Fragment wished to make contact with a Mature Artisan in Caution it is likely that the Fragment would go about it differently than when making contact with a Young King in Passion. Sensitivity to these aspects of Overleaves can gain much in understanding between Fragments, which is one source of genuine Essence Contact. Where the "mathematics" are compatible, the contact may be established more easily. Just as the polarities emphasize reciprocity, so the mathematical balances reveal the presentation of the Fragments, by which we mean that the true personality establishes reciprocities within itself. Where this does not occur, we speak of Overleaves that abrade inwardly, just as we have often pointed out the problems of Overleaves that abrade between individual Fragments. These inward abrasions are occasionally perceived as neurotic aspects of a personality, and there are certainly times that we would agree with that assessment. But when such Overleaves are chosen, they are intended to make certain experiences and lessons possible. The inward balances and reciprocities can be used often to determine what other Fragments respond to in any individual.

We will discuss the case of a seventh Level Mature Warrior in the Observation Mode with a Goal of Growth, an Idealist in the Moving part of Emotional Center with a Chief Feature of Stubbornness. That can be expressed as a King Level Scholar Cycle Warrior in the Scholar Mode, Priest Goal, Sage Attitude, King part of Slave Center, Scholar Chief Feature. In numbers, a seventh Level fourth Cycle three in the four Mode, six Goal, five Attitude, seven part of one Center, four Chief Feature. As you can see, there is a strong likelihood of autocratic attitude here, which we would agree is valid.

To add to this, however, this is the fifth cast Fragment in the fifth cast Cadence of this Fragment's Entity, which lends a very Sage/five air to this Fragment who often appears more flamboyant than is usual in Warriors. This strong reinforcement of Sage/five-ness in part accounts for the lifelong fascination this Fragment has had with the theater, although his work is not in any theatrical area and is, in fact, more concerned with sports than the stage. Many persons encountering this Fragment would assume they are dealing with a Sage with an unusually blunt manner—Sages, being natural diplomats and negotiators, are adept at "the soft answer that turneth away wrath"—which is, of course, the Warrior at work.

Often this complexity of responses is present when there is a strong diversity in the Overleaves. What reveals this interaction of Warrior and Sage qualities is this Fragment's tendency to create situations that are challenging. The creating of situations is from the Sage/five influence: the challenge, as you are aware, is what the Warrior nature seeks. We have told you before that the universe is more vastly ordered than you find possible to imagine, for it is far easier on the Physical Plane to perceive the chaos, which is an essential part of the Physical Plane, than to perceive the order. Of course, that order extends far beyond the Physical Plane and is present in all aspects of evolution, from the emergence of species on your planet to the tides between the galaxies, to the reuniting of Entities and Cadres, to the vast synthesis of the Buddhic Plane or the all-encompassing knowledge of the Akashic Plane. That order is present as we have described it to you, and the interaction we describe as the weaving of the tapestry comes from that ordered interaction.

This in no way abrogates your choice. It is always possible to choose Overleaves, lives and situations that encourage the personality to express itself away from Essence and casting natures. In fact, almost all Fragments do make such choices many times in order to bring all lessons to bear. Let us provide you with such an example, and in this case, a fairly extreme one. Let us discuss a fourth Level Young King in the Perseverance Mode with a Goal of Submission, a Pragmatist in the Intellectual part of Emotional Center with a Chief Feature of Martyrdom. In Role terms, this is a Scholar Level Warrior Cycle King in the Warrior Mode, Warrior Goal, Scholar Attitude, Artisan part of Slave Center, Warrior Chief Feature. Since the King and Warrior Essences are on the Action Polarity, there would be a tendency to see this Fragment as very much a Warrior, and it should not surprise you to learn that this Fragment is a physician working at an isolated hospital in Africa—this gives both the King and Warrior aspects an opportunity to work. Also, this Fragment is an ordinal Fragment, the first cast in the sixth ordinal Cadence, which is the Slave position in a Priest Cadence. This Fragment is working very much in harmony with his Overleaves, has been able to burn twelve karmic ribbons and to gain philanthropic karma as well. He is, incidentally, a puzzle and something of a disappointment to his family, most of whom are very successful businessmen and publishers. While his humanitarianism is praiseworthy, in their eyes he has definitely overdone it.

This King has as a Task Companion a seventh Level Young Warrior in the Observation Mode with a Goal of Submission, a Pragmatist in the Moving part of Intellectual Center with a Chief Feature of Stubbornness. This Fragment, a woman, works with seriously disturbed children in Europe. She is very capable and focused in her work. Both of these Task Companions reveal the protective nature of the Action Polarity which is as strong as the forceful side. While neither Warrior nor King is aware of the other in their waking lives, both have "dreams" which are their explanations of their Astral contacts. The metaphor that the Warrior perceives is being alone in a grand hall with a tired man in courtly robes. The King dreams of visiting a military field tent and talking with a tired woman in armor.

To contrast, let us take as our example a second Level Young Slave in the Passion Mode with a Goal of Acceptance, a Cynic in the Moving part of Intellectual Center with a Chief Feature of Stubbornness. In Role terms, an Artisan Level Warrior Cycle Slave, Priest Mode, Sage Goal, Warrior Attitude, King part of Artisan Center, Scholar Chief Feature. In numbers, a second Level third Cycle one, Mode six, Goal five, Attitude three, seven part of two Center, four Chief Feature. As you perceive, there is a greater diversity in this Fragment than in the Task Companions discussed earlier. This Fragment operates and maintains farming equipment in rural Argentina, which is not inappropriate for these Overleaves. It is interesting to note that often in the past this Fragment has been an armorer and cannon-maker, and to this day finds armor, guns and weapons fascinating. This Fragment has as his Essence Twin a third Level Young Scholar in the Passion Mode with a Goal of Retardation, a Spiritualist in the Moving part of Intellectual Center with a Chief Feature of Self-Deprecation. This Fragment is an Ursuline nun and was for two years the school teacher of the Artisan above. To express the Overleaves in terms of Roles, she is a Warrior Level, Warrior Cycle Scholar, Priest Mode, Slave Goal, Priest Attitude, King part of Artisan Center, Slave Chief Feature. To express this in numbers, a third Level third Cycle four, Mode six, Goal one, Attitude six, seven part of two Center, one Chief Feature. Both of these Fragments are ordinal, and as you perceive, are examples of the seventh time when referring to the six times out of seven that Essence Twins are the same Essence.

These two Fragments have had more than the usual number of past associations—two or three per Cycle is about average for Essence Twin contact—and have known each other in fifteen of their past lives. For such Young Souls, this is a very high incidence of contact.

Often among cardinal Essence Twins there is less contact: among ordinal Essence Twins, there is more contact. Conversely, among Task Companions, of course, since one is always cardinal and one ordinal, there is no pattern differential. We know of several very ordinal Essence Twins who have spent fully a third of their lives in contact, whereas we are also aware of very cardinal Essence Twins who have spent as little as ten percent of their lives in contact. Because the positive pole of ordinality is responsiveness, there is less tendency to reject the contact of Essence Twins. Cardinality, especially high cardinality, often finds the experience of true equality perplexing and unfamiliar, which is one of the many reasons why we have indicated that for most Fragments the relationship with the Task Companion is more comfortable than the relationship with the Essence Twin.

We have indicated that this planet is approaching the fifth Level of the Young Cycle, which, as you will understand, has to do with expansion. You have already seen the beginnings of this in the advance in technology and the possibilities of expanding exploration beyond the planet itself. But thus far we would have to say that there has been more of the negative pole of five—that is, adventure—than the positive. It is not unlikely that within the next fifty years, assuming that no irremedial steps are taken that render the planet largely uninhabitable, contact with other Fragments from other planets will occur to a greater or lesser degree. That does not mean that flying saucers filled with little green men will land at major "tourist attractions" speaking English and knowing which fork to use. By contact, we mean received signals from a locatable star system, that can be verified in other parts of the planet. At this point, it is apparent to us that most of the Fragments extant on your planet are ill-prepared for this eventuality. After all, you already share the planet with another ensouled species— the cetaceans: whales and dolphins—and you have yet to validate this connection with recognition. While we do not wish either to encourage you or discourage you, we would think it is not unreasonable for you to learn that simian mammals are not, in fact the "beau ideal" of the universe. Perceiving Essence and Overleaves beyond the "packaging" could be of great use to all of you, should you decide that you wish to enter the positive pole of the fifth Level.

Of course, since the positive poles are the access to Essence, we would wish to comment on gaining access to these poles. This is most often accomplished by what we have called "hands across" or, in the case of Scholars, "hands through" the polarities. Let us explain this to you. Each of the polarities has cross-influences. The Artisan/Sage, Slave/Priest, Warrior/King polarities can be used in this way: if an Artisan is trapped in the negative pole, artifice, it is possible for the Artisan to bring this to an end by examining the positive pole of the opposite Role, that is, Sage. The Artisan, in effect, asks what it is that the Artisan wishes to express, and that in turn allows access to the positive pole of Artisan, which is creation. By the same token, if the Sage is caught in the negative pole—oration—the pattern can be stopped by examining the positive pole of the Artisan— creation—and determining what it is that the Sage wishes to create, and that in turn can lead to expression.

In the Inspiration Polarity, if the Slave finds itself in the negative pole of bondage, the hands-across technique to the positive pole of Priest, which is compassion, makes possible the positive pole of Slave, which is service. The Priest, likewise, can end the negative zeal by determining what it is that the Priest desires to serve, and by that, come to compassion.

The Action Polarity experiences the same change: if the Warrior is caught up in the negative polarity of coercion, determining what it is that the coercion is supposed to master leads to the positive pole of persuasion. The King, by the same token, if it is in the throes of tyranny, can break the pattern by discovering what it is that it wishes to persuade others to do, and by that, enter the positive pole of mastery.

Scholars, being in the neutral position, have access to all positive poles to bring them from their negative pole of theory to the positive pole of knowledge. What the Scholar must determine is what area the need arises from—is the theory/knowledge a matter of Expression, Inspiration or

Action?—and then to address the positive pole of whatever Role is most appropriate to what the Scholar desires to achieve. This flexibility gives Scholars a great range of experience and abilities as well as reinforcing the Scholar studiousness, which can occasionally appear to others as a lack of involvement, or being slightly removed from the situation, which is not an invalid perception. In most instances the numbers of the polarities add up to seven, which in the positive pole brings inculcation, the exception, that of the Action Polarity, is compensated for with the interaction of Warrior and Scholar—three and four—Essences, and the nature of the mid-Cycle, which is reflected in this interaction. The "hands-across" and "hands-through" techniques can work for all the Overleaves.

For example, if "how" you are doing a thing does not appear to be working positively, then the polarities of the Mode are where the hands-across or hands-through techniques will be most efficacious. In this instance, the neutral Mode—Observation—is the source of the "hands-through" technique. If "what" you are trying to do is the problem, then the Goal is where the "hands-across" method may be most effectively applied. The neutral Goal, we remind you, is Stagnation, and that Goal is the source of the "hands-through" technique for the Goals.

If "why" you are doing a thing appears to be the problem, then the Attitude is the Overleaf to approach the "hands- across" from, with the "hands-through" originating from the Pragmatist Attitude. Since two of the Centering Overleaves are not routinely applied, the method is not easily employed in Centering, and all but a few advanced students find the technique at the Centering Overleaves too complex a problem to use successfully. That does not mean that we think it is "wrong" or "right" to attempt such a technique, and we do not say this to issue a general challenge, but we believe that most Fragments will have greater success in approaching this problem through other Overleaves.

In the matter of the Chief Feature, we point out, as we have many times before, that there are no good Chief Features, and that all Chief Features block progress. Nevertheless, the positive pole is a less limiting pole than the negative one, and for that reason, the "hands-across" and "hands-through" technique can work even there. Stubbornness is the neutral Chief Feature, we remind you. Of course, the polarities of cardinality and ordinality may also be used. A cardinal Fragment caught up in fruitless activity—that is, the negative pole of cardinality—would do well to examine what response is desired, and thus to come to the positive pole of lucidity. With ordinal Fragments, if the passivity of the negative pole has become the focus of the ordinality, the Fragment is well-advised to consider what it desires to be lucid about in order to gain access to the positive pole of responsiveness.

When undertaking the "hands-across" and "hands-through" techniques, it is of help to keep in mind that in the polarities, the ordinal Role has the cardinal number and that the cardinal Role has the ordinal number so that, for example, if an Artisan is connecting to the Expression pole of Sage, the Artisan is also connecting to the expansion of the five as well as the responsiveness of the ordinality of the five. By the same token, the Sage connecting to the creation of the Artisan also has access to the stability of the two and the lucidity of the cardinality of the Artisan number.

The same is true for all the Roles in Essence as well as the rest of the Overleaves. It is not impossible for Fragments to turn this "hands-through" and "hands-across" technique, through understanding of the interaction of the number/Role cardinality/ordinality into genuine mastery, which brings great growth and insight to the Fragment and often aids in the extinguishing of the Chief Feature, which is perhaps the greatest single accomplishment for any Fragment on the Physical Plane where Essence evolution is concerned, and a thing so rarely accomplished that it is a seductive trick of all Chief Features to propose to a Fragment that extinguishment of the Chief Feature is possible, and then bludgeon the Fragment for failure to accomplish this task.

The most easily accomplished "hands-across" is accomplished, of course, with the Task Companion, given the reciprocal nature of the relationship. In fact, we are aware of many instances when the relationship of Task Companions was a continuing exercise of the "hands-across" or "hands-through" techniques. Often Monads between Task Companions emphasize just this technique.

With the Essence Twin, the experience is not as easily managed, largely because the Essence Twins are so much the same Fragment. It is not incorrect to say that the Essence Twin brings the Fragment more fully into Essence and the Task Companion brings each Fragment out of itself. The practice of the "hands-across" and "hands-through" techniques, with understanding of the number/ Role cardinality/ordinality function practiced within the self, can benefit, either directly or indirectly, both Essence Twin and Task Companion. When either Task Companion or Essence Twin is not extant on the Physical Plane, it is not unusual for that Astral Fragment to aid the earth-bound Fragment to develop this internal technique during incarnation, for it tends to make recognition less difficult when both are extant on the Physical Plane at the same time. When all Fragments are extant on the Physical Plane at the same time, then that assistance is not as strong, but just as valid, especially when there has been contact and the recognition is validated. If it would help to have an image of the evolution of the soul as well as the numerical function of the Overleaves, we would suggest that the image of interlaced helices is the most easily grasped. The helix expresses both growth and reciprocity and the intertwining reveals the tapestry. While we do not intend this literally, the metaphor is both easily visualized and appropriate as well as free from social or mammalian stereotyped expectations. All that most Fragments expect a helix to do is to spiral. What the Essence does is evolve.

[*January, 1989*: The assumption that there is a "secret" to what you call Michael-Math is perhaps misleading. We are using known concepts in an application that seems unfamiliar to you, and that lends it an "exotic" aspect that we assure you is more your perception than ours. As we have mentioned, the process of evolution proceeds from its own nature, and Fragments on the Physical Plane adapt their Essences and casting to the manner in which they choose to manifest their particular phase of evolution by establishing a template for that evolution in the form of Overleaves. By assessing the Overleaves in all their descriptive possibilities, we would think that a more comprehensive perception would become accessible to you all. Of course, there is no compulsion applied that you should choose to pursue this, or any, perception, but we would think that the more tools at your disposal that can be brought to bear in regard to recognition and validation, the more readily comprehensible our information can become.]

CHAPTER NINE
Continuing Conversation: Jessica, Camille and Leslie

Leslie is medium height, chunky and energetic. She bustles into Camille's living room, tossing her purse onto the table and her scarf over the back of a chair. "Sorry I'm late," she says as she takes her seat on the sofa. "Bad traffic."

"'When shall we three meet again,'" Camille quotes, holding out a wineglass and indicating the open bottle on the coffee table. "White zinfandel."

"Anything," Leslie sighs, pouring some into the proffered glass. "And I don't think I like being compared to Macbeth's Three Witches."

"Well," Jessica says carefully, "there are plenty of people out there who wouldn't hesitate to make the comparison."

"True." Leslie toasts the other two and takes a sip. "So, what have you been talking about?"

"Everything," Camille says comprehensively. "Feel free to talk about whatever you like."

"How about the price of a herd of cattle in an area where there has been serious livestock disease the previous year?" She grins at the other two. "Right," she goes on briskly. "Never mind livestock. On to Michael."

"Somehow, livestock might be less enervating," Jessica sighs. "Sometimes just thinking about all the information we've got over the years exhausts me."

"Getting the information exhausts me," Leslie declares. "Gives me the trots, too, if I overdo it—and I usually do."

"That's happened to me a few times," Camille admits, coloring slightly. "At first I didn't see the association, but when I'd been channeling for about two years, the pattern was pretty plain."

"Hell, I figured it out in six months," Leslie says, turning to Jessica. "What about you? Does it ever keep you up nights in the bathroom?"

"Once in a while," Jessica says. "Especially when the information has been very dense, or when it's been something I disagree with or about a subject I have to work hard at keeping my opinions out of." She shrugs, smiling a little. "Not quite half the time, I guess."

"God, I wish Larry would get through the infamous Fourth Monad and start channeling—we all could use the help." Camille leans back against the well-stuffed chair cushions.

"How's he coming?" Leslie wants to know, taking another sip of wine.

"Give him six months to a year and I think he'll be ready." Jessica glanced toward the window. "It was handy when Craig was here to help out, but with his practice and . . ." She makes a dismissing gesture.

Leslie finishes for her. "The Impatience didn't help, either. You know it, I know it, and Craig knows it, though he hates to admit it. He's got a vested interest in many of the people he asks about, too, and that gets in the way."

"Impatience asking about patients," Camille observes with wicked innocence.

"That was really awful," Jessica tells her mildly. "You've done better before."

"Short notice," Camille offers as an excuse.

Jessica nods and straightens up. "I was reading over the material you got the last time you were around," she says to Leslie, obviously determined to get the conversation back on information channeled.

"Which bit?" Leslie inquires, not objecting to this. "I was most interested in the answer to the question about the nature of reality."

"That was a good one, wasn't it?" Leslie says with a reminiscent smile.

What is in effect here is the difference of perception of the personal realities and the World Truths or realities and, of course, the great Universal Truths. What is being perceived is the difference between the experience of the individual Fragments in comparison to the "real world" which is, of course, the validity of the Physical Plane. We would stress here that the experience of the Physical Plane is valid to those incarnate upon it, while its validity is not as strong for those who have evolved beyond it, or who are between lives on the lower Astral Plane. We would also wish to point out that reality is part of the rule of maya, that is the rule of illusion, that has been influenced and clouded by perceptions and validations of individual Fragments extant upon the Physical Plane. The question of individual Personal Truths in relation to World Truths is the basis of almost all of what you call science and art. Understanding that existence is the bearer of "reality" in all phases of evolution is a worthwhile realm of inquiry for those inclined to pursue it. All aspects of Physical Plane existence are valid, with or without souls. What is a virus is valid, no matter what your Overleaves might be, and how you choose to perceive or not perceive the virus. But what is Good Work is dependent on your Essence and soul Level as well as your other Overleaves. There is no real conflict, of course, between these Levels, but the definition between them is the major occupation of all extant on the Physical Plane on this and all other planets and "worlds" of the Physical Plane. When the dichotomy is truly understood and perceived, then the Fragment has learned the lesson of the Physical Plane and will evolve beyond it.

"Sounds so easy," Camille agrees with an insouciant wave of her hands. "Just keep straight what's really you, what's really everyone else, what's really going on, what's just illusion, and what it all applies to. Piece of cake."

Jessica isn't as blithe. "That's a good bit of the problem in a few words, but when I think of the magnitude of what it implies, it scares me. I know being scared isn't Good Work, but damn it, I can't help it."

"Hey, I didn't mean to make it sound easy." Camille is far more serious now. "But if I let myself get caught up in how enormous the whole thing is, it tends to stop me. If that's the difference between Self-Dep and Arrogance, or Scholar and Sage, so be it. If it's the difference between Growth and Dominance, so be that, too."

It is, of course, a combination of responses, but the Chief Feature is the primary culprit. Let us suggest that there is no requirement for you to grapple with this or any of the other problems of the Physical Plane. That is a choice that every Fragment makes sometime during the life, and usually quite early in the life—that is, whether or not to become involved with things arcane. Overleaves help quite a lot, or tend the Fragment to put attention into other aspects of life. Let us remind you that all concerns with life are equally valid. Those in occult or spiritual studies are no more "advanced" than other Fragments who are spending time studying chemical engineering or acrobatics or the breeding of long-haired sheep. In fact, there are those Fragments who seek spiritual teaching as a means to avoid the very real tasks at hand for a life. It is easier to escape into meditation and chanting than to learn how to bandage a diseased hoof or decontaminate industrial tubing, or graft fruit trees. It is always Good Work to keep in mind that the lessons of the Physical Plane are, in fact, learned on the Physical Plane. While there are those of you truly driven to spiritual studies, those whose Overleaves, casting, and past experiences tend toward more such exploration, that does not mean that the lessons of the Physical Plane are to be set aside. It is, in fact, quite the opposite—spiritual studies for those on the Physical Plane are most successful when applied to the life being lived rather than to removing the attention from the Physical Plane. You are on the Physical Plane to deal with the Physical Plane, not to avoid it. Those who ask about such things as rest and the Overleaves of their job associates and how to purchase the best automobile are, in fact, pursuing their spiritual teaching on the Physical Plane, which brings the lessons to bear so that validation can occur.

This is not to say that we do not see importance in perceiving Universal Truths. We are aware that such perception is of the highest spiritual attainment. But it is worthwhile for all concerned to tackle the Personal Truths and World Truths and get a reliable understanding of the difference between World and Personal Truths before more esoteric studies are attempted. We do not mean to discourage any of you from approaching this or any other endeavor: we would wish only to stress that you are in your life to live that life, not to avoid living it, and that World Truths and Personal Truths have more bearing on your lives through such things as gravity, sunlight, physical health, nutrition, environment, body type, and all the laws of physics, than the world experience can encompass in a single lifetime. The Universal Truths are just that—universal. They will remain unchanged for all you can conceive of as eternity. They will transcend the Physical Plane and all other Planes of existence. There is no part of your evolution, from casting to the return to the Tao, that will not be part of the Universal Truth. The World and Personal Truths can only be experienced on the Physical Plane, and for that reason, avoiding those truths prolongs the process. Perhaps we should point out that time, as you understand it, is another World Truth and has little or no bearing beyond the Physical Plane.

"I wonder if that's supposed to cheer us up?" Leslie muses.

"Well, doesn't it?" Jessica asks, not quite seriously.

"In a way," is Leslie's equivocal answer.

"Have you noted how Michael continues to emphasize that the important things are choice and really living the life you're in?" Camille remarks. "I've been going over my transcripts and the same things come up over and over and over again—that we're here to choose and the purpose of the choice is to live with what we choose."

"That has an ominous ring to it, somehow," Leslie says, but not too harshly. "And I know what you mean. I've done enough channeling to be aware of how much Michael will do to avoid telling anyone what to do, or even what they might want most to do, just to keep from interfering with choice."

"That frustrates some of the people I've done private readings for," Camille says. "They want a blue print and an iron-clad guarantee, with names and dates, and there's no way I can give them."

"Say, do you have trouble getting names?" Leslie asks.

"I'm terrible getting names. And while I can get Overleaves pretty easily, it's very hard to get casting order."

Both Jessica and Camille nod sympathetically. "Names really frustrate me," Jessica concurs.

"Names are the hardest. I've been able to get them on occasion, but very, very rarely," Camille says. "Once in a while, I'll be confident, but it doesn't happen more than two or three times a year, and when you figure that I do readings twice a week, between these sessions and the private ones I schedule for Alex, that means a lot of Michael material and very few names."

"I know what you mean," Jessica adds. "I've been channeling for more than ten years, and I don't remember getting more than a dozen names in all that time."

"That's better than what I've been able to do," Leslie says. "I can't get them at all. Or at least I never have."

"But I've had times when the person has an impression of a name and Michael will validate or unvalidate it," Jessica goes on. "What is it about names?"

Names are not only insignificant in many instances, they are not part of the validation of Essence. On the other hand, it does make research of the past easier. Names change from age to age and from culture to culture. For example, the Fragment who is now Camille was once a distinguished Korean diplomat. We would think it would not be possible for any of you to properly transmit the name unless working in trance, and possibly not then. Those Fragments who have memories of names can occasionally recall enough to make the identification possible, and we would much rather validate than try to point the Fragment in any particular direction. For example, a Fragment may be born in Poland of a Russian Jewish background. The name given the Fragment may reflect both cultures and be equally difficult to interpret for someone lacking a daily knowledge of both Russian and Polish naming systems. The Fragment who is now Jessica was once born in Tunis of Greek parents, who were slaves. Given a Tunisian name by her owner, and a Greek name by her parents, she was sold to a merchant from Persia, who gave her a Persian name. Which name would be the accurate one, we wonder, and which would be the most valid?

What of the cultures that give different names at different stages of life? What of the cultures with private and public names? What of the cultures that refer to its members with deed names that would roughly be translated "the third son of the leather-worker who shot the most game for the birth of the king's son"? What of cultures that give names that are deliberately not words but a combination of sounds that have no specific meaning so that evil magicians cannot gain control of the individual Fragment? What of the cetaceans that identify themselves and one another with a progression of notes rather than "words"? What of cultures that establish genealogies with names, such as the old noble Spanish and Scandinavian traditions— although both cultures arrived at this technique through different means? What of cultures where it is most wise to name children after rulers and then refer to them by nicknames, as has happened in many of what you call pre-Columbian cultures?

There are many reasons why names are unreliable and these are only a few of them. It also should reveal why getting the names is difficult when channeling. Also, where there has been valid recognition, then the obtaining of our validation is a much simpler thing, and for the individual Fragment with the recognition, the name is the least of it, and the least significant aspect of the recognition. What is recognized is Essence. The name that is attached is at best a "convenient" label.

"That's one of the things that people new to the teaching always find disappointing—they want not Overleaves or comments but names," Jessica says with a shake of her head.

"And some of them can be . . . unpleasant when they find out that they won't get names, at least not from me. They say they want the name of their Essence Twin and Task Companion and the rest doesn't interest them at all. Instead, Michael gives them the Overleaves, the approximate age, occupation, sex and geographical location of the Fragments and leaves it at that."

"But I think it's exciting when someone makes that connection." Camille looks at a stack of notebooks on her dining table. "Most of the group members feel the same way."

Leslie chuckles. "I remember when I first got involved in the group, before I started channeling, I had asked about a person whose work I admired and that I thought was . . . speaking to me. I knew little about the person—I still don't know very much—but I had a sense that the work he was doing had some bearing on what I was doing. That should have given me the clue, but it didn't. I got his Overleaves: second Level Old Scholar, Passion, Growth, Idealist, Emotional of Intellect and Arrogance. Very complementary with my Overleaves, and that didn't give it away, either. As I said, I was new to the group. I didn't know how to ask the questions yet, and how to follow them up. Well, a couple of years later, I asked for my Task Companion's Overleaves and some comments. Lo and behold, they were the same Overleaves and the occupation was the same. I took the plunge and asked if the man whose work I admired and my Task Companion were one in the same."

We were wondering when you would notice.

"Those connections are hard to figure out, sometimes," Jessica says. "And you're right about asking questions. That's half the trick, figuring out how to ask the questions so that you get the information you want. Asking questions is one of the most difficult aspects of the Michael teaching."

"Have you noticed a pattern with students?" Camille begins. "I mean, over the years, there seems to be a progression of questions that almost everyone goes through. I know I went through the pattern myself, and Leslie did. When you first come into the group, you ask for lots and lots of Overleaves, and you store up questions about everything. Then you start asking 'what was it all about' questions, when you stop assuming that every relationship or experience is riddled with Agreements and Monads and karma. After that, matters of deep personal interest come out. Would you say that's the usual progression?"

"I think so," Jessica says. "Certainly the endless Overleaves are the start."

The obtaining and understanding of Overleaves is certainly the first step to validation, and very much at the heart of what we are communicating to you. If the perceptions of Overleaves are faulty, then it is likely that other information is not accurately perceived. The Overleaves are the means by which each of you decides to experience your life. As you have seen, it is possible to experience the "flavor" of all Essences by selecting Overleaves that provide that quality of experience without shifting the nature of Essence itself, or the casting imperative. If the Overleaves are not understood, much of what we teach will make little sense. This is not to say that there can be no progress or that inquiry would be futile, because what is learned and understood is as much a matter of choice as the Mode, Goal, Attitude, and the rest of the Overleaves are choices that are part of life. When Overleaves are set aside as having little bearing on the life, then the rest of what is asked will necessarily tend to be sketchy at best. It is difficult to gain insights from the recognition of a past life if the Overleaves of that life—as well as the current life—are not understood or dismissed as unimportant. We would wish to put forth this metaphor. If the life is the building, the Overleaves are the blueprint from which the building is constructed. The choices along the way are the modifications that are made, and the conditions of the life are the materials used. Obviously when the materials are not up to the standard of the blueprints, then many difficulties can arise that were not anticipated in the blueprints. What is done with the modifications and adaptations is the results of choice and the ramifications of those choices that are made during the life-the construction of the planned building. To undertake to understand this material without a grasp of the Overleaves would be to try to understand architecture without any grasp of the specifications of building materials, and the plans from which the buildings are made. Certain appreciations are possible, but at best limited.

"And after the endless Overleaves, and the assumption that everything is filled with complex meaning, then the shifts begin." Camille rises. "I'm going to get some cheese and crackers."

Not all relationships are based on Agreements, Monads, karma or even simple body-type attraction. Some relationships are simply intriguing, some are compatible Overleaves, some are just convenient. While it is tempting to think that each relationship has a well-established pattern behind it, we would remind all here present that what you decide to make of a relationship, no matter how much or how little contributes to it, is your choice. A relationship may be rife with karma, past associations, body-type attraction and even Cadence ties, but if you do not choose to explore it, the relationship will be minor at best. Where a relationship has little to fuel it beyond your desire to associate with the Fragment, your choice gives it validation that creates the relationship. That does not mean it is any more or less valid. The choice is what matters in this as in all other things.

"I'll tell you what drives me crazy," says Leslie. "It's people, not just those in the group, but others as well, who call themselves Michael students before Michael calls them Michael students. It seems to me that they miss the point by a mile."

When Fragments have truly recognized and validated the nature of their own existence, then we refer to them as students. This does not put them in a more favored position, or mark them as superior to other Fragments, but it does validate their validations. Those who choose to call themselves students without such confirming validation are usually disinclined to do the kind of work toward self-awareness that we perceive as studenthood. While there is no error in designating oneself as our student, it does indicate a lack of comprehension of what we are striving to impart.

"I know what you mean," says Jessica. "Tony Hammond—you know, he comes to sessions about four times a year—keeps calling himself a Michael student, although he has only the fuzziest comprehension of the material." She shakes her head. "We can't change him, or his grandstanding. It's his choice."

"Yeah," says Leslie, "but I don't have to like it."

Changing the subject, Jessica goes on, "I've noticed that once the first Levels of Overleaves and all the rest of the basics have been done, that the people who continue to come to sessions develop an ability to take more risks in their lives. I don't mean that they're more irresponsible, just that they're willing to extend themselves a little more where others are concerned." She looks at the other two women. "Have you had that experience?"

"You bet," Camille says at once. "And some of the results are amazing. No matter how many doubts I have about the material, the way that people in the group are able to make connections always convinces me that something's going on."

"Yeah," Leslie agrees. "And there's more willingness to accept others on their own terms. I've found that people who stay with the teaching are more . . . forgiving is too judgmental a word, but more willing to see the other person's side. I guess that describes it best."

While we do not advocate tolerance—or anything else—as such, we are always aware that where true tolerance is present, growth is more likely to occur. By true tolerance, we do not mean a condescending attitude that all too often passes for tolerance, but a genuine acceptance that every Fragment has its own choices to make and its own life to live and that beyond a certain level of concern, each Fragment is responsible to and for itself. By this level of concern we speak of the ability to perceive others as as valid as oneself. To be willing to release expectations, of oneself as well as of others does much to advance tolerance.

"Easier said than done," Jessica says, a bit wistfully. "If I could release expectations without giving up hope, well, I think my life would be much different than it is."

"I try to keep the idea in mind," Camille says with an upward tilt of her chin. "I try to remember that it's all right that I don't like everyone and that everyone doesn't like me, and that no one is at fault because of it, but it's hard."

"Self-Dep doesn't like it, Arrogance hates it," Leslie says. "I remember Michael saying that Arrogance is the source of true shyness, and I can't help but think about the miserable time I had in college. I was told that the awkward stage was over and now I'd blossom, and how terrible it was."

Each Chief Feature is based upon an underlying fear and can result in behavior that reflects ways of dealing with the fear.

Those with Chief Features of Impatience are often considered charming—one expression of the positive pole of audacity. Impatience is very hard for the Fragment who has it to live with, but many find it exciting and intriguing. Those with Impatience are basically afraid of missing something.

Those with Chief Features of Greed are rarely trusted by others, and often rightly so. On the other hand, there is a style to the positive pole of egotism, and often this is manifested in a personality that is self-centeredly attractive. When the Fragment is a public figure, the Chief Feature of Greed makes dealing with attention both easy and "satisfying" for the Fragment. Greed stems from a fear of loss or want.

The Chief Feature of Arrogance creates the only true shyness. Since Arrogance stems from a fear of vulnerability, the Fragments who possess it are likely to wish to avoid anything that smacks of exposure, and the behavior that results is often shyness. Occasionally the Fragment will go out of its way and develop a very strong public image so that the true personality need not be exposed.

Those with Chief Features of Stubbornness—fearing new situations— often go out of their way to make others comfortable and welcome so that nothing unanticipated is likely to occur. This can lead to very fine social graces and good entertaining.

Those with Chief Features of Self-Deprecation show this in self-effacing behavior that can appear "unspoiled" and modest. Those with Self-Deprecation often learn early to bring others "out of themselves" in order to be able to accommodate the expectations of others. Self-Deprecation arises from a fear of inadequacy.

Those with Chief Features of Martyrdom often put themselves at the disposal of others. They are more than willing to stay up half the night arranging flowers, or will volunteer their kitchen for making the neighborhood summer feast. This can endear them to committee chairmen who will go on heaping tasks on them as long as the martyr will accept the tasks. Of course, those in martyrdom feel they have failed if they say no, since the underlying fear is the fear of worthlessness.

Those with Self-Destruction are often inclined to avoid social contacts and can be thought of as difficult. They tend to be authoritarian, since the underlying fear is a loss of control. Those with Chief Features of Self-Destruction are more likely to doing their socializing in very controlled situations—company luncheons, family reunions, cocktail parties or on very limited bases. The intimate dinner for four is about the largest gathering a Fragment in Self-Destruction can comfortably handle, as it is possible for some degree of control to be kept under those circumstances.

"Both Jessica and I have Arrogance," Leslie says with a shake of her head. "I've learned to get over being shy, or at least I've got so that I don't appear shy, but there are times I still want to drop through the floor."

Jessica does not agree entirely. "I don't like to push my luck that way. Every time I think I've been able to get around my Chief Feature, it gets even with me, and I hate it."

"You guys better help me eat this cheese," Camille warns, then adds, "I know the feeling. Self-Dep runs me around the block any time

I try to keep it from taking over."

We remind all Fragments that the Chief Feature will strive to distort perceptions when it senses a threat to its existence. If it reacts strongly, it is generally because the Fragment has been able to get along without it, even for an instant, without disaster. The Chief Feature will not let this happen if it can help it. Again, the Chief Feature is not an external, although it is not truly part of the personality. Observe the circumstances that cause the overreaction in the Chief Feature. There is often a useful pattern to be discerned that will lead to much insight.

"Have you noticed how careful Michael is to avoid using language that sounds like giving instruction? I've done private readings when all the person wanted was for Michael to tell him or her what to do and then promise them how it would turn out. We've all three been in that situation before."

Camille tosses her head. "And what to say? I've wanted to get one of the 'choice' lectures Xeroxed so that I can just hand it to the person asking the questions and say, 'Read this' without having to get it fresh all over again."

Camille looks up at Jessica. "You've been doing this longer than I have—you must feel it much more keenly."

"Sometimes," Jessica says. "There are times it's good to get a choice lecture again, because it's a good reminder for everyone. Michael certainly harps on choice, and that's important."

"I usually tell people who want answers like that to go to some other teacher. Michael isn't the Delphic Oracle or the Prophets of Old. It doesn't make them feel any better, but at least I don't think they're getting conned." Leslie pauses. "Some psychics seem to be pretty good at picking upcoming events, at least near future ones, and I know a couple of astrologers who are damned uncanny in their ability to assess upcoming influences. But none of them give the kind of foolproof prediction that many people seem to want. No one can tell them that they will meet a tall, auburn-haired woman, thirty-nine years of age from Columbus, Ohio, who will introduce them to a thin, balding man who wears glasses and was born in Saskatoon and now lives in Miami who will offer a deal that will net all three of them fabulous sums of money no later than the fifth of August on the following year."

Both Jessica and Camille are laughing, and it is difficult for either of them to speak in response. Finally Camille wipes her eyes and says, "Saskatoon was inspired."

"It's a funny word," Jessica agrees, perilously near laughter again. "I know what you mean about astrologers. I'm very cautious about most of them, even those who appear to be sincere. But there are a few—Davina, who used to be in the group, is a fine astrologer and she has an excellent record for her updates. She's also been keeping records of Michael students to compare with their charts. She does a wonderful and thorough job. She's not the fastest stargazer on record, but she gives good detail and very conscientious assessments of her material."

"I like the way she describes the influences as being kinds of available energy, or unavailable energy, and emphasizes the cyclic nature of the influences," says Leslie.

"She calls in questions from time to time," Jessica goes on. "And you talk to her on the phone, don't you, Leslie?"

"About once a month, yes." Leslie leans back. "I've recommended her to some of the people I know, and most of them have been very favorably impressed. She did some very worthwhile work for a woman who came to me to find out about scheduling surgery—for hemorrhoids, poor thing. Michael was very specific in his suggestions to her, and the first thing he suggested was that she consult a competent astrologer."

We would agree that this procedure, while not urgent, is necessary, and we would recommend having the affected tissue removed, as it cannot be isolated and treated. In general we do not endorse surgical solutions when other possibilities are present, but where they cannot be avoided, then we would think that "stacking the deck" in your favor of a desirable outcome, as many ways as possible, is a prudent approach to any such procedure. In this instance, the risk of infection is high, but this is low-risk surgery. The condition itself is due to early nutritional imbalances predisposing the body to such problems. In preparing for the surgery, we would suggest that you buy and use goldenseal and comfrey root as teas regularly. Analgesic salves will ease pain temporarily. The liquid content of the body would be best kept at a high level during this time. The recovery period from the surgery itself is indeed painful and unpleasant, but the alternative could well be worse. In order to strengthen the body and improve its overall tone, we would recommend the wearing of light weights on ankles and wrists before the surgery so that the stamina level is high. Discretion in food and drink would be helpful, as well. Before the surgery, it would be wise to consult the surgeon on diet and make recommended adjustments. As tension and anticipation increase, B vitamins intake would be best if increased. The use of tryptophan in such instances is not unwise. Rest is beneficial, and we do not mean lying in bed staring at the ceiling while chewing fingernails. With problems of this nature, there is often a slight decrease in the body's absorption of protein, and increased intake of fish and fowl would not be amiss. If there is additional muscular tension, additional calcium and magnesium can alleviate the problem. Perceptions gained through the entire surgical experience should not be discounted in terms of your work. When the surgery has been finished, much rest is very wise, and the very mildest forms of yoga for exercise as soon as it is possible to move without serious discomfort. Because bedrest can be enervating in itself we recommend massage to keep the body limber. However, it would be wiser to hire a professional massager than to ask your spouse to do the job, for that would tend to trade one tension for another.

"She said that the surgery and recovery went very smoothly and well and she had none of the horrible experiences she had been warned about by others who had had similar surgery. The fifth day after the surgery, she started doing yoga, she was sent home two days earlier than originally planned. She began walking inside the house for fifteen to twenty minutes a day on the tenth day after surgery, when it was clear that the incisions were healing, and by the third week after surgery, she was walking just under a mile outside. For what had been done, this was a very rapid and successful recovery. The day she had chosen for the surgery was selected with help from her astrologer—Davina—and she paid close attention to the information from Michael as well as what Davina suggested." Leslie pauses. "Mind you, this is not a recommendation for everyone under every circumstance, but the experience that this woman had was aided by Michael. She is convinced of it, and so is her very bemused surgeon, who thought the whole thing was strange but not unreasonable. When she said that she wanted the surgery performed on a certain day because of the advice of an astrologer suggested that this would be the best time, the surgeon said that if it made his patient feel more confident and relaxed, he didn't care what the source of the information was as long as it did not run contrary to medical good sense."

"How does that make you feel?" Camille asks. "I know you get the best medical information. Doesn't it ever worry you when you're asked about health conditions?"

Leslie frowns. "Yes. There are times it scares me. There are times I don't want to deal with such questions. But for some reason I tend to be able to get more of what's there than you or Jessica can do, just as Jessica is better at getting geographical information, and Camille is best at getting relational and personal questions answered. Michael has explained that it has to do with where we are in casting, as well as our Roles in Essence, and I'm willing to believe it. I don't understand it, but I will believe it, largely because I can see it going on all the time."

"That's also what Davina has mentioned in terms of where there are strong emphases in our charts. Two of us, by the way, have twelve house natal suns, which she says inclines us to this kind of work,"

Jessica remarks, adding, "I've done some studying in astrology in the last five years. I'm not anything like an astrologer, I haven't the experience and I haven't nearly enough education about it, but I do think I've reached the level of well-informed student."

"That's more than I have," Camille exclaims. "You've got to understand about this Old Scholar," she goes on, nodding toward Jessica. "For her, anything less than an advanced degree level of expertise counts as well-informed student. She's a book-reading fiend and she has very eclectic interests."

"So does Leslie," Jessica responds, a trace of defensiveness in the straightness of her spine. "That's part of being Old, I think. Or maybe it's just being over forty."

"What does that have to do with studying?" Leslie asks, puzzled. "Besides, from what you've said about your childhood, you were born studying."

"Well," Jessica says, and then changes the subject. "Michael did tell us that astrology—"

"Very neat," Camille applauds.

"Thank you," Jessica acknowledges primly. "And to go on, Michael agrees with Davina; he has said that astrology measures the areas of available energy or lack of energy programmed into a life—all part of what they call programming the bio-computer—and occasionally good at spotting major vectors in a life."

"Ah, yes, vectors," Camille enthuses. "Where would we be without vectors?"

"We'd be pretty much nowhere," Jessica answers far more seriously than Camille asks. "But sensing the things, that's what's difficult to learn to do."

"And trying to explain them," Leslie protests. "I've never been able to work out the best way to describe what they are. Michael has an explanation, but it creates more questions than it answers. Typical."

When we refer to vectors, we speak of the results of choices that bring two or more Fragments into "alignment" with each other. In other words, when one Fragment makes a choice that tends that Fragment in a certain direction, one of the results of that choice is that the Fragment will then tend to encounter other Fragments whose courses intersect the course of the Fragment. These intersections are not all the results of Agreements or Monads or karma, but simply part of the repercussions of choices. For instance, a Fragment may choose to change not the work it does, but where it does it, and accordingly moves a considerable distance.

That move, in turn, brings about contact with other Fragments, and some of those Fragments will have importance in the life of the Fragment who made the move. The move itself created a vector and those with whom important contact resulted from the move are those with whom the Fragment is on vectors. Of course where there are strong and compelling aspects behind the contact, the vectors stand to have greater strength in the life of the Fragment. Those with certain sorts of psychic gifts—and the Fragment who is now Davina is one such—can sense the "drift" of Fragments and the resulting vectors. Those Fragments with "psychic gifts" that enable them to interpret cards or tea leaves have an ability to perceive the vectors and to interpret them with some degree of accuracy. When a Fragment is "on vectors" with another, there is often a sense of facility and ease that is part of the energy of the vector itself. We should caution you, however, that being "on vectors" does not guarantee that the contact will and must be made. It is possible for the vectors to shift.

For example, we know of one Mature Scholar who had agreed to appear at a professional conference to give a talk on specific information. In agreeing to do this, she put herself "on vectors" with four other Fragments, including two members of her own Entity, one of whom had not planned to attend the conference until he heard that she would be speaking and found himself wanting to hear what she had to say. All was in motion and the arrangements were going well. The day before the Mature Scholar was to leave for the conference, her oldest child, a girl of sixteen, was seriously hurt in a boating accident. The Mature Scholar—quite understandably—canceled the conference engagement so that she could be with her daughter at the hospital. The vectors with the four Fragments who attended the conference were not fulfilled, but there is no reason that they cannot be renewed at another time.

Vectors often have two or three means of being put in motion when there are compelling reasons for the Fragments potentially involved to meet, such as Agreements, Monads, karma, Entity ties, Configuration ties and the like. Vectors are important "shifting points" in the life and as we have said, are often perceived by those with psychic abilities and in many cases, great skill in such studies as astrology, palmistry, and similar disciplines.

This does not mean that all meetings are the result of shifting vectors, but shifting vectors often result in meetings. When major vectors are converging, it is not unusual to find Fragments with Chief Features of Impatience in motion and waiting—impatiently—for the vectors to converge. We do not intend to give the impression that vectors turn the life around, or that they are of great significance in the life. There are times vectors lead to the simple pleasure of potential contact, such as meeting old friends from the past during an otherwise boring party. Many of you have had the experience of feeling that although you do not usually enjoy a certain form of social event, entertainment or similar occurrence, that in a specific case, it would be worthwhile to go. In many instances what is being felt is the converging vectors that can lead to contact.

"I have one client who comes to me for private readings," Camille says wearily, "who is convinced that every meeting in her life is the result of karmic vectors. This woman cannot believe that everything that happens to her is not filled with greater meaning. Well, she is a Priest in Passion, and she does both those things very well. It's not easy to get her to accept that she is not living out some sort of clockwork enlightenment that is based on profound significance in every aspect of her life. She's a fatiguing woman."

"She's probably fatigued, as well," Leslie suggests.

"No." Camille shakes her head. "No, this woman is looking for something overwhelming to throw herself into. She's found Michael rather disappointing, in fact, because Michael does not provide her the chance to inundate herself. On the other hand, Michael is more reliable than any of the other teachings that she's forever trying out, and so she keeps coming back. She wants all the fireworks and the brass bands and the angel choruses, but so far she's been willing to settle for reliable information."

"I know how that can be," Jessica says. "From time to time over the years we've had people come to sessions who were looking for those . . . brass bands and angel choruses and wanted the whole thing packed in pink lace, but Michael doesn't go in for that."

We do understand that there are those who prefer to have a teaching as glamorized as possible, but that is not our purpose. If there is desire for such ornamentation, there are those who will provide it. A student would do well to examine its hopes and expectations about a teaching before entering into it. We are not here to coddle our little group but to provide information, and we will present the information as clearly as we are able to. Belief is not required, acceptance is not required, faith is most certainly not required. If what we provide aids validation, then evolution occurs on all levels, including ours. That does not mean that you, as students, must validate. If the validation takes place, then the growth is shared by all. But that is the case in all growth. Validation and contact are the means to evolution in all Planes of existence, for those are the tools of love. And by love, we do not mean the syrupy sentimentality mixed with body-type attraction that most often passes for love in your cultural constructs, but the whole-hearted acceptance of another as he or she is. We do not mean uncritical acceptance, but whole-hearted, or as the present parlance has it, "warts and all".

"Not really what the general client wants to hear," Camille says philosophically.

"I've always found the questions that are hardest for me to get answers to are those that have to do with why something didn't work, such as why a contact was abdicated or denied, or what went wrong in terms of vectors that did not converge." Jessica pauses, then goes on. "Part of it is that I hate getting information that says 'you blew it,' because no matter how many times Michael says you can't blow it, most people are certain—thanks to Chief Feature—that they can and do, and part of it is that my Arrogance hates to appear fallible. When I get information about a potential contact, I don't want to have to retract anything."

"But since Michael doesn't predict—" Leslie begins.

"It doesn't matter. I still want it all to go well. The Pragmatist in me demands it. This stuff isn't any good if it doesn't work, and disappointments always make it seem that it doesn't work."

"That's not true," Camille objects. "If it were, then there wouldn't be any real choice."

"That doesn't change how I feel," Jessica says. "I'm not disagreeing, not really, but . . . oh, I can't explain it sensibly. I don't want to let anyone down."

"Neither do we," Leslie interjects.

Little as you may wish to acknowledge it, Jessica, you do not control others. Dominance would appreciate validation in having those Fragments who come to you for information and channeling get perfect results every time. But contact between Essences is not quite the same thing as a cake batter mix, where you need only have the proper ingredients and follow instructions to get the cake. In Essence Contact, genuine recognition is necessary for validation to occur, and there have been times when the Fragment who asked for your channeling did not permit the contact to occur.

For instance, one Fragment who has been in our little group for some time was aware that he had the opportunity to contact a member of his quadrate while he was traveling abroad. To that end, he arranged to visit the place where this Fragment would be staying. He even went so far as to visit the location. But once there, he did nothing but meander around the place, taking pictures, in the hope that the other Fragment would recognize him and take that agonizing first step, something Americans are much more culturally inclined to do than Europeans. He was not willing to face the possibility of rejection and therefore did the rejecting himself, albeit passively, and was then able to convince himself, and you, that the other Fragment had failed to permit him to make contact.

This is not unusual, and we do not suggest that such action is in any way "wrong". It is perhaps sad that the contact was rejected, and it is sad that you believe that you are in any way responsible for the rejections. Each and every Fragment on this or any other Plane is responsible for its own actions. Unless karma is to be created, that is the only Fragment for whom any Fragment is responsible—itself. We wish to remind you yet again: no one is keeping score, no one is judging you, no one is in charge other than the Fragment itself. No matter how much you may wish for the validation to happen for other Fragments, it is not and cannot be your responsibility. The only time you might be said to have bearing on the actions of another Fragment would be if you deliberately provided incorrect information, or represented yourself to be channeling when you were not. That comes close to the process called "mind fuck" and leads eventually to karma.

"I love Michael's little pep talks," Leslie says.

"So cheering," Camille agrees.

"Shut up," Jessica tells them amiably. "You've had a Michael wrist-slap from time to time."

"God, yes, not that Michael calls it that," Camille admits. "And richly deserved. And that is not Self-Dep talking. I went through a period when all I wanted was to get information that was reassuring, thinking that it would be more helpful. That really wasn't my choice to make, and it took an evening with you, Jessica, to get myself straightened out on that with Michael."

We perceive the desire to aid and succor as being strong in Camille, and the impulse is commendable as far as creating a climate of acceptance goes, but it does not permit the Fragments consulting you to understand what factors have led to the current state of existence. It is not helpful to withhold the hurtful or negative information because it leaves too much unexplained and does not aid the Fragment to make considered choices. The Fragment, in consulting you, has already indicated a willingness on some level to know what has gone before and what influenced the current life. We would agree that many Fragments do not enjoy learning that the past has had much karma, but if that pattern is to be avoided in future, the knowledge of the karma can do much to bring understanding into the current life. What the Fragment does with the information, including disregarding it entirely, is the choice of the Fragment. Tact and diplomacy are the natural arenas of Sages, and it is "natural" for you to try to sugar-coat the most bitter pill, but it is not Good Work to withhold it altogether. [July, 2000: We have discoursed on the hazards of "scripting," and those hazards extend to the "perils" of this work, for providing only positive information can easily be turned to "feeding" the script by what is often perceived as reinforcement of the script in question. One of the Fragments who consults you, Camille, a Mature Scholar with an inclination to what is sometimes called obsessive/compulsive disorder, tends to see all-positive information as supporting her marked tendency to script. This perceived "endorsement" of her choices can and does make it difficult for her to break the patterns that have contributed to many difficulties in her life. While we agree that a steady diet of negativity would not do much to ameliorate her situation, allowing some of the material we have provided of a less than glowing nature could, in time, provide this Scholar with a less perfectionistic view of her life, and allow her to choose less restrictively than is presently the case. Of course, this does not mean that you are "responsible" for her scripting tendencies, but it does point out that her experience of this teaching is not what you conceive it to be, and that blocking negativity, while as valid a choice as any, is not providing what you intend it to provide.]

"That's another one of those 'thanks, Michael' situations. I try to keep it in mind when I know that the information I'm getting is not very welcome to the Fragment in question, that's true, but such information is often the means to validation. I get that. I hope I've learned that lesson, but I know I have to watch my tendency to gloss over the unpleasant parts."

"But, Milly," Leslie reminds her, "you've got information for me that was decidedly unpleasant, but very, very helpful. I think that sometimes that unpleasant stuff is even more important than the positive information. It seems to me that the lives that were unpleasant can show where questions are not yet resolved and there are lessons to learn."

It is not uncommon for those in the grip of maya to cling to pain because it is so reliable, and to avoid the occasion of joy because they are likely to appear more transitory. There is also the leftover condemnation of pleasure that is common in the Christian and Jewish religions. These patterns reinforce the notion that pleasure is to be avoided because it is frivolous, while undertakings of an unpleasant and arduous nature are to be hailed as noble and worthy. Some of these beliefs are likely to occur in times and places when survival is difficult and harrowing. Joy is not easily found during a barbarian invasion or a smallpox epidemic. That does not mean that lives spent in danger or poverty must of necessity be void of joy, for that is not the case, and we do not mean the pallid and neurotically smug self-congratulation that comes from masochistic austerity. Joy is the natural product of recognized Essence Contact. The only goal of Essence is joy. The only goal of love is joy. Joy banishes fear and as such is a great threat to the Chief Feature and the rule of maya. Where true joy is present, the positive poles of all the Overleaves are easily experienced. It is never wise to underestimate the healing of joy.

"So there," Leslie says, hitching up her shoulder. "Somehow, it's tough to feel virtuous when you're having a good time," Camille remarks.

"My seriously Christian relatives would be very upset to hear this."

"Your seriously Christian relatives aren't likely to read a Michael book," Jessica says dryly.

"True enough," Camille allows.

"Sort of takes the fun out of self-flagellation," Leslie says.

While there have been those Fragments whose Overleaves allowed them to learn to transcend pain and to achieve joy, most of those who inflicted pain on themselves and others for "the good of their soul" and "the mortification of the flesh" found not joy and not transcendence but a psychological hunger for destruction, which is the final triumph of the Chief Feature that locks the Overleaves into the negative poles. Once this has occurred, it is rare for the pattern to be broken. These Fragments experience what we have described as the "rapture of fear," and for that reason seek out events, occurrences, persons, and "predictions" immersed in fear. Even the presence of the Essence Twin, Cadence members, and/or Task Companion are often not enough to break through the barrier of fear that continuing pain erects. You put on flesh not to be mortified but to be mortal. There is no shame in being mortal. The Essence cannot and does not feel shame. Only the false personality, the acculturated personality and the Chief Feature can experience shame. This does not mean that the personality has no real shame, because, of course it does, as most of you have experienced to a greater or lesser degree in this and other lives. That shame does not carry over from life to life, although it is possible to feel a degree of chagrin at the immaturity of the former self. While this is not the same as the "true" shame, it has echoes of it. When past lives are recalled, it is well to keep in mind that the lessons of the past have been learned in the past and that it is appropriate for the past to have been filled with learning lessons that are now validated. If this were not the case, the Cycles and evolution would be unnecessary and "ridiculous".

"I once read some material a previous 'I' had written," Jessica says awkwardly. "I remember thinking how he had missed the whole point of what he was trying to say and that I felt embarrassed for the lack of perception in the writing."

This recognition was Good Work, although the embarrassment was the interpolation of the Chief Feature and an attempt to disguise the realization that the previous life had no direct bearing on this life beyond that the lessons learned in that life are valid in this life. Preoccupation with a previous life is often an attempt to avoid the lessons of this current life by staying on the safe ground of lessons and experiences already safely behind you, and in a personality that is not currently involved in living. While there are lessons to be learned from the past, reliving the past is not one of them, unless the reliving is done with the purpose of releasing the past, so that the current life may be lived more fully. For those at the sixth and seventh Levels of a Cycle, a more complete recognition of the past may occur as part of the validation of the harmony and the inculcation of the lessons of the Cycle, but that recognition is part of the lesson, and accepting that the past is past is part of the lesson such recognition brings to bear. Validation of the past serves many useful purposes, not the least of which is the freeing of the current personality from the "holdover" from previous experiences. At the same time, release of the past advances the life. While we are aware of the draw to understand what has gone before, and we see Good Work in the perceptions, we also wish to remind all here present that you are living your current incarnation. The greatest gift the past can give to any of you is the present.

"Michael amazes me, sometimes," Leslie marvels. "I think that they're talking in circles, and according to them, they're talking in helices, or other kinds of curves."

"I think I understand most of what Michael's getting at," Camille ventures. "It's one of those cases when the past is and isn't important. Something like the way childhood is and isn't important. What we were as children and the experiences we had really colors the way we are as adults, but as adults we have different experiences and our lives are an outgrowth of the childhood, not a repetition of it."

"Not bad," Jessica says, nodding her agreement. "I get the impression that Michael doesn't see any inconsistency in continuity and disassociation. I wish I could get the hang of it."

That perception is valid, Jessica. However, we would express it in this manner: the integrity of the Essence continues through the diversity of the personality. Personality is a changeable factor, constant only in the degree the Overleaves are manifested in a given life. The Essence, of course, is intrinsically itself, unchanging in any way you can perceive it. If you wish to think of your incarnations on the Physical Plane as the childhood of the Essence, there is some validity in that. Just as childhood goes through many stages until the Fragment is an adult, so the Essence goes through many stages of evolution that permit growth and experience to bring about the evolution of the Fragment back to the reuniting of the Entity and then the Cadre. In terms of the Physical Plane, this Fragmentation and reunity is what you mean by infinity.

Jessica stretches out her legs and crosses them at the ankle. "Michael has a touching belief that we can all grasp what they're saying if they can just say it clearly enough."

Of course: because you can.

"If we choose to," Jessica and Camille say in unison; Leslie leans back and grins at the ceiling.

CHAPTER TEN
Michael On Recognition and Validation

If this teaching is to have any direct bearing on the lives of individual Fragments, it is through recognition and validation that the lessons are perceived. Recognition, of course, is the crystallization of insight that brings into sharp focus the various impressions that are part of the insight. That recognition can be a minor or fleeting awareness that, for example, the roof of Saint Paul's Cathedral in London used to be different. The validation comes when through exploration—simple research in this case—which reveals that the impression or recognition was accurate. In terms of the example we have proposed, the roof of Saint Paul's Cathedral was destroyed in the Great Fire of London in the year one thousand six hundred sixty-six, common reckoning, and was rebuilt, along with a fair section of the city, in the years that followed. From such an experience, it would be reasonable to assume that the last life spent in that part of London ended before the Great Fire.

Of primary importance in recognition is the true realization as compared to what you would call wishful thinking. Most Fragments tend at first to wrap the process of recognition and validation in a rosy, romantic glow that is as misleading as it is glamorous, and we mean both words very literally. This slows down the real recognition and makes validation almost a disappointment at first. Some of our students have described recognition of a sensation of "where were we before we were so rudely interrupted?," a sense that they already know the other Fragment—which, of course, is valid to a point—and are merely resuming a relationship rather than initiating one. This is Good Work and the beginning of progress toward validation. That sense of being with an old friend usually indicates some sort of connection, even if it is little more than body-type attraction or highly compatible Overleaves. All these factors play a role in validation. There are those Fragments who use supposed recognition to block the validation rather than aid it. They would prefer to dwell on the past than to deal with the present, and therefore spend time trying to identify what has gone before rather than dealing with what is occurring now. This is a very seductive trap, and, of course, the subtle work of the Chief Feature and fear. Tempting though it may be to try to recall just how grand a time you had before, let us recommend that turning the attention to the grand time in this life is Good Work and the validation that results can be very rewarding as well as helpful in overcoming the hold that Chief Feature exercises on the personality. We remind you that what we call Good Work is anything that contributes to the completion of the Life Task.

Because you as Fragments are incarnate in separate bodies, the process of validation can be an arduous one. We would think that those of you who have attempted it are aware that there are many distortions that can and do enter into the perceptions. For example, a Fragment in this group had occasion to meet a colleague in a field related to her own. He was somewhat familiar with this Fragment's work, and anticipating the matter, she armed herself with his Overleaves and a basic review of what this Fragment had accomplished in recent years. The meeting went well and a somewhat "off-beat" friendship developed. Out of curiosity, the Fragment in the group pursued the matter, especially after having a dream in which she saw this Fragment as a Nazi officer who ended up biting out his own tongue. Since this Fragment was not a Nazi in his youth, our student assumed that she had stumbled upon something from the past, and asked us about what was to be made of the dream, or whether it could be ignored. Since she had chosen to ask about the dream, we were able to point out that she had perceived the past in terms of what she knew in this life. The image of the Nazi regime reflected the sense and experiences of a past life when this Fragment who is our student had been officers of a very restrictive and limiting royal court that was heavily allied to the most repressive elements in the Church and therefore reflecting the stringent policies of the clergy. This recognition was expressed through images that were understandable and familiar, and might have been thought to have no direct bearing on the nature of the origin of the friendship, had not our student decided to pursue the question and determine if she had actually experienced such a life.

Upon learning that this man had been an official censor in that former life, the reason she saw him biting out his own tongue became clear. The past contact was validated for her and revealed much to her in the nature of the friendship she continues to enjoy with this Fragment. This is not the only way to perceive the past, but by far one of the easiest. Dreams give access to many experiences and can be used to understand current developments as well as the resonances from the past.

Of course, dreams are often couched in symbolic events and personages, but if careful attention is given to what is dreamed, then the differentiation is possible, and from that, much can be learned and developed.

Let us digress to the extent of discussing dreams in general. Dreams describe many occurrences that take place for the most part during sleep. The word "dream" is used to describe many events and experiences, and not all of them are the same thing, no matter how they are perceived. We are aware that a great many older souls Astral-travel a great deal while "dreaming" and what they assume is the image of a friend in a dream may in fact be a visit to the friend via Astral travel and Astral projection.

Let us give you an example of how such dreams work. A Fragment "dreams" that he has visited the home of a friend that is at a considerable distance. He perceives the friend either at rest or in activity, and takes note of the setting. Upon waking, the Fragment thinks of the friend and perhaps misses him. This could lead him to choose to contact the friend. The Fragment could then test his Astral perception by asking about the place his friend is living. This is one of the easiest forms of validation there is, but not always socially acceptable. Astral contact is not considered socially acceptable to most Fragments extant on the Physical Plane, and would prefer to think such events are "dreams".

There are Astral contacts between Fragments extant upon the Physical Plane that are made entirely on the Astral Plane, and although we have touched on this before, we will discuss it again.

Two Fragments, in this case, Task Companions who have not actually met face to face in this life, have maintained close Astral contact for most of their lives. Each has the sort of dreaming we have discussed before—that of consistently repeating images. The Fragment in this group has the image of a man putting on clown makeup before a cracked mirror. The other Fragment has the image of a stone mason at work on the wall of a large building. As is probably apparent, these two are Sage and Artisan, and have had many associations in the past. The pattern of contact is always the same—only the matters discussed are changed, and are usually of importance to the Life Task. That is one way to recognize this sort of continuing Astral contact: the patterns and images do not change, but the information exchanged does. Most often the setting is a very limited one, and the circumstances are private. Often these patterns are established very early in life and continue through all the years. If one Fragment dies, the contact can continue from the Astral Plane without significant interruption.

It is of interest to note that those who develop an ability for this sort of contact generally come to "see" the features of one another quite clearly and it is not unusual for Fragments, after prolonged periods of Astral contact, to recognize each other by facial features when contact is made on the Physical Plane.

Dreams of past lives are not uncommon, although they are often not well understood. We have already described a dream where the recollection was distorted, but there are times when the memory is clear and without "adaptations". These dreams are quite often markedly unpleasant, for often the clearest memory from the past life or lives was in the departure. For example, the Fragment who is now Emily has had for many years a recurring nightmare of a fire in which she sees Fragments running from buildings with their garments in flames, hair charred, and dreadful burns on their skins. The clothing she perceives is ancient, and the buildings are not familiar to her. In her desire to understand what had transpired, she began to research through various sources many of the fires that have become famous in history. This memory was of a fire in the city of Rome in what you call the first century when several "blocks" of "low-income" housing burned to the ground, killing many who were trapped in the levels below the street, and causing severe hardship to many of those living in that part of the city which was not far from the warehouse district of the city. Incidentally, this is not the best-known of the Roman fires, the one attributed to Nero, which destroyed a much larger portion of the city; it is an earlier one, during the reign of Claudius. This dream remains with the Fragment who is now Emily, and it is generally recalled when circumstances cause her to feel untrustful of her surroundings.

Another Fragment in our little group has a recurring dream of a man, stocky, wearing Byzantine armor, standing at the window of a luxurious building. It is night, and the man is reading a document which issues orders. He, being an honest and faithful officer, is committed to carrying out the orders, but he is aware that the orders are "wrong" and that what is being required of him is a grave error and one that will haunt him all of his life. Which, in fact, it did. The officer's career, up until that time a very promising one, was thereafter disappointing and unsatisfactory. The officer died a decade later during combat. This life was the one in which the important Mature Soul Monad of honorably serving a corrupt master was accomplished, and to this day, when the high principles of this student block perception and advancement, the "dream" reminds the Fragment of what it has already learned and brings the lesson to bear in the current life.

Dreams of this sort are not subject to intrusions of images nor do they change in any detail. The Fragment discussed in the previous example is aware of the minute details of the surroundings of the officer's rich quarters, even to the movement of the fine linen curtains over the windows, and the smell rising from the street below. These are the sorts of details that mark memory dreams and they do not change from one instance to the next. Such dreams always have a high level of such detail, and a very real sense of the body occupied during that life. For example, if the body occupied had a limp, the Fragment, in a memory dream, would be aware of that limp as if it were its own, and the "reality" of that body, that life, those Overleaves, would be very present.

Dreams that are concerned with converging vectors are less specific but often recall friends from the past in current settings, as preparation for actual contact. When this occurs, it is not uncommon for a "conversation" to take place that reminds the Fragment of the impending meeting and the nature of the vectors. These dreams are often ignored or dismissed because there is so little to identify them with "real world" conditions.

This is not to say that dreams always and necessarily reveal such information as we have indicated. Many dreams are the images of the mind and speak a curious and symbolic language of the turmoil that is experienced by all those in the throes of maya and who are caught up in the perplexing troubles of life on the Physical Plane. We would not encourage anyone to dismiss the more traditional interpretations of the psychological and mystical teachings, but that while these disciplines are being recalled, the workings of the past and of Essence are not forgotten "in the shuffle". If you wish to use your dreams for development of your perceptions, it can be done with perseverance and practice, and this is what we call shaped dreams. Many of you do shaped dreams now without awareness of what is being accomplished.

Let us make a few recommendations to guide those of you who choose to explore your lives in this way: A shaped dream is most effective in cases of memory dreams, especially when the memory is traumatic. It is somewhat less effective but equally valid in vector-sensing dreams in which some greater sense of awareness can result from the shaped dream. There are several ways to shape a dream and we will explain them to you. First, the dream would be concerned with changing the impression of a traumatic event in a past life, although it will work equally as well with symbolic dreams. What is necessary is to identify what has actually happened sufficiently to appreciate the bearing it has on the current life. By this we mean, if a Fragment has had a repeated and disturbing dream about "something awful happening on a flight of stairs," it is of use to get as clear an impression as possible of where the stairs were, why the Fragment was there, and what happened. Then, having established as much as possible and validated for yourself through a teacher or meditation, that the event has bearing, the dream must be deliberately repeated, sometimes more than once, with a deliberate decision to alter what occurs.

Assuming that the dream is of the dark stair, the Fragment must first identify the stair—for example, a staircase in a tavern in Poland roughly two hundred years ago, or the steps on a Mayan pyramid, or the narrow steps in an Incan city. Since the first example applies to one of our little group, we will focus on that one. The Fragment at that time was a servant in the tavern and had surprised thieves in the process of robbing one of the guests. In an effort to stop the thieves and to alert the people in the tavern, the servant was found out by the thieves who stabbed him and threw his body down the stair.

Having perceived this clearly, the Fragment may then choose to accept the validity, but now returns to the tavern in the dream and walks down the stair without harm. As we have indicated, this occasionally must be repeated several times to bring the Fragment away from the trauma and to establish that the events of that life are not, in fact, events of this life. After repeated returns to the tavern, the Fragment will realize that the past life, while valid, does not intrude in this life. Such differentiation is Good Work and does much to promote growth in the Fragment attempting the shaped dreaming.

[*September, 1998:* This kind of shaped dreaming involves a type of concentration that is not easily sustained while asleep, and it often takes a fair amount of "practice" before the technique is actually grasped and applied without difficulty. There is no "failure" in this, for the discipline is demanding, and expectations can and often do interfere. What is sought here is the capability of releasing the hold of the past, not to change it, but to allow your understanding of its being over to reach fruition. The one time when shaped dreaming tends to be most difficult to sustain is during an Age Spike, that is, when the Fragment has reached the age at which a major trauma befell the Fragment in a past life that is significant to the present one. The period surrounding an Age Spike—usually a year in each direction—tends to overwhelm the process of shaped dreaming, and to bring about a much sharper awareness of the trauma, rather than its diminution.]

The second form of shaped dreaming is concerned with vector sensing and the recognition of those with whom one is on vectors. This is not as easily accomplished because, of course, it is still heavily subject to changes by choice and those choices can shift vectors even moments from actual contact. Nevertheless, let us outline the most effective method of shaped dreaming in the case of vectors. With this caveat: vectors are not the product of wishful thinking or wishful dreading—vectors are the products of choice. Those who have a vague and persistent daydream or fantasy of meeting a person of notoriety because of that person's fame, or the desire of great recognition or accomplishment being heaped upon a person, either oneself or others, such as spouses or children, are not, in almost all cases, sensing vectors. Shaped dreaming will gain nothing for the Fragment who is caught up in fantasy and scripting.

Shaped dreaming will be useful to those who are truly on the vectors. We do not therefore say that shaped dreaming should not be attempted, but we do caution you that should you choose to do it in these circumstances, that you exercise a little sense in its application. When shaping a vector-sensing dream, it is generally not possible to foresee the actual conclusion of the vectors, but it is possible to address those with whom you are on vectors. Here is an example for you. You have sensed that you are on vectors with two other Fragments, and have an ill-defined impression that these two are not known to each other. In the dream, these figures are not truly recognizable.

First shape the dream by attempting to "see" the other Fragments or Fragment. This is not always possible, and occasionally what is "seen" is the face that you knew on the Fragments the last time you met on the Physical Plane. Some of our students have described the sensation of such perceptions as "I didn't recognize you with that body on". One of the Fragments is likely to be more easily "seen" than the other, and it is not amiss to address this Fragment first. This is done in the dream by the simple expedient of walking up to the more "seen" Fragment and introducing yourself. A conversation may ensue, and it is possible to learn where that Fragment thinks it is going, or what it is planning to do. It is not always possible or particularly advisable to force more specifics of the impending vector intersection because requiring too much information can limit the perceptions of when and how the actual meeting is able to take place.

You may determine that this Fragment is going to be at a particular sporting event that you now plan to attend. But the "game is called on account of rain" or you buy your seat on the other side of the stadium from where the Fragment sits. You are so disappointed that you decide to stay home or not to attend a gathering in the neighborhood, and therefore are not in place for the vectors to intersect. When attempting to learn about converging vectors, it is useful to know the general area in which the geographical meeting is likely to take place, and it is often useful to determine in what context the meeting will occur, but again we would suggest that you avoid a too-rigorous inquisition that might keep you—and the other Fragment, for that matter—from making the connection on the Physical Plane.

Often, incidentally, it is easier to approach the Fragment who will facilitate the meeting than the Fragment with whom the meeting is planned. It would not be valid to assume the Fragment you speak with first is necessarily the crucial Fragment in the vector where you are concerned. This is not unlike the social custom of the host introducing guests.

A word here about scripting. Scripting is a common "failure" of Fragments on the Physical Plane, and one of the most persistent and insidious. We use the word failure advisably, since in general this is too strong and judgmental language for our purposes, but since the scripting almost always renders true contact impossible and reinforces the Chief Feature at the same time, it is not too strong a word for it.

Scripting is what we mean when a Fragment, anticipating an event or contact, works out in its mind, in meticulous detail, precisely how that meeting is to go. The Fragment devises dialogue for all concerned parties, determines what is to take place, where, how, and what the outcome will be, and prepares to deal with the event in precisely that form. The occasion then arrives, and to the horror of the Fragment who has scripted, no one else appears to know their lines, or the way the scene is to go. The Fragment with the script becomes confused, angry and frightened and refuses to continue with the interaction, for the script has made improvisation largely impossible, and the Fragment with the script is left "dangling". The possibility for recognition and validation has been lost, and the Chief Feature has been given a greater hold on the personality through the reinforcement of the underlying fear.

Some Fragments do a variation of this, which is not nearly so negative, which, when anticipating what might be a difficult occasion, work out in advance all that might possibly happen, all questions that might be asked, all situations that might present themselves, and decide on a means to deal with them. This, while we must again issue warnings about limiting a contact, is obviously less hampering than scripting, and for many Fragments, gives a sense of ability to deal with difficult or awkward situations. We would only suggest that if a Fragment chooses to indulge in this kind of "war-gaming," that the Fragment deliberately strive to make the anticipated scenarios as wide and as varied as possible, with as many variations as they can bring themselves to imagine. So long as one scenario is not preferred over another, the exercise is not likely to block too many perceptions.

Scripting and shaped dreams can have an unfortunate reciprocal aspect that makes breaking the pattern even more difficult than it would be with only shaped dreaming or scripting functioning. Shaped dreaming, if used wisely, permits the Fragment to be prepared for certain changes and contacts. If it is used to make the perceptions more limited, then it defeats its purpose. An obvious example is someone who senses that they are on vectors with another, begins to make Astral-dream contact with the other Fragment, and then decides that it is going to be a great romance and immediately imbues the whole vector with a rosy glow and the insistence that there be instant body-type attraction. When the Fragment turns out to be a ten-year-old child who has an Agreement with this Fragment for gaining instruction, problems can arise, and it is not unlikely that the Fragment with the rosy dreams will abdicate the Agreement because it has not lived up to unfounded, scripted expectations.

Let us suggest that if shaped dreaming is done with vectoring, that actual Physical Plane contact be left to when it occurs on the Physical Plane. One of our advanced students uses vector-sensing dreams very well, by enforcing the contact during the dream without defining it, and then deliberately making the same gesture to the other Fragment at the end of every shaped dream. When contact actually occurs on the Physical Plane, this Fragment repeats the gesture, which, in fact, is a friendly sort of wave, one that is not unusual or "unsocial" or that would be thought inappropriate in most meetings, and therefore serves to aid the meeting without making it so outre that the other Fragment rejects the entire contact. This student has done fairly well with this technique, and it strikes us that it is not an inappropriate way to use this sort of shaped dream.

The third sort of shaped dream we would have to call collaborative, and one that is generally based on a prior Agreement that for some reason cannot be realized on the Physical Plane directly. These occur mostly between Old Souls and in special circumstances, such as when a past experience is brought to bear in the present life with the recognition that it is past. In circumstances of this sort, the illusion of reality in the dream is really quite strong.

As one of the two mediums represented in this writing by the figure "Leslie Adams," has experienced, dreams of this sort have great influence in the waking life and do much to reconcile a Fragment to the current predicaments that are operative in the life. This Fragment had an Agreement with a Fragment of her own Entity—we should perhaps mention at this juncture that one of the mediums in that combined identity is male, the other female—that had some bearing on the life before last. The secondary Agreement for assistance in that life was abdicated and the primary Agreement, with the Fragment with whom the Agreement was made, was made incompletable in that life by the death of the other Fragment. In this life, some of the sense of loss remained, as it had in the immediate past life, and it was appropriate for the work at hand for the Fragment who is now the female half of "Leslie Adams," to transcend the problems of that life and get on with the tasks at hand, which is why that Fragment has a Goal of Growth in this life.

Since geography and monetary limitations made direct contact difficult for these two Fragments, and the Fragment with whom "Leslie Adams" wished to contact was aware that his current life was likely not to last much longer, a shaped dream was agreed upon after Astral contact, and was carried out with good memory on both sides. Now "Leslie" met the other Fragment on the street of the city where he then resided and where their previous life together had been lived. The other Fragment conducted the Fragment who is now "Leslie" on a tour of the city, ending up at the place where the Fragment who is now "Leslie" had been killed in the life before last.

The purpose of this admittedly unpleasant visit for the Fragment who is now "Leslie" was to bring to bear the passage of time. This time, the other Fragment escorted her through the places where the end of that previous life had taken place, with the constant reminder that this time the Fragment who is now "Leslie" would not be left alone. The streets and other locations were traversed, all without incident, barring a modern traffic jam. The Fragment who is now "Leslie" was able to recognize and validate that the experiences of that past life were no longer valid in this life and that who she has become is not who she was. The Fragment who participated with her was able to discharge most of the Agreement through this rather unorthodox method and the Fragment who is now "Leslie" was able to bring those lessons to bear. Upon awakening, the Fragment who is now "Leslie" was able to recall most of the dream in sharp detail, and had the good sense to contact a journalist friend to discover what the weather had been like in the city she had dreamed of during the last three days. What she learned was that what she had perceived was consistent with what she had seen. Of especial interest was the information of a worse-than-usual traffic jam at the location she had observed during the shaped dream.

As we have already remarked, dreams of this sort are comparatively rare and generally are operative with Old Souls. Some Mature Souls have similar experiences, but more often with the purposes of identifying a Fragment from the past rather than putting the past behind them. If you will examine the nature of the Mature Soul, you will perceive why this is most often the case.

Dreaming is a great tool for those interested in increasing self-awareness, no matter what Cycle and Level they are living at this time, and for those who choose to do so, we would suggest that keeping a log of dreams is an excellent place to begin work on the perceptions and validations that can be achieved. Upon awakening, it is most effective to record at once any and all impressions as completely as possible. This serves many purposes. It establishes a habit of recollection. It makes possible the least interpretation before recording. It also enables the Fragment to tend to this before the tasks of the day intrude on the "consciousness".

It is indeed possible to learn the difference between dreams of Astral contact, dreams of shaping, dreams of symbolic content, dreams of memory, both from this life and other lives, and dreams of messages.

These last are what most of those who study the art of psychiatry mean when they embark on understanding dreams, for these are the ways by which the personality sends perceptions to the waking state. Most of these perceptions have to do with misperceptions and misunderstandings from the past, both the immediate past, and from past lives, and it is of use for the personality to be aware that these dreams have as much significance and validity as the dreams with more arcane content. Of course, most recognition and validation occurs directly on the Physical Plane and in a face-to-face manner. Those who have experienced such recognition are aware that the encounters are not always pleasant, nor do they inevitably result in fast friendships or enduring contact. Abdication and rejection of contacts are not uncommon, and we would point out to you all that when such events occur, it is not Good Work to assume that the entire validation is an accomplished fact. Recognition does come before validation, but that validation is part of the process of living the ramifications of the contact and perceiving the function such contact has in this life, and has had in others. Of course, the greater use such contacts have is in the current life, and for that reason alone, we would remind you that the current life is the life that has the greatest importance to Essence at any time. Let us suggest an exercise for those who suspect that they have encountered someone with whom they have past associations.

First, it is not unwise to ask yourself if, in fact, this Fragment reminds you of someone—your grandparents, your first-grade teacher, the neighbor up the block, the most obnoxious kid in the fifth grade, your best friend's cute cousin from Ohio, the movie star you had a crush on, the scout leader, the cutest cheerleader, the postman, the oldest secretary at the office, your pediatrician—and identify this Fragment, if such is the case. This identification is also part of recognition and validation, and is Good Work. If no memory is stirred from this life, then consider the past. Knowing what is not contact is as valuable as recognizing what is.

In what context do you see this person, even if it is very different than what is the current context? For example, is the Fragment currently a librarian, but, unaccountably, makes you recall sailing ships? That may be an indication of a past association. In this case, a shaped dream of the past that permits you to explore what happened and what bearing it has on the present is not inappropriate, although if such a shaped dream is not possible, meditation can do much to bring such validation to the conscious mind. What may be difficult is to discern in what way your previous self interacted with the previous self on this Fragment. We remind you yet again that personality does not continue from life to life, and what you in the present might find friendly and fascinating, the you in the past might find distressing and hostile—and vice versa, of course—and that these realizations are part of the recognition. Let us offer an example. A friend of one of the students in this little group had occasion to meet a Fragment who brought up many unaccountable reactions in the friend, who, in desperation, talked about it with the Fragment who is now Brad, who in turn inquired of us on the other's behalf. The friend in this life is a professor of an active and inquiring disposition. The Fragment he had met was a guide, hired for the summer to assist in a "dig" for bones of extinct animals. The professor, who usually liked the guides, found this

Fragment upsetting, but for no "sensible" reason. He began having dreams of oppressive circumstances, of being forced to labor to build a stone structure, and of being furious with the overlord who had required that he do this. He felt himself to be hostile and rebellious, two emotions that do not often occur to him in this life, and he resented the presence of this Fragment. He was also aware that the garments he wore, and that were worn by those around him, were those of two to three centuries previous and that there was no sign of any modern conveniences. Haulage was done by horses and oxen and mules, the food they were provided was salted meat and cheese, and the beer they drank was stronger than beer the professor was familiar with.

Upon his return from the "dig" he admitted to the Fragment who is now Brad that he had had a peculiar experience, and since he was aware that the Fragment who is now Brad was "into the occult," confided the details.

What had taken place, of course, was the memory of a past life, when the Fragment who is now a professor was living in what is now Germany during what you call the Thirty Years War. This Fragment was forced into service building fortifications under the command of the leader of the mercenaries that had been hired by the regional overlord. The Fragment who is now the guide had been the leader of the mercenaries and had been a severe task-master. The Fragment who is now the professor had been a dyer in that life, and the task of building walls and fortifications, no matter on what cause, lost him business, income, and caused much resentment, since his religious beliefs were not consistent with the predominant religious beliefs of his small city. The dyer was killed when one of the stones being set in the fortification fell, crushed his hip and broke three ribs.

It would be surprising if any recognition had taken place that was not unpleasant and distressing to the professor, especially since he specifically does not "believe" in reincarnation and past lives. Information was sought only when all "sensible" avenues of inquiry yielded nothing but frustration.

[August, 2002: Of course, not all dreams have bearing on past lives. In fact, most do not. But those that do stand out for their consistency, their mundanity, their ordinariness, and their coherence. Most dreams are concerned with "decompressing" from daily events, and present all manner of images to accommodate the decompression process. The more stressful the daily life, the more "necessary" dreams are, not only as a means of releasing the most habitual stresses, but as a means of giving definition to all the subsidiary factors that contribute to the stress. These dreams are full of symbols—many of which are incomprehensible in the waking state—and of surrealistic "events" that allow the Fragment to cope with what is causing stress. And we wish to remind you that not all stress is negative. The disruption of major positive occurrences brings about as much stress as most negative ones. Even nightmares, which usually have a major Chief Feature component, serve to release stress by providing the Fragment a "known" source of distress to be employed as a "vent" to compounded fears. The only exception to that is a past life dream that is not only articulate, but horrendous as well.]

It is not uncommon for Fragments to resist the recognition, or, once it has been made, to deny it. Recognition is a frightening thing, and many Fragments have no concepts of how to deal with it when it occurs, and therefore prefer to do nothing or ignore it. There is nothing "wrong" in this. Let us emphasize that again. Denying or resisting recognition is not "incorrect". We would add, however, that it is generally a case of fear getting the better of love, and insights being blocked. Nevertheless, all reactions or lacks of reactions are choices, and choice, and the ramifications of choice, as we have said many times before, is the "purpose" of ensouled life on the Physical Plane.

Recognitions are most easily sustained when the memories are pleasant, the current contact has minimal stress and the Fragments are able to be face-to-face most of the time. Recognition at a removal of distance or emotional boundaries is possible, but less complete and more difficult to validate. That is not to say that recognition cannot be accomplished by an exchange of letters or a series of telephone calls, but it is not likely to be as validated as eye contact. As many of you are aware, avoidance of eye contact is often indicative of refused contact in other ways. Many Mature Souls find eye contact difficult where there is little understanding or trust. Others are prone to assume prolonged eye contact is an invitation or an invasion.

[February, 2004: As regards recognition and validation with a Fragment with whom karma has been burned, we would have to say that this recognition and validation is a most "useful" one, in that it also allows for recognition and validation for the completion of the karmic ribbon. When this contact occurs, there is often a sense of "relief" on the part of one or both Fragments, and occasionally, a feeling of accomplishment as well. By recognizing and validating that the karma is, in fact, behind them, the Fragments involved can bring about a strong and "enduring" bond that can be rewarding to the Fragments concerned.]

Because this country is a Young Soul country in a Young Soul world, resistance to validated contact is very strong. That does not indicate that the contact is not possible, only that there are more social pressures to overcome than would be the case on a late Mature or Old Soul world. In such places, eye contact or its equivalent is not only socially correct, it is a "natural" thing to do. On worlds where there are predominantly Baby Souls, many social strictures against contact of many kinds are common, and it is not unusual for such worlds to have complex codes of behavior and courtesy to keep everyone at a "reasonable" distance.

We do not mean to imply that those who are comfortable with more contact are necessarily older souls, but to indicate that in a social setting where proper conduct requires certain behavior, those who do not behave in that way by general inclination are likely to be reflecting their familial patterns, or the inclination of their soul Level, or perhaps the social patterns rewarded by their educational institutions. To take an obvious but worthwhile example, a Mature Soul from an Italian family who was educated in an "Ivy League Prep School" would be likely to exhibit some unusual behavior patterns that differed to some degree from those around him in any particular setting. Many of these influences distort Essence and Overleaves, particularly if the Fragment is inclined to take on the coloration of its surroundings—through such things as passion Mode or a Goal of Acceptance or Submission.

What we have been describing in part is, of course, what we call the false personality—the person you were taught to be instead of what the Essence has chosen to be through the Overleaves. With so much hindering recognition and validation, it is not uncommon for Fragments to avoid such insights throughout life, or to postpone them until after the Fourth Internal Monad, when the Overleaves come to grips with the false personality. The Fourth Internal Monad recognizes the Family Icon—that is, the person the Fragment was raised to be—as just that, a sacred image, and one that many not fit in any significant way with the life the Overleaves support. We have pointed much of this out to demonstrate that much of what is perceived can be misleading, and that reinforces resistance to recognition and validation. It is not our purpose to discourage you with these remarks, but to point out where difficulties may arise and interfere with what is being sought. Recognition is very much a breakthrough, an affirmation of the positive poles of the Overleaves and through it much realized growth is possible. Of course, growth will occur in any case, but with recognition and validation the growth tends to be more rapid and less terrifying.

Let us also point out that not everyone you meet and respond to must necessarily be someone from the past. There are many reasons for such a response, and to dwell overmuch on such aspects of a possible relationship is an excellent way to keep the relationship from developing, and while in pursuit of recognition and validation, through preoccupation with it, to lose the opportunity to experience it.

While recognition and validation most often occurs between individual Fragments, there are other means to achieve them, such as the example we have already cited, of the roof of Saint Paul's Cathedral in London. There have been Fragments who have had past lessons brought to bear through visiting locales known in the past. As we have already pointed out, this is often not an enjoyable experience, but a valid one. Upon occasion, the experience is quite pleasant.

To give you some sense of this, we offer an example of each sort of recognition. First, an unpleasant recollection: a Mature Artisan who has had some dealings with this little group was traveling in Europe for the first time in his life, and visited the city of Venice. Being an artist as well as an Artisan, he spent much of his time sketching, fascinated by the buildings and the water. He was sketching on his second day in that city when he had the unmistakable sense of extreme danger and he had to resist the urge to flee. He also had the impression that he knew what was behind him, although he had not explored that part of the city and was relying on maps to find his way. He sensed that his fear was not the usual sort, and decided to draw what he thought was behind him. When he had completed this sketch, he turned to compare it to the building and found that, aside from a third story of obviously more recent vintage than the rest of the building, he had indeed drawn the front of the building correctly. Assuming that this was a fear from the past, upon his return he consulted the Fragment who is now Camille for a private reading of this experience. It was, of course, a recognition from the past and his fear was sparked by seeing the place where he had been stabbed to death roughly four hundred years ago.

To continue with a more pleasant example: a Mature Priest, also occasionally involved with our little group, had the opportunity to visit the People's Republic of China and while there traveled extensively. While traveling in south-central China, she and the party she was with visited a temple. This Mature Priest, who has always had a love of Chinese art, asked to be permitted to explore the temple. After some arranging, she was granted permission. Although she had a guide with her, she soon was telling the guide about the temple, describing the grounds as they had been six centuries before, and remarking on the changes that had occurred since. She pointed out the pedestals that were left in the old part of the gardens and described the statues that had been there, as well as discussing the devotions of the monks. The guide was impressed at her scholarship and assumed that she was a professor with an extensive academic background on the subject. The statues, which were in severe disrepair, were kept in a university not far away, and when that university was visited, the Mature Priest expressed dismay that the statues should be as badly damaged as they were, and described again how they had stood in the temple garden. By this time, the guide had asked a number of questions and learned that the elderly lady was not a professor of oriental history or art and that, coming from a French and Scottish background could hardly be expected to know about the arrangements of statuary in Chinese temple gardens.

Of course, this Mature Priest was recalling a life when she, then he, served in that temple. It was a contemplative and gentle life that was filled with benefit and growth, and visiting the temple again exercised a calming and happy influence upon her. Validation can be made when this sort of recognition occurs by the process of research and study. For example, the Mature Priest who came to us for validation might also have gone to the library and read about life in Chinese temples and monasteries. That would have revealed that what she described was indeed correct. It would also have been possible to consult with those who are genuine experts in the field to find out about such things as garden statuary. It would also be possible to examine the records of that time to learn how life was lived, and what place the temple occupied in the life of the society. We encourage all Fragments to augment our information with more "standard" research, so that the range of validation may be embraced, and its validity made more comprehensive, should you choose to do so.

There are those who assume that past life memories are not that, but "subconscious" recollections of material that was already learned. While we do not necessarily disagree with this out of hand, for there are times that such factors do play a part, it does not account for such things as a schoolboy in Memphis, Tennessee, who "knew" the procedure for denouncing a suspect person to the Inquisition in Spain. There were no books that this serious young Methodist might have read that described this, and certainly no one in his family or those around him had knowledge of this. It had not been discussed in school. There was nothing about it on radio, record or television. Of course, this Fragment had once been a familiar of the Inquisition and had earned much karma in that life. Because he had an Agreement with a Fragment with whom he had a ribbon from that life to burn, the recognition was much "closer to the surface" than it might have been under other circumstances. However we do not discount the possibility of acquiring information without being aware of it as a factor in cases like this one. There are many ways that Fragments learn information that do not always register in the standard educational way. Certainly skepticism is a very healthy attitude when such claims are made, and a thorough check of various influences is a wise precaution, but if other inquiries lead nowhere, then it is not unreasonable to assume that the influence of former lives is being brought to bear in the present life. We believe that the rule known as Occam's Razor is a sensible guideline to follow in these instances.

Those of you who are eager to explore the past have much to learn. We have often cautioned our students that there are lives that will not bring you satisfaction or delight. Much of what has been done has been the result of fear, and as such reflects an attitude that can cause distress in the current life. Again, this is not said to discourage or encourage you, but to remind you that there are likely to be events and occurrences that will not be joyous to you. There are also likely to be some that are joyous, but for those who expect untrammeled satisfaction, it is fairly certain that what is learned will be disappointing. We would have to say that many questions asked of us and Mid-Causal teachers like us have to do with past lives that were in turmoil rather than those that were steady and pleasant. This is not to say that all lives recalled were unpleasant but that the recollections of trauma were more easily touched than those of enjoyment. This, once again, reflects the tendency to find pain and suffering more "real" than joy. As the pattern is learned in this life, so it was learned in past lives, often under more arduous conditions than the conditions of the present life. Most western thought predicates a joy that is acceptable only when found in very limited and approved expressions, such as religious exercises and pleasure at the presence of offspring. Joy that is not "sanctified" is suspect. When the past is recalled, it is often highly colored by this assumption.

There are other cultures, those of some of the Pacific islands, those of certain African peoples, that permit joy to be attainable and commendable far more readily than most do. While it is not our intention to alter behavior—that is a matter of your choice, and your choice alone—we do wish to remind you that other perceptions and behavior are possible and that the past is apt to reflect this more than you appreciate at this time. There is a shock not unlike what is called culture shock that can enter into these recollections and distort what is perceived.

We recall one Fragment who had experienced a very powerful recognition while visiting the grounds of a famous European castle. Being a proper woman from a strict family, and married to an equally strict man, this Fragment was more distressed by the awareness that as a courtier in that castle she had regularly defecated behind the curtains—as did most of the courtiers during that period—than by the awareness that as that courtier she had beat a servant to death with a cane.

Occasionally recognition and validation occur after the fact, usually, but not exclusively, in connection with Agreements. A Fragment who "never" does a certain thing will do it quite naturally and then wonder why later. For example, a teacher who "never" tutors will agree to take on a private student for a limited period of time, and do the teaching with ease. When the task is completed, the teacher wonders why he permitted himself to break his own rule. The answer, of course, is that the student had an Agreement with the teacher, the period of instruction fulfilled the terms of the Agreement.

There can be a similar reaction when an Agreement is abdicated, in that the Fragment may be troubled that rule or no rule, perhaps it "ought" to have done a specific thing for a specific Fragment. There is rarely any stronger sensation than this if the Agreement is a minor one, and by minor we do not mean insignificant, but ill-defined and hence can be completed in a number of ways. When the Agreement is a major one, that is one with a certain degree of specificity, the reaction is commensurate with the scale of the Agreement.

The desire to recognize and validate is perceived by Essence, of course, and those with access to the positive poles of the Overleaves are more apt to respond to the pull. Essence does not compel the personality and there is no "error" if there is no response, no "error" if there is no recognition or validation. Just as there is no "error" in reading the "Iliad" in translation or not reading it at all. To continue the analogy, life is not necessarily better or worse for reading the "Iliad," either in archaic Greek or translations, but there is an added dimension that can be the result of adding the tale to a Fragment's life. The same is true of recognition and validation—there can be an added dimension in life when it is done, if the Fragment chooses to permit the dimension to function.

Recognition and validation can be used to enhance the perceptions of any given life, and in many instances this makes it possible for the Fragment to decide actively to pursue the plans made at the onset of life. Certainly the process of recognition and validation can add to self-awareness as well as positive access to the Overleaves. Should the Fragment choose to do so, much perception of the tapestry then becomes possible, and the aspects of choices can be more clearly understood, both in light of the current life being led and in terms of the lives that have gone before.

For those active in what you on the Physical Plane call the arts, recognition and validation can come about through the art being practiced even though the artist may be unaware of this recognition and validation in the rest of its life. This in part accounts for the dichotomy perceived between the quality of the art of an artist and the quality of the life led by the artist. An extreme but obvious example is the mid-Cycle Mature Artisan who lived as Vincent van Gogh. That Fragment spent that life in intellectual and emotional torment while producing paintings of great and undisputed quality. The perceptions were brought to bear in the work, but were blocked in the life.

Most Fragments rely on "flashes" of insight, which we do not disparage, for this is often the only way that recognition is permitted to function for a Fragment. There is a tendency to believe that the insight cannot be grasped beyond that momentary flash, and as a result many Fragments choose not to attempt to garner more from the insight than what little is glimpsed in the flash. If this is all that a Fragment desires to do, there is, of course, no "fault" in such a choice. Should the Fragment prefer to learn from the flashes, we would suggest that keeping a notebook of the impressions, dating them, and verifying them in follow-up comments might be an orderly method for such study. The advantage of writing down the impression is that it aids the mind in focusing on what the flash actually conveyed as well as bringing to bear the awareness that the flashes are "real." for example, a Fragment who has a flash one early Saturday morning that its old college chum needs cheering up might make a note of it in the flash notebook, marking the time and the date. Perhaps, should the Fragment decide to pursue the matter, it would either call the old chum or make contact in other direct or indirect ways. As a result, the Fragment might learn that at the time of the flash, the old college chum had been notified of the serious illness of a parent. In time, should the Fragment continue this practice, whatever ability is possessed can be honed so that some comprehension of the nature and scope of the flash can be established when the flash is happening rather than determined in retrospect. We are aware of many Fragments who are particularly adept at sensing flashes and tend to put the most dire interpretation on them. This is often the result of the Chief Feature combined with a love of the dramatic.

There are recognitions that are based upon not the response of Essence and Overleaves, but upon the perceptions of the mammals that you are. The rising of hair on the neck, while it may be in conjunction with the recognition of Essence is also a mammalian recognition, just as the low growl of a dog is a mammalian response to what may be a threat. We would also point out that one of the few truly reliable gauges of pleasure is the purr of a cat. For most Fragments, the mammalian response is more likely to be a growl than a purr when encountering recognition and its validation. Of course, since you are mammals as well as ensouled, many of your responses come from "mammalian" impulses. The dichotomy between Essence and species is one of the principle lessons of life on the Physical Plane. We would have to say that recognizing and validating the "truth" of both no matter now apparently contradictory they may seem, is the Cyclic task of the Old Soul, which is why the Cycle has to do with being.

It is of use to remember that whether or not the recognition is shared by another Fragment, it is still valid. You may recognize, perhaps, a member of your Cadence, and validate this close bond while the other Fragment chooses to block the recognition and to reject the contact. This does not in any way invalidate the contact. The recognition is not "repudiated" because one Fragment validates the recognition and the other does not. The validation is a matter of individual perception. Of course, if the recognition is mutual and shared to a greater or lesser degree, then Essence Contact is likely to be attainable, which is, of course, good work. However, we must emphasize again that your experiences are valid as being your own, and that in itself is a recognition that is worth validation in your life. When recognition has been made, the recognition cannot be rescinded. It can be distorted or denied or ignored, but it cannot be canceled. Most recognitions are "commonplace" in their impact, even when what is being recognized is the Task Companion or the Essence Twin. If the emotion inspired is lustful or syrupy, then it is most likely that body-type attraction or even hero worship are functioning, not recognition.

Some students have described recognition as something "clicking into place": bells, soft lights and fireworks are far more likely to indicate infatuation of one sort or another than valid recognition. Most recognition, where it is not linked to karma, is, for want of a better word, friendly. Fragments on the Physical Plane tend to be far more intolerant than those who are not currently incarnate, and that intolerance most often extends to themselves as well as to others. When recognition is abdicated, it is not unusual for one or both Fragments to become highly critical of the other. This is the work of fear and one of the many ways that the negative poles of the Overleaves are put into play. If this occurs, then the lessons of the recognition have much difficulty in being brought to bear in the current life and are put aside until the next incarnation. Many Fragments react to rejected recognition as to a "slap in the face," which we would have to remind all here present, contributes only to the rule of maya. If it is possible for a Fragment to choose not to reject the recognition for itself because another has rejected the recognition, then there can be much growth as well as some opportunity for validation at a later date in the life.

We are aware of many Fragments who yearn for recognition almost as vehemently as they deny its possibility. Such ambivalence is not remarkable or unexpected, but it is sad to see so much energy put to the use of inward stalemate. This is not to say that such a stalemate is useless, for there are lessons to be learned through it as well as through any and all other experiences in this and all other lives. Let us repeat that nothing is wasted. No matter how frustrating or dreadful, nothing is wasted. The crux of recognition and validation, of course, is recognition and validation of yourself. Those Fragments who truly know and accept their Overleaves, who recognize themselves and validate themselves by the choices in their lives, are far more likely to be able to recognize and validate others in their lives. Without this initial recognition and validation, the rest is apt to be "spotty" at best.

Those Fragments who yearn to be Old and "exalted" and who are aware on many levels that this is not the case will find it difficult to perceive the rest of life with any degree of accuracy. While individual Overleaves are very much a Personal Truth, they are perhaps the most important of Personal Truths, and those who cannot understand this will find it almost impossible to make contacts with validity. We do not intend to discourage any of you, but to provide you with insight into why it is that the recognitions are often difficult to complete. We impart this to you so that you will be able to perceive the "payoff" for your self-recognition and self-validation.

When we speak of unconditional love as the goal of Essence, we include love of self in that unconditional love. We certainly do not intend to advance egotism or vanity, but instead, the awareness that the individual Fragment is indeed part of the larger whole, and that love offered the larger whole must of necessity include love of self if the love of the larger whole is to be valid. That does not mean that we imply that complete and unquestioning approval of the self, because that is based on expectations, as is all approval. Approval is the reward offered to Fragments who do what is expected of them. We would think that love offered for the self and the larger whole is the ultimate integrity in the most literal sense, and that its accomplishment would show the way to all the positive poles of the Overleaves, from which Essence has access to the personality.

Recognition and validation perceive the open door and then walk through it into the experience. There is much Good Work in this. In fact, a great portion of Good Work stems from and is part of the process of recognition and validation.

CHAPTER ELEVEN
Questions and Answers

Over the years, Michael has been asked a number of questions on various subjects and not always in the context of general sessions. The following questions and answers are dated by month and year and by the medium channeling the information.

August 1974: What would Michael say is the greatest deterrent to growth?

Without doubt it is the Chief Feature, not only for the distortion caused by its influence, but because it is caught up in fear and the instrument of Maya. (Medium: Jessica)

December 1977: What gives the Chief Feature its strength?

Fear, of course, and the resultant maya that clouds the perceptions and cloaks them in questions and suspicions. We remind you that the only forces at work on this or any other Plane are love and fear, and that little as you trust it, love is the stronger. (Medium: "Leslie Adams")

July 1978: Michael has said that "photographing" the Chief Feature is a good source of understanding. Would he explain how this is to be done and what can be gained?

By photographing, we do not mean using a camera to immortalize on film the action of the Chief Feature, but the process by which you come to recognize the action of the Chief Feature in life. For example, when the Chief Feature is Stubbornness and the Fragment with this Chief Feature can be reasonably certain that the Chief Feature will be brought into play because the Fragment is dealing with a new situation, the Fragment can prepare to observe when and how the Chief Feature manifests its control, with the added warning that the Chief Feature will do all that it can to distort what is perceived, both during the manifestation and afterward. The awareness that this is a danger can alert the personality to the efforts of the Chief Feature, so that as soon as the Chief Feature "clicks in," the Fragment can then monitor its behavior under the influence of the Chief Feature and recognize—as far as possible—the very negative effect that the Chief Feature has. To understand that the Chief Feature is a survival mechanism, and the isolation of the moment which gained it the control it now exercises is worthwhile work. This recognition can make clear how and what the Chief Feature seeks to control as well as the manner in which it is done. Once that is recognized and validated, the Fragment may do much to identify the situations under which the Chief Feature is most likely to operate and to take measures, should that be the Fragment's choice, to contain it. We warn you that if you choose to contain its activity, it is likely that the Chief Feature will "rebel" against what you have done and attempt to distort even more your perception of the actions without its presence. Once the gross manifestations are recognized, work on its lesser forms is possible. To those here present, it may appear that this is a thankless task, and in certain respects this is not an invalid perception. However, when it is realized that the Chief Feature has created fear where, in fact, none need exist, then breaking its hold becomes a distant possibility. Remember that the Chief Feature is a very persuasive element of the personality. (Medium: Jessica)

December 1982: I've been attempting to photograph the Chief Feature at work and to keep it from controlling me. Would Michael care to comment on my headway, if any?

Yes, we would wish to point out that frequently progress made on the Chief Feature is not discernible by the Fragment until a period of time has passed, and even then the progress is perceived and noted more as a matter of relative "ease" in areas wherein discomfort was experienced before rather than any definite and concrete "achievement". We would also point out that such is the case here, in that progress is indeed being made, however months are likely to pass before you perceive progress in any tangible way. We would commend you and hasten to add that the best work is yet to come if you choose to stay centered and focused on the exercises and activities we have described. We might also suggest that your faithful execution of the work at hand is perhaps the "best" choice you can make in terms of a steady and persistent "attack" on the Chief Feature. Remember that what you have accomplished in realizing the hold of the Chief Feature is Good Work and there is no "failure" because you cannot change it overnight. The Chief Feature is never more in evidence than when it does its best to convince you that it is not there. (Medium: Camille)

June 1983: Is there any reason I can't identify my Chief Feature? Michael has said that it is Self-Deprecation, but that doesn't appear to be the case with me.

First, we would suggest that a review of the polarities is not inappropriate. As you recall, the positive pole of Self-Deprecation is humility and the negative is abasement. You often rejoice in your humility, congratulating yourself on your ability to avoid the trap of egotism and keeping what you call your "perspective" on what you have accomplished. We would wish to remind you that the Chief Feature is seductive, and never more so than when it is challenged. In questioning the Chief Feature, you have served notice that you are aware of its influence, and therefore intend to notice when it influences your life. The Chief Feature will find any number of ways to discourage you, and the distortion of its perception is one of the most effective. (Medium: Jessica)

October 1984: My grandmother often referred to the clinging to negative characteristics as "hugging your cactus". Would this be similar to the hold of the Chief Feature?

The image is not incorrect, and certainly the influence of the Chief Feature is similar to hugging a cactus. There are many who embrace their Chief Feature as if they were shipwrecked and the Chief Feature an adrift lifeboat. To continue the analogy, the lifeboat is empty of life, of food and water, and it is drifting into unfriendly seas, where the current would carry the Fragment a few hundred yards to a safe harbor, food, warmth and protection. But the rule of maya is like a fog bank that hides the friendly shore, and instead the lifeboat, which is in many ways a death trap, appears to be the only salvation. We ask our student to remember that he has died at sea fifteen times. Our images were not chosen at random. (Medium: Camille)

September 1981: I've noticed that Michael calls only a few of us students. What determines the student status in Michael's eyes?

We are aware that many here present are "window shopping" and not seriously interested in pursuing the contacts or the information. There is nothing incorrect in this and we do not for an instant discourage it. Nevertheless, there are those who actively test and validate the information we impart, and they are the ones we call students. Until the validation is undertaken, the recognition of the task at hand and the Role information can play in it remain more an object of curiosity than a factor in the choices made in the life. (Medium: Jessica)

January 1984: What is the relationship between what Michael calls the tapestry—how everything weaves together—and the workings of Michael-math? Michael has indicated that they are part of the same thing, but could they clarify that statement?

We would think first of all that on a rather obvious level, the more a Fragment knows about the structure of anything, the more a Fragment can perceive the whole. Any self-respecting Artisan could tell you that without blinking an eye. However, further exploration of these "details" will provide the benefit of allowing a Fragment to know at what point the Fragment is placed—and here we are using the word point in a transcendent sense, for the multitude of dimensions in which we mean this is beyond the understanding or grasp of those on the Physical Plane who live with the illusion of time—this is not unlike the pirouette of the ballerina in the sense that the entire universe can be taken in from one point and on many levels, but almost too rapidly for the "eye" to follow—and other senses as well, we might add—to take it all in. It is always of value to understand as much as possible about the path and the paths to the Goal in order to ease the journey, if that is what you wish to choose to do. We might add that the value differs for each Essence but is equal in "weight" in the sense that the knowledge contributes equally to the possibility of propulsion along the path and the paths to the goal. To relate this to the tapestry specifically, let us say that the weaver makes more progress when he or she perceives the final pattern to be obtained and as in all things, there cannot be too much attention paid to the detail which may be "the moment" or the task at hand, or the bit of information gleaned about the larger picture to be presented. At some point, a quantitive perceptive leap can propel the student onto a higher level of understanding which can accelerate the progress even further and in a significantly different way, so that what was known before is seen and understood in a new "light" and with an enhanced appreciation of the complexity.

This principle, we might add, applies to many different areas of endeavor and cannot be taken too seriously, whether one is studying the cosmos or the proper setting of wood screws. Each Fragment here present could do much to accelerate progress with just this simple adjustment in the life view or general outlook. As usual, of course, the Chief Feature is the key obstruction to advancement, and it is the Chief Feature that clings to previous understanding with dogmatic tenacity rather than gives way to increased comprehension. (Medium: Camille)

July 1976: It seems to me that there are new potentials opening up since I've completed the infamous Fourth Monad. Would Michael comment on this?

We would think that impatience in this regard will do little to further matters, although, in fact, there are several avenues of potential development with regard to your work, not in the least is a chance to progression the Life Task—which has to do with communicating a method for differentiating the personal from World Truths—professional contacts need not exclude even seemingly remote possibilities that are part of your desired but unadmitted advancements. It may appear at this time that you have truly scaled the heights, but if that were the case, Essence would be bored long before the life came to its planned end, and life would be likely to "bog down" in the eddies of disappointment and restlessness that often results from Essence boredom. At its greatest height, incidentally, Essence boredom can lead to severe depression, among other things. At this stage of life, there has been a casting off of chains, accomplished through the completion of the Fourth Monad. Now that you have established your true personality, there is every chance for clearer and more precise perceptions as well as greater chances for intimacy, should that be what you choose to accept. There are contacts that might be followed up at this time to the mutual benefit of all concerned. (Medium: Camille)

December 1981: Would Michael be willing to discuss a little more what he or they mean by intimacy? It has something to do with Essence to Essence Contact, doesn't it?

Yes, we would suggest that there of course are many ways for the Essence to Essence Contact to be fostered and we would further suggest that all here present are well aware of those moments when such contact has been made, that that is generally the duration of such contacts—moments. When such a contact has occurred in a personal sense for two Fragments, there is little need to stop and ask what it is. However, we can give some general indications as to how such contact is arrived at, that is to say, experienced. First, and most obvious are those moments when the Chief Feature is disarmed and we would point out that this occurs through long and intensive work beginning with the photographing of the Chief Feature, which in terms of the quality of life can be the most important Overleaf, for it can subvert all the others. This does not require psychic studies to accomplish, incidentally. When one is in the presence of trusted friends, especially when the friendships are of long duration, the Chief Feature dissolution can most easily occur. Work of this nature provides momentary insights, forever, for Essence Contact of longer and more lasting duration, the entire gamut of false personality will be attacked. Again, this can be accomplished in a variety of ways, and if often described as a "peak experience" in a particular life, one that is remembered in vivid detail through all the rest of the life, and held up as an example or a standard for other experiences and contacts. Of interest to some here present is that this is often accomplished for self and other Fragments through music, which provides access to the higher Emotional Center. However, there are those who find such contact more easily verified in direct physical contact, such as sports and sex. The unifying principle or guideline is found in the dissolution of all those factors connected to the Physical Plane while in the presence of another, receptive, Fragment for whom the same has occurred. This, incidentally, is one of the attractions of "religion," which is not to be entirely ignored, for in its truest spiritual sense, it can accomplish this, although such contact is rare. (Medium: "Leslie Adams")

March 1984: Michael has said a lot about the advantages of the positive poles of the Overleaves, but not very much about how to get into the positive poles of the Overleaves. Apparently this takes some doing— would Michael care to comment on this and give a few pointers?

The question is, of course, an entree into a rather complex mechanism which we shall nevertheless attempt to unravel. Unfortunately, the ultimate starting place lies where you have suggested, which is to say within the mechanism in operation in the negative poles, which are the domain of the Chief Feature, for this is, in fact, the source of what you refer to as fear and as we have said before, it is the fear which stands in the way of the experience of Essence through the positive poles of the Overleaves. However, when the Chief Feature can be relaxed, even slightly, it is possible to catch glimmers of the experience of love—or, in other words, it is through those moments that the positive poles of all the Overleaves and attributes of the Overleaves can be experienced.

This in turn allows the barriers of the Chief Feature to be dropped somewhat and again allows love to be experienced a bit more, and again this affects the perception of the positive poles of the personality, even the false personality. It is interrelated and interwoven on many levels, but let us assure you that chinks anywhere in the vast armor of the Physical Plane do open up possibilities for chinks in other areas, and no positive experience is ever lost, no matter how minor or fleeting it may seem to be. For many souls, as we have recommended, the art of photographing both the positive and negative poles is an excellent beginning point and one which should not be overlooked for its power and efficacy in this matter. We would hasten to add that most on the Physical Plane are prone to point out negative poles in themselves and others and, while this is not all "bad," it would serve you all well to make note of those instances when positive poles are active also. This is definitely a case of practice helping to make perfect. (Medium: Camille)

April 1978: Michael has told me that I have a karmic debt to burn, and then added that the debt is one with reduced responsibility. Would he be willing to clarify that and explain what it means and why my responsibility is diminished?

Karma, as we have indicated before, is the result of removing another Fragment's ability and/or right to choose life choices for itself, and is a profoundly compelling tie between Fragments until the karmic ribbon has been burned by equal payment. We have said before but we will reiterate, you do not get karma for bad manners. In this case, this Fragment was the chief officer in a Greek village which was threatened by an invader who captured the chief officer and presented him with the choice of the execution of his family or the execution of the entire village. The chief officer wanted very much to commit suicide but was warned if that was his choice, everyone in the village, including his family, would be executed. This was no longer a simple question of the chief officer's requirements, but one of response to stringent conditions laid upon him, and while he was responsible for his decision, he nonetheless was not entirely responsible for making the decision since he did not create the situation which brought about the karma.

In cases of this sort, the standard must almost transcend the Physical Plane. It is what is meant by "the judgment of God," and demands that the Fragment perceive with full realization, recognition, and validation, where the true path lies. While we would not say that this Fragment achieved that state, we will remark that the choice was the least damaging—he sacrificed his family rather than the forty-six families of the village—given the circumstances, and one which two of the family members accepted and understood at the time. Where such situations occur, there has usually been a choice made for the course of the life to deal with difficult problems.

This was also a case of the Mature Soul Monad of honorably serving a corrupt master, in this case the corrupt master was the leader of the invaders and the Mature Fragment was the chief of the village who was put in the intolerable position of making one of two wholly unacceptable choices. Because the leader of the invaders had an Agreement to make the village leader his vassal, the contact resulted in a karmic ribbon between the two of them, for the leader of the invaders had not agreed to make it a life-or-death issue, as he did in fact. This is another one of those debts that come under the definition of "mind-fuck," requiring that the Fragment lose touch with itself in order to accommodate the demands made. Whether because of brain washing, manipulative religious conversion, or this sort of action, the karmic debt is the same.

Let us remark again that karma is a very serious and binding action that requires restored balances in the lives of the Fragments caught in its toils. Those who assume that a beneficial relationship is the result of a karmic ribbon are very likely incorrect. Most pleasant relationships are from Monadal associations and Agreements, as well as from body-type attractions and from Entity relationships and the bond of compatible Overleaves. The tendency of many Fragments to see karma everywhere does not clarify the perception, nor does it recognize and validate the weight of karma and its role in the evolution of the soul. (Medium: Jessica)

October 1975: Michael says very little about the Higher Intellectual and Higher Emotional centers. Why is that? Why is no one centered there?

We did not say that no one was centered there, we said that Fragments are given access to those Higher Centers usually during periods of extreme stress or extreme pleasure, and no Fragment on the Physical Plane that we are aware of—on your planet or any other—is in a position to sustain such an experience more than fleetingly. We do not mean that it is therefore impossible to have the experience at all, but that there are no Fragments, not even those few truly enlightened souls extant on your planet, who are capable of fixated Centering in the Higher Intellectual or Higher Emotional Centers. The only Higher Center to which there is constant and relatively easy access is the Moving Center, which is the cardinal polarity of the Sexual Center.

We perceive, incidentally, that there are those here present who misunderstand our use of the word sexual in this context. If you would prefer another word, the physical excitation center would have something to do with it. Sexuality is not confined to such things as genital contact and carnal appetites. Sexuality is pervasive in all Fragments possessing sex.

In your society, there are very few Fragments Sexually Centered because the society does not acculturate for it. However, the extension and therefore the exaltation of the Sexual or Physical Excitation Center is the Moving Center, which applies the stimulus, as it were, to some form of action.

As to the Higher, Moving Center, and we address this center first because it is accessible to Fragments on the Physical Plane in a fixated or routine sense, and can be described in some degree of accuracy. When the Moving Center is in its positive pole, it creates a stamina that carries through in all things, not just the body. There is a certain kind of high that some athletes experience—and we do not mean the masochistic euphoria that results from pain and exhaustion that leaves the body tired but extended. Dancers experience it more often than more traditional athletes. So do those athletes who work with animals, such as equestrians and lion tamers, where the action of the body and the rapport with the animal become a continuous interaction. The same thing can take place in the intellectual sense in the Higher Intellectual Center, which has telepathy as its negative pole and integration as its positive pole.

Consider what this can mean. There are those of you who experience something quite indescribable when reading fine poetry or excellent prose, something that is beyond words to explain, although you are responding to words. This understanding that is beyond explanation and transcends words is a glimpse at the Higher Intellectual Center.

Some writers and poets enter it from time to time during the completion of a work and therefore the work appears to be more than what it is. Of course, the Fragment who was William Shakespeare was able to do this with some regularity, and was, in fact, unaware that he had done anything unusual. He associated many of these insights as being the result of performing, for, first and foremost, to his understanding, he was an actor. Some actors, particularly those actors who are not Sage Essences, experience the Higher Intellectual Center when acting, in that the Role seems to do itself. The experience is exhilarating and occasionally frightening. The Chinese poet, a Sage cast fourth in his Cadence, Li Po also had many experiences in the Higher Intellectual Center and became so sensitized to his surroundings that he became an alcoholic to dampen his sensitivity.

The Higher Intellectual Center has to do with words, with the intellectual, left-brain part of the "mind". The Higher Emotional Center has to do with emotions, and with feelings. It is evoked most directly with music, although there are times when a truly superb meal can touch it as well, or an entrancing storm. The negative pole of the Higher Emotional Center is intuition and the positive pole is empathy. Again, those working with music, either composing or playing it, have a more direct access to this Center than do others. Listening to it, in live performance, of course, can cause a contact high that will permit those attending to gain access to the Higher Emotional Center. One of the reasons that musicians are drawn to this teaching is that it is similar to the process of what they do, but can be accounted for with words. Music is by far the most abstract of the arts and as such relies on its practitioners to be more willing and able to reach the Higher Centers. It is no accident that most well-regarded conductors are in the Moving Center—that is, the cardinal center of the Action Polarity—and can gain access to the Higher Intellectual Center or Higher Emotional Center while leading their musicians.

For those Fragments who desire to achieve these Centers, determined wishing is hardly the most effective approach. Higher Centers are achieved by opening to them, not by demand that they open. For all but a very few Fragments, the Higher Intellectual and Higher Emotional Centers cannot be sustained for very long, and can prove exhausting, although the outward experience is more apt to occur in instances of stillness than during frantic activity. You are more likely to enter a Higher Center while lying in a bubble bath listening to Bach, than in dogged pursuit of "enlightenment".

Of course, as we have indicated before, the Higher Centers are also possible to reach in times of stress—William Bligh relied almost entirely on his Higher Intellectual Center to navigate his open boat, by memory, across almost three thousand miles of open sea—and agony. Those who claim to have glimpsed something "important" during agony are not entirely trying to escape their distress. Some Fragments, but not all, can find the resources to sustain themselves in their Higher Centers in prolonged insights – which are most often measured in minutes, not hours – that no other part of the Overleaves can muster. (Medium: Jessica)

November 1984: Last September, while I was traveling, I was invited to attend what was called a Michael group. Since the person inviting me was unaware I was part of a Michael group, I was curious to find out what they were getting. I was very distressed by what I experienced and I felt that what was being done was misleading and manipulative. The person who claimed to be channeling had very narrow views on relationships and religion and everything that was channeled reflected those views. The person also said that Michael required certain behavior from his students and outlined a very austere way of life for them. Can Michael give me some idea of what to do about this situation?

First, it is the choice of those attending such meetings to be there, as it is your choice to be here. However, we would suggest for you that it would be wise for you to steer clear of such "misguided" souls who choose to frequent this source. If you even suspect that the channeling is amiss, or the information misleading, then examine what is being said and done in the light of what you have learned from us. This does not mean that you are dealing with "heretics," for belief is not required. Some groups of this and similar sorts can and do cause harm to many, often with the "best possible" motives. This, of course, encourages all here present to take care in selecting their metaphysical associates. Others have a deep-seated need to influence others to behave in ways that reassure the influencer.

How can you tell the valid from the invalid? This is an excellent question, and is the very center of the issue of choice, for it "overlaps" into all aspects of life, and makes it "apparent" when insights are subjected to "spiritual review". There is no correct way to have an insight; if a teacher should claim otherwise, then we would think you might want to examine both the teaching and the motives of the channel. Careful attention to your inner guidance is the first step, of course, to comprehension. However, there are several more obvious cues, namely, that such characters often have a tight group of noisy and self-interested followers. Secondly, they sometimes have an affected and flamboyant attitude which calls attention to themselves and to their "teaching" by obvious and blatant favoritism and similar methods. Such self-proclaimed masters often demand complete devotion of others while indulging every whim on their own, punctuated by demands for proof of devotion in the form of subservient behavior and lavish gifts of appreciation. Thirdly, they often charge exorbitant fees for very little work, and couch their teaching in vague and esoteric language that implies much and explains little.

Often such "teachers" create discord and alienation between people and promote feelings of intolerance and superiority rather than the understanding that each Fragment is only that—a Fragment of the larger whole. Of course, such self-proclaimed masters do not encourage questioning or testing of their information. We, and all true Mid-Causal teachers, urge but do not require—for we require nothing—our students to question, to recognize and validate or reject as they choose. However, incidents such as this one should alert all of you that all is not well in "The Land of Oz," and that it takes more than ruby slippers to get "home". (Medium: Camille)

June 1980: Recently I met a person who disturbed me very much, and who seemed disturbed by me as well, although I have no reason to feel this way. Was this a Chief Feature attack, or something else? Will Michael give me some insight into what was happening?

To begin with, the Overleaves abrade badly, body types are not compatible and your last past association was as political rivals. If that were not enough, you resemble his former spouse to a degree that embarrasses him. This sort of antipathy, while unfortunate, is hard to avoid in circumstances of this sort. Let us suggest that if you choose to, you "chalk it up to experience". (Medium: "Leslie Adams")

August 1979: Michael, I've been having back problems and the doctor has not been able to find out what the trouble is. He's prescribed drugs for the pain, but I don't like taking drugs all the time. Do you have any suggestions?

Let us recommend that different shoes be purchased with care taken to be certain that the arch is high enough and that the area for the toes is wide enough. Shops that cater to shoes for nurses and other professionals who must be on their feet a long time might be a good place to begin the search. Also, regular foot massages could help ease the discomfort experienced. (Medium: Jessica)

February 1983: When I was a child, three and four, I had a number of "imaginary" playmates, and most of them I was aware, even, that I had made up. But there was one that didn't seem to be like the others at all, and who didn't seem nearly as imaginary. He wasn't the same sort of thing, of personality, as the others. What was he, Michael?

Children are often open to Astral contacts, either from those currently extant on the Physical Plane or those with close Entity ties on the Astral Plane. This Fragment was and is a member of your Cadence and has had many past associations with you. The contact as an "imaginary" playmate was the easiest and most direct means of access this Fragment could find in order to communicate with you while still in the Astral interval. Your assumption that the "personality" was different was a correct perception. This Fragment is now extant on the Physical Plane and it is not unlikely that your paths will cross before the sojourn is over. Incidentally, we do not mean by this that all children with imaginary playmates are necessarily indulging in Astral Contact—most imaginary playmates are just that: imaginary. However, there are instances when the Astral Contact is the function of the contact and this was one such instance. We would think that this recognition can aid in bringing certain lessons to bear in this life. (Medium: Jessica)

May 1982: Would Michael indicate what they feel are the greatest hazards currently threatening the world, and why?

Of greatest importance is the entire matter of overpopulation. Most of the other problems stem from this basic fact. Given the current use of resources, there are too many people living on the Earth at this time. The hazards of famine, plague, war, pollution, and the other major ills are the result of this problem.

Coupled with the current dilemma, there has been, for some time, and we believe we have discussed it at length in the past, a shift in worldwide weather patterns. This happens periodically on this and all other planets, and when it occurs, there are always serious results to those Fragments currently incarnate. The immediate hazard, where the weather shifts are concerned, has to do with the growing of food, and that has immediate and far-reaching significance for much of the population of your planet. The problems experienced in parts of Africa are likely to spread over the next decade and eventually bring suffering and drastic changes to this continent. But that is what you might call the "tip of the iceberg," for the weather patterns are not just influencing the agricultural lands of Africa, but the agricultural lands all over the planet. The shifts are apt to make themselves felt more slowly, but they are taking place nonetheless. From that the problem of food distribution results, and that has always been a problem. Now it is very likely to become worse in the next ten to twenty years. *[Has this happened? Yes, it has in Africa, and India as well as parts of the Middle East.; growing patterns in the southeastern US are feeling the shift, as well. It has been more than twenty-five years. We have about another twenty years to go before the new cycles are established. AIDS has, however, had major impact. Yes, we can do something about AIDS if we choose to do so, but we're kind of stuck with the weather.—CQY]*

The danger of war brought about by famine, especially minor wars, is a very real possibility, and one that probably cannot be entirely avoided no matter how much such avoidance is desired.

The problems of the potential for nuclear war are, of course, well known, and the specter has loomed over this planet for more than forty years. For what little consolation it may be, we would wish to point out that most planets that have destroyed themselves with such weapons have done so within a generation of their discovery, and you are into your second [now third] generations since the discovery. However, the leaders are not of these later generations and are not truly cognizant of the shadow such weapons cast over those who have learned to read since the year one thousand nine hundred forty-five, common reckoning. What is particularly distressing is the continued urge to test the weapons. Whether or not the detonations occur where the hostile nations are, or over "empty" areas, the particles released into the atmosphere are genuinely harmful, no matter how they were regarded by those setting off the detonation. With the increase of such particles in the atmosphere, there are ever-increasing risks for cancers, mutant births, sterility, and all the other fruits of contamination. The same risks may be observed by those working with plants to generate nuclear power. While this may provide needed power that would not be possible otherwise—which we doubt—it also cannot help but contaminate many Fragments with the effluvia of the process. A comparison of the cancer rate in children born near such plants in comparison to those not born in such an area would reveal much. We believe that there is a place in Ireland that has done some research on the matter. *[The threat of nuclear weapons now seems to be from them falling into the hands of fanatics—groups or countries.—CQY]*

Along with the "cavalier" attitude toward nuclear substances and their various applications, we would mention the entire question of environmental contamination, whether from toxic wastes, the release of hydrocarbons into the atmosphere and similar matters, or from the problems of untreated sewage and contaminated wells that are prevalent in less technologically sophisticated societies. This, as we see it, is the single greatest problem after overpopulation that can be perceived on your planet at this time.

There are many areas of the world that are now not truly safe to inhabit and will not be safe again for many generations, and this is from the poisons that have been released in an irresponsible way.

What is ironic and tragic is that much of this need not occur at all. There are sources of energy that, if studied with the same devotion as nuclear power has been studied, would provide as much if not more power for considerably less money and would not harm the environment. You are aware already, we believe, of solar power, of wind power and other adaptations of old generation techniques. There is also geothermal power, which is an excellent source of energy. The harnessing of tides to generate power would not be difficult if the problem were approached pragmatically and investigated with diligence. Improvements on batteries and storage techniques would render all these "natural" methods more efficient and less costly, and would introduce almost no damaging elements to the environment.

Let us also point out that the power for transportation need not rely on fossil fuels. Steam power and solar power for transportation is not the least impossible, and the use of hydrogen as fuel is another prospect, and in regard to what such fuels could power, it need not mean quaint little carts that move around slowly with one or two passengers.

What continues to keep the current problems in operation is the aspect of profit and prestige. The manufacturing of weapons is an important political and financial occupation, and those who are active in it enjoy great power in the world of politics. The offshoot of power and industry also is controlled by those eager for political and/or financial advantage. This current system prolongs the difficulties, and serves only to make them worse. Should the overall philosophy shift so that profit and prestige went to those who ended conflict and toxification, then those who seek power, profit and prestige would be motivated to take actions toward ending these problems. In general, however, those with power are admired for their power and given more. This is not unusual on worlds populated primarily by Young Souls, such as this one. (Mediums: Jessica and "Leslie Adams")

March 1984: Michael has talked in the past about the problems they perceive in the entire notion of marriage. What's wrong with marriage, anyway?

We did not say anything is wrong with it, simply that the way it is perceived is generally unrealistic. For one thing, it is assumed that it will endure for most of an adult lifetime, through the raising of children and into old age, and always provide a perfect complement between partners. If this were described as the terms for a business partnership, they would never be possible, and business partnerships need only be sustained in working circumstances, if that. Marriage, as conceived by this and other societies, was evolved out of the capture of females for the purpose of getting children. As the concept of clans grew, the purchase rather than the capture of brides became the usual arrangement, and this continues in a muted form to this day.

Marriage is generally for the convenience of the male. It is supposed that the female will make the necessary changes and concessions for the pride and comfort of the male. Most of the institutions of your societies—political, religious, economic—have gone to great lengths to reinforce this pattern, so that at this time, when it is not truly necessary that families produce eight or nine children so that three will live into adult life, at least not in the technologically advanced countries, the pattern of marriage continues to be presented as if this were the case. The worth of females is generally established by the familial connections she possesses, her worth in terms of prestige or finance, and her asset worth in terms of skills and attractiveness.

It is also assumed that once the relationship has been formalized, it need never again be reviewed, and that the terms of the partners as understood in their youth will remain unchanged until the end of their lives. That series of assumptions is at best foolish. We do not believe that marriage under these conditions does much to advance understanding, either between the Fragments married or those around them. The added assumption that the two Fragments of a marriage partnership will always be able to be all things happy and desirable and helpful to the other, has little to do with what actually occurs.

Let us suggest that the most critical element, and one that is almost never discussed, is trust, and that where trust is lacking, the relationship is likely to fail. For any relationship that is by nature involved on so many levels of life relies on a level of trust that is quite remarkable. The trust, if genuine, is Good Work. There are more times when there is a semblance of trust and a denied sense of desperation and injury that result from the fiction.

We would think that a regular, scheduled review of the nature of the relationship and its function, with a referee, if necessary, might do much to begin to reevaluate this institution and to bring a greater balance into the institution, both for the males and the females. Certainly we do not advocate the ending of the institution, for that is a matter of individual choice. However, we do believe that examination of marriage, its conduct and conditions, might be a useful step for those wishing to remove some of the difficulties from their domestic arrangements. (Medium: Camille)

July 1979: I am going to be visiting Europe in a couple of weeks. Does Michael have any suggestions about places I might want to see while I'm there?

Undoubtedly the city of Prague should stir some memories from the life before last, and there would be a possible connection to be made in the area of Vienna.

We would think that the northern lakes of Italy would be pleasant, though crowded. We would also suggest that, should you have the time and inclination, that the Greek islands, particularly Rhodes, might be of interest. We do not necessarily believe that travel should be indulged in to gain access to the past, but it is a relatively direct means and one that offers compensations if the contacts are not made and the memories do not bring forth much information. In the case of these plans, it might be wise for you to avoid Spain as, in the last two lives you lived there, you existed in poverty and died violently. Such recognitions, while valid, are not a very pleasant way to spend your travel time.

While you have no strong past associations of note with Norway, the Task Companion lives there and, provided you do not script yourself into believing you must meet this Fragment, you could find the fjords beautiful and the population pleasant. Let us point out that you have chosen to travel for the pleasure of it. There is nothing the least "wrong" in this. We would hope that you do not feel duty-bound to devote all your time to your former experiences because you have already had those experiences and lived those lives. It is not inappropriate to have and enjoy this one. (Medium: Jessica)

October 1981: I am scheduled for surgery in a week. Does Michael have any suggestions about the operation or the aftermath?

First we would recommend that if your physician has not yet put you in contact with a therapist for this emotional trauma, that you request that he do so at once. We would have to say that the disease is indeed present and that the surgical removal of the affected tissue is the wisest course at this time. We are not aware of other areas affected and we do not recommend that greater damage be done to the body through the ingestion of poisonous chemicals, no matter what is recommended. Let us instead point out that there are those who have had excellent results with alternative treatment in other countries, and that what has been done in Europe, especially in cases like yours, is most encouraging. You have indicated that you are prepared to seek out another physician in another country if it is necessary, and while we are not giving instruction to that end, we do agree that you are apt to get a better recovery and more complete restoration to health if you are willing to consult one of these physicians other than your current one. We also point out that this is not a popular suggestion and you may decide that you would prefer not to take that chance, and spend so much time and money. Whether you do or not is your choice and for what it may mean to you, a fair degree of recovery is likely in any case. (Medium: "Leslie Adams")

September 1982: I've been told that my blood pressure is too high. I take medication for it and I've been on a diet to lose weight. Does Michael have any other suggestions?

For the loss of weight, we would recommend that you take a tablet of amino-acid complex between meals twice a day, preferably with citrus liquid, and restrict your consumption of red meat to once a week, being sure to have wine when you have the red meat. Then, for protein, let us suggest that poultry and fish are excellent sources and that they are more preferable than, say, cheeses. As to the condition itself, we would recommend that you consult a competent herbalist and follow the recommendations that Fragment makes. While this procedure will not work for all Fragments and we do not recommend it for any student but you, the program will not interfere with what your physician has already suggested. Rest, of course, is also useful when the blood pressure is high, but that does not mean lying down to fret. (Medium: Jessica)

November 1980: My brother just "came out" and the whole family's upset. Can Michael give me any suggestions as to what I can do to ease us through the crisis?

While your concern is natural, the task of "easing them through" is not yours, and although Warriors are very protective by nature, this is not one instance when that protection can serve much use for anyone. As to the brother, this Mature Priest made his sexual preference choice, as all on the Physical Plane do, before he was three years old, and there certainly is no reason or method to try to change that choice now. This Fragment has been aware of his sexual choices for well over a decade and has denied and avoided the issue until contact with the Mature Sage who shares his home. These two Fragments have an Agreement, and being lovers is one way to accomplish that Agreement. They also have very high body-type attraction to urge them on, and they have seventeen past associations of note. What the rest of your family does about this is, of course, a matter of choice, and it is not appropriate for you to try to shepherd everyone through. If you believe that you must make your position known, inform your brother first of your decision and ask if that would cause him more distress than your silence. Remember that Priests do not respond to difficulties as Warriors do, and he is not nearly so inclined to confront the problems and grapple with them as you are. If he would simply prefer your silence and friendship, then it might be wise to be content to give that, for although you can choose to act in any way you wish, your desire to pour oil on troubled waters might backfire if you do not take a few precautions. (Medium: Camille)

January 1981: Michael has said that to some degree clothing reflects Essence. Would they care to elaborate?

We begin by remarking that taste is an acquired thing and is much influenced by socialization, level of society, and parental patterns. However, yes, there is a distinct degree of influence that is particularly apparent after the Fourth Monad. Slaves in general tend to be utilitarian in their choice of clothing. It may be very expensive or very inexpensive, but the key is appropriate and utilitarian. If the utilitarian choice is a pin-striped suit, then that will be selected; if it is jeans and boots, then that will tend to be chosen. Artisans are often great clothes-horses and find themselves attracted to very new or avant-garde styles. Many high-fashion models are Artisans: this sense of fashion sometimes takes on the aspect of costume. Warriors view clothes, as they view most of everything, as part of a strategy. They tend to be sensitive to what is the correct uniform and to wear it, often with dash. Warriors are usually hard on shoes. Scholars often ignore clothes or tend to the relaxed styles that need little attention. However, if what they have chosen to study is clothing, then they will be turned out to the nth degree with great attention to detail. Sages, as you might expect, are the most extravagant dressers around, and dress for a definite effect. They can wear extremely elegant clothes so casually and naturally that one would think they dress that way always. Clothes are costumes for the Sage. Priests regard clothing as vestments and look for what is the "right" thing to wear, often preferring simplicity and durability to the more dashing, so long as the clothes have "elegance" or "impressiveness" about them. Kings tend to set the standard for what everyone else wears, and they appear quite correct no matter what they wear or where they are. It is not unusual for others to copy the dress of Kings, just as they tend to wish they could copy the flamboyance of Sages. This is not intended as absolute gospel, for obviously an Old Priest in Retardation will have a much different style than a Young Priest in Dominance. These are some very simplistic guidelines as to what might hint at Essence in the manner of dress. (Medium: "Leslie Adams")

January 1985: Would Michael give some insight into the origin and nature of depression?

We would have to say that depression does not describe any specific condition, but a number of conditions that result in similar behavior, and that tend to be regarded as the same condition. Depression can stem from such problems as fatigue—physical, psychological, professional, emotional, spiritual, esthetic, and several other varieties—and boredom, which is a common factor in all Chief Features. We would encourage you not to underestimate the power and danger of boredom, both in terms of what is called depression and in terms of other "disorders," both of the personality and of the body. There are some Fragments in whom the depression is a matter of physiological chemical imbalances, that can be corrected with proper analysis of the body chemistry and the proper correction. In this case especially, we do not believe that medication does much to relieve the basic condition, although it will mitigate the outward behavior of the sufferer, just as a bandage applied to the abdomen will do little to aid a ruptured appendix. The characteristics of depression are so well known that it is not often the condition is evaluated as to type, with the possible exception of the depression that is part of what has been called "job burnout". We would also wish to observe that there are times when depression is an appropriate response to the circumstances of life, and that not to be depressed would be an avoidance of emotion rather than a valid expression of emotion. It is not much use to try to "jolly" a Fragment out of depression, for that only reinforces not only the sense of loss, but adds the implication that the Fragment is making too much of the loss, is overreacting, is self-dramatizing or in general making a nuisance of itself. For a depressed person, this accomplishes little. Let us suggest that instead of such reaction or the too convenient use of drugs—except when the source of the depression is physiochemical—it be discarded in exchange for as much stressless rest as possible, as well as finding ways to provide some sense of advancement or gain instead of the loss. Incidentally, the advancement or gain will be more effective if not in the same area as loss, for trying to fill in the same area as the loss only serves to remind the Fragment that the loss has occurred. Let us caution you that such conditions take time and patience to endure. (Medium: Jessica)

October 1982: I've been very worried about the relations between the United States and the Soviet Union, and from what I can see, we're going from bad to worse. Would Michael please comment on this?

Some of the problem lies in the linguistic structures of the Russian and the English languages. In English it is quite simple linguistically to express a double conditional—if such and such, then perhaps this or that—but in Russian these constructs require major linguistic feats. The communication between the leaders is made worse because of Overleaves: one country is run by a fourth Level Young Sage in the Aggression Mode with a Goal of Acceptance, a Pragmatist in the Emotional part of Intellectual Center with a very marked Chief Feature of Greed. The other country is run by a fifth Level Mature Scholar in the Observation Mode with a Goal of

Dominance, a Realist in the Moving part of Intellectual Center with a Chief Feature of Arrogance, exacerbated by failing health. Political and economic differences are valid to a point, but the misunderstandings rise from much deeper roots. Of course, the United States does not in general understand the internal problems of the Soviet Union, the extreme diversity of its peoples, the very real and extremely serious agricultural limitations of the arable land in relation to the population at large, and the matter of district politics which in fact are far more extreme than what is usually experienced in the United States. We would also have to point out that the Russian tradition of mysticism does not mesh well with the pragmatism of the United States. We would agree that the misunderstandings are grave indeed, but not insurmountable, if the semantic barriers can be scaled to some degree, and the abrading Overleaves of the leadership recognized at some levels and made allowances for by those working around them. (Medium: Camille) *[Of course, there is no Soviet Union now and the entire Cold War was probably based on misperceptions, albeit the base cause was the result of predictable tensions between two world powers that had been suspicious of one another for nearly a century.—CQY]*

June 1980: I'm an Old Slave and I've been puzzled by how many others in the group appear to feel the need to seek out certain sorts of contacts and activities. I don't think I have these sorts of needs, or if I do, I'm not aware of them. Would Michael give me some insight on this?

Unlike all other Essences, Slaves do not need special conditions to fulfill themselves and their "purpose" on the Physical or any other Plane. The Slave serves the common good, which needs no special circumstances in life to be realized. Whether the Slave shares a music stand as you do, shares straw in a stable, makes hamburgers for a scout troop, answers questions, answers phones, or rules a country, the Slave is serving the common good in whatever circumstances the Slave encounters. A Slave can be physically incapacitated and still be capable of serving and fulfilling the Essence Role and the Life Task. This is true of no other Essence. For that reason alone, the Slaves tend to pass more quickly through the Levels, and do so with less wear and tear than the other Essences.

An Artisan always requires a structure to work with, if the Essence is to be fulfilled. The Warrior always requires a challenge, the Scholar always requires a study, the Sage always requires "wisdom" and someone to impart it to, the Priest always requires a higher ideal and the means to impart it, the King always requires a mandate and a kingdom to act upon it. It is not surprising that you do not share the drive that you perceive in the other students here present. That does not mean that you lack "ambition," but that you have chosen to serve in a way that ambition is needed to accomplish, and so you are ambitious. Those on the Action Polarity are perceived as being ambitious simply because action is required of the Action Polarity. Those on the Action Polarity act. Those on the Inspiration Polarity, which, of course, includes Slaves, seek to inspire, which a Slave can do by little more than "passing the salt". (Medium: "Leslie Adams")

November 1984: I've been watching *Reilly: Ace of Spies* [a 1983 television mini-series] and I've been very much struck by the story. They claim it is largely the truth. Would Michael agree?

For the most part we would say that what is presented tallies with what is known about the Fragment who was known as Sidney Reilly. This Fragment was a most successful spy and one who lived with far more visible activities than most successful spies do. The Fragment who was Sidney Reilly, incidentally, was not a double agent except in one instance when his double agency was the result of blackmail. This particular production, other than taking care with the material and the historicity of the events, has one other aspect "going for it" in terms of our perceptions. The Fragment who was known as Sidney Reilly was a second Level Mature King in the Passion Mode with a Goal of Rejection, a Cynic in the Moving part of Intellectual Center with a Chief Feature of Impatience. The actor playing the Role is a fifth Level Mature King in the Observation Mode with a Goal of Acceptance, an Idealist in the Moving part of Emotional Center with a Chief Feature of Arrogance. There are very strong resonances from actual man to actor— and for those who wonder, no, they are not the same Fragment, since so much growth in so little time would be next to impossible—and this is reflected in the "validity" of the performance. (Medium: Jessica)

Let us comment on this a bit longer. In general, when performer is matched with creator by polarity or Essence, there is a stronger resonance than otherwise, for there is access on many levels to the "purpose" of the creation. That is not to say that no other performers can do the work "properly" or "as well" but that there is likely to be an additional element in the art that will be realized by many. For example, a King or a Warrior performing and/or conducting the works of Stravinsky might find more material in the music and be able to realize it in performance than another Fragment of different Essence might. A Scholar actor performing Shakespeare might have a greater sense of what the purpose of the words is than many others, although this does not mean that Scholar actors are necessarily better performers of Shakespeare than others, for this is patently not the case.

What we imply by this is that when the Essences or polarities of the performer and creator agree, an added resonance is possible, and hence a stronger quality of "veracity" to the work. This does not mean that we believe that only Sages should perform Lizst or read Dickens, or that only Warriors should sing Bellini or act in the plays of Pirandello—there are no "shoulds" that we perceive at any level and in any circumstance at all that are valid—but we point out that when this is the case, more insights are possible, no matter what the outward critical success of the performance or the critical success of the creation may be. (Medium: "Leslie Adams")

August 1978: There are times I get the impression that what Michael does during half of these sessions is remind us of things we've forgotten.

That is all we ever do. (Medium: "Jessica Lansing")

CHAPTER TWELVE
Michael and Me

In the following pages, members of the Michael group will tell you in their own words what they have got out of their association with Michael and the Michael teaching. They will be identified only by Essence and Cycle. These people have been in the group for as short a time as a year and for as long as thirteen years. They range in age from mid-twenties to mid-seventies. Some are educated, some are not, some have been satisfied with what they have learned from Michael, some have been disappointed. Two of the people contributing to this section are no longer active in the Michael group.

The only people dealt with in this book, as in *Messages From Michael*, are those of the group that meets with Jessica Lansing and Camille Rowe and the dual identity in "Leslie Adams". Any other group claiming to channel Michael or any other Mid-Causal teacher is not represented in either book. My only dealings are with this group and I do not endorse or debunk any other group or their claims. However, I view most such groups with many reservations.

A word about the persons represented in the first chapters as part of the group—with the exception of the two mediums, all the characters are constructs, fictionalized versions of two or more members of the Michael group—if you feel you are sure you have figured out who "Emily" really is, remember that Emily is a combination of three Priest Fragments, and only two of them are women. This was done for the protection of the privacy of the group members, at their request.

Now, for what the group members say about "Michael and me".

MATURE ARTISAN: The Michael material makes a lot of sense to me, but I think it's kind of silly to ask Michael for advice, since that might take the fun out of it. I like to know the Overleaves of my friends, and sometimes I'm curious about the people I admire, but the rest of it seems like a waste of time, in a way. Michael keeps saying that we're supposed to know what we're doing, deep down. We'll probably just do it anyway. The times I've asked Michael's advice, it hasn't made much difference, it just put a different slant to the problems.

MATURE WARRIOR: Although I have been aware of the Michael teaching for several years and have read *Messages From Michael* three or four times, I've only had the opportunity to participate in the sessions of the Michael group for a short time. They are fascinating and eye-opening. The material is so complex, so many-layered, that it will take a long time to achieve anything approaching a real understanding of it.

Yet even over the space of a few group meetings, I can see some profound and exciting effect that Michael is having on my life.

One welcome effect is the opportunity to get in touch with a metaphysical part of myself that I'd been neglecting for much too long. The mechanics of earning a living and coping with everyday demands were taking all my time and energy, with the result that my life was feeling constricted and binding. It is refreshing as well as enlightening to consider the larger issues and perspectives that Michael presents, and Michael is one of the factors currently in my life that help me feel that a logjam within me is finally breaking up. One of the most important things I've learned so far is the great extent to which I limit and undermine myself. I am beginning to discover how fear operates within me (it operates very effectively, even seductively, with skill born of long practice). Even better, with Michael's help, I am learning to recognize the fear and to acquire some tools to help overcome it. I have a lifetime's worth of work ahead of me in this regard, of course. But Michael's greatest gift to me so far is a lot of hope and a little more confidence that, with diligence, it can be done and will be worth it.

Do I believe in Michael and the teachings? In truth, I'm not sure. I certainly believe that something happens in the sessions that is beyond the scope and power of the members of the group, individually or collectively. The teachings appeal to me because they are as logical and sensible as any belief system I've encountered, and a good deal more so than many. I have long been of the opinion that all systems of belief and thought—religions, philosophies, sciences, and arts—are attempts to answer the same questions. Like the blind man studying the elephant, each system is trying to describe the whole from its knowledge of a very small part (and some are better than others at acknowledging that all they've got is a small part).

Michael seems capable of understanding and describing a fairly large chunk of elephant. It may be that Michael is dealing only in metaphor. (In fact, it may be that all teachings, whatever the source, are metaphors, and that given us mortals' limitations in the way of language, intellect and good sense, metaphor is the only way we can approximate an understanding of the truth.) If so, Michael's are practical, useful metaphors that can help one make progress toward understanding and loving oneself and others. With that result, it almost doesn't matter whether Michael is real and true.

MATURE SCHOLAR: I have been going to Michael sessions on and off for at least five years, and I feel that I'm finally starting to make some progress on controlling my Chief Feature. Starting! That's how strong a hold it had on me! At first the answers I got served mainly to identify feelings about situations or people. I could understand someone better by knowing their Overleaves and past associations I had with them. Meeting my Essence Twin was a strange experience— obviously we had some strong connection, and when I heard about Essence Twins in the group I knew without doubt who mine was. That was a big help in dealing with him. Even though Essence Twins have a strong tie, it doesn't mean that knowing one's Twin is always comfortable or can work out smoothly.

After going to sessions for a few years, I started to realize what my Chief Feature was really doing to me. I could start to identify the feeling that Arrogance gives me when it's acting up—for me, that feeling of being struck, immobilized and basically unable to act effectively. I would want to hide in my room under the covers and just know that I could do wonderful things, without actually doing anything!

The other area in which labeling helped was knowing about my Fourth Monad. It's a killer! But I was also doing a Level transition at the same time! [*Something that happens very, very rarely, and usually under great stress.—CQY*] Anyway, just knowing what was going on helped a lot. And now I've just ended the Fourth Monad and can really see how my Overleaves work. As soon as the Monad was over, I started a huge project that keeps me busy about fifteen hours a day. Quite a change for a lazy bum who wallowed in Arrogance for a few hours a day and never got much accomplished in reasonable amounts of time.

OLD SAGE: One of the convenient things about a "true principle" is that it works; you can verify it with your own experience. Take, for example, a simple principle in physics like leverage. There is a large industrial moving and construction company whose motto goes something like this: "Give us a place to stand and we'll move the Earth". I like the philosophical implications of that optimism (although the fact that some people might apply such truths literally can be somewhat disconcerting) because in the deepest and most central part of myself, I, like many, have been searching for that place to stand; that perspective that is all-encompassing. My earliest experience of "truths" as a child were of God, until the rules and dogma which accompanied religious spiritualism became too cloying. Later in my life I studied mathematics and physics, but science was so limited by the assumptions of language and linear thought, so lacking in poetry and scornful of anything which its circles did not enclose.

Throughout my life I have read numerous philosophical and religious doctrines, each with its own questions and answers, but each building as many walls as doorways and windows. For me the problem has always been that floating around in the middle of nowhere, with no clear idea of who I was, why I was here, or what I was "supposed" to do, was like being tethered by a fear and ambivalence which severely limited my sense of freedom.

The Michael teaching has served not only as a "system" of thought but as a comforting pair of shears with which to "cut myself loose" from that tether. Michael has managed to weave a tapestry (or, more accurately, describe a tapestry) in which my own perceptions of spirituality, intellect, science, art and relationships all find themselves interwoven. I have found a great amount of strength and comfort in realizing that it is possible to attempt to "describe" the experience of life in a way that does not inherently establish limits or create an "in" group who "know the way"—the point being that there is no one way, but rather a complex and beautiful dance of growth and choice.

Robert Frost wrote: "Something there is that doesn't love a wall, that wants to tear it down." For me, Skeptic that I am, the debate over "truth" has become secondary to the practical question "does it work?" If it does, I will use it until it ceases to be useful. Right now Michael has helped me to accept the validity of so much that I have always "known" but been unable to completely believe in, and thereby provided me with that place to stand from which to begin finally dismantling the walls.

MATURE KING: I think that the information in Michael is very valuable and useful, but it disturbs me when people ask about such trivial things as the need for glasses or whether an antique is authentic. Information of this sort seems to me to be too important for such inconsequential application, and although Michael doesn't seem to mind, I sometimes do, especially since there are questions of much greater significance that have not yet been addressed. I do understand that everything is chosen, including what is asked of

Michael and what use it's put to, but I can't help feeling that a lot of solid energy is being wasted on very minor considerations.

MATURE SCHOLAR: If I had to sum up in one word what I've gotten from Michael, it's perspective. Of all the many forms of tyranny human beings have managed to create, the most insidious—precisely because it is universal—is the tyranny of the ego: the illusion of separateness and all of its attendant miseries. Through a looking glass which is at once completely nonjudgmental and totally compassionate, Michael offers a perspective of a truly extraordinary cosmos, which on every level challenges one to overcome the handicaps of ego and maya. However complicated Michael's perspective may seem at times, it is linked inevitably with freedom and responsibility: in ways we can scarcely comprehend, we are free to choose our own paths, and we are completely responsible for the choices. It sounds a little strange to say this, I know, but the greatest gift Michael has to offer, other than his knowledge, is his indifference. To me, the most extraordinary thing about Michael's knowledge is not the content, but the fact that it is offered without the slightest trace of coercion, manipulation, bribery, shame or guilt. Take it or leave it: he does not care. More than anything else, Michael teaches about freedom, and it is precisely his indifference which allows me to use his teaching as I see fit, and which frees me to shake loose, as best I can, from the constraints of ego and to chart the course of my spiritual evolution.

OLD PRIEST: I don't attend sessions often, but I always get something interesting out of it when I do. I'm not really sure that it matters in the long run. Michael himself says that we will evolve with or without any real awareness of the evolution, and the evolution happens because it happens, which makes sense. If it didn't work that way, it wouldn't be evolution but a system of rewards of some sort or other. Michael has a clean, to-the-point style that appeals to me, and he doesn't require ritual or awe for his messages, in fact, that seems to turn him off. I like the mediums, too. They're good, down-to-earth people who aren't too tied up in what they're doing. I feel that we get minimal distortion through them, and that Michael is able to get his point across as much as the limits of language will allow. Having the Overleaves my kids chose helps sometimes, because I've got a better idea what's going on in them. I don't know if I handle them any better for knowing the Overleaves, but I'm pretty sure I don't handle them any worse. That's worth a lot, over the years, and it gives me some hope that maybe my kids won't end up the way so many of their contemporaries have.

One of them's young and very headstrong, the other's Mature and a little like a volcano—quiet for long periods of time and then pow! an explosion—and I've always known that they needed something different in terms of their relationship with me, but with the Overleaves I've got a better idea what it is. There's still a lot of time left in this life, I hope, to check Michael out. Maybe in twenty years, I'll be able to tell what kind of influence the teaching has had in my life, but until then, it's really too soon to say.

MATURE SCHOLAR: To me, the most fascinating aspect of Michael is the enigma of his/their personality. "His," of course, is merely a response to the use of a masculine appellation. "Personality" is also an arbitrary designation, referring as it does to a composite of what were once many hundreds of individual human egos. And herein lies the fascination: just how can these fused and depersonalized Entities such as Michael project pseudo-personality for purposes of intelligible communication? How can their massed souls assemble in this fashion to form one recognizable and intelligent, intelligible unit?

The necessity for this is obvious, if its purpose is communication with ordinary human beings, but the methodology is beyond my comprehension. Who or what orders this phenomenon? Is it governed by mass control or does it represent an evolution to another level where other laws determine function and performance? I suppose I am asking the same questions that a unicellular protozoa would address to a multicellular organism, whose form and activity would be similarly incomprehensible to the simpler organism.

Trying to "understand" is perhaps a mistake. I tend to feel that accepting is a better course. But acceptance of such a condition entails rejection or renunciation of individual ego and there is the rub. Apparently I have still quite some distance to go.

But with Michael's guidance I hope to continue the journey towards awareness. I think that what he's trying to tell us is that true knowledge is love.

OLD WARRIOR: I regard Michael as a kind of road map. It can show you all the ways to get there but makes no guarantee for your choice or direction of travel. You may only be driving around looking at the scenery, you may have something specific in mind, and the map gives you an idea of what the route is like. For example, it showed you a river with a drawbridge, but does not indicate whether or not the drawbridge will be up or down; it makes no allowances for traffic jams or for detours or for the weather or the condition of the road.

That's your part of the travel. Michael can be consulted for information and advice, but he can't and won't tell you how to get where you're going, to tell you what you have to drive to get there. In fact, Michael lets you—no, insists—that you choose the destination, route and vehicle for yourself. Michael's information has very often shown me that the way others see the world and the way I see it are not the same, and that's perfectly okay. These various points of view, infuriating at times, still are a necessary part of where we are and what we are doing. There have been many times when this concept has kept me from becoming needlessly frustrated with my co-workers, and made it clear to me that they were not acting to drive me crazy, but simply being what they are, and that the craziness I felt was my own dissatisfaction with what I had permitted to happen in my life. This is a very freeing understanding and prevents many disappointments.

The information Michael has given me on finding new work has been very useful and has kept me from feeling more strain than was already on me. I've had a chance to review what it was I set out to accomplish and what I was doing to accomplish it—not very much— and to make some realistic and workable plans to get back on the track again. I don't pretend to understand it, but I've had enough experience with the material now to know that it works. Over the last six years or so, I've seen what it can do, and how it can help a person through a difficult time. It doesn't stop the difficulty, but it often gives a person a handle on what has taken place so that you don't have to flounder around as much. Michael has made this point better than I could, but it means a lot to me, and so I'll mention it: Michael makes it clear that it's all right to be what we are, to be doing what we're doing, to be going where we're going. That's a tremendous load off my back.

OLD SCHOLAR: It is not easy for me to limit my description of my "Michael experience" to any normal length or content. Looking at my Overleaves, it is easy to see that many of them (Old Spiritualist Scholar, Passion, Acceptance) line up perfectly with the Michael experience. All my life I've been looking for such a thing, and in so doing I've looked into rather a lot of the available options (Presbyterianism as a child; a lot of Eastern stuff during college; meditation, Seth, and positive thinking more recently) all of which seemed okay for a while (I forgot *Course in Miracles*). Many times I have longed for a "person" to be my teacher or guide in the largest sense, but I have been naturally wary of the guru-at-large style (Oh, I forgot Rashneesh). So I've been hungry but very picky.

In the Summer of '83, at one of the arts festivals, I was staying with a friend, had an afternoon with time to relax and found, while scanning his bookshelf, *The Tennis Murders* and *Messages From Michael*, at the same time, and typically, began them both immediately, and finished them soon after. A member of the Michael group was at the festival [actually, there were two members of the Michael group at that festival], and I vaguely remembered her mentioning something about all of this Michael stuff the year before, so I went to her and began to ask her about her experience, and if I could come along and visit for myself. She went to the group, the group checked out my Overleaves and talked it over, and I was invited, and that, as they say, was that!

Since then, it is not an overstatement to say that my life is centered on Michael work, and that everything of importance I do or ever think about is related immediately and at length to Michael concepts. I have been searching for many years for my career, with a large pile of frustration, anxiety and pain left to show for it. The most obvious and concrete benefit that the Michael material has given me is solving that convoluted riddle in one stroke: instrument-making. That whole burden is simply gone, and although I am aware that the working out of the new direction will be a long and complicated proposition, the internal feel of now knowing what I'm doing (and actually beginning to do it, instead of spending most of my energy pulling my hair out about what it was to be) is tremendous. As I said, that is the most obvious improvement in my life from my Michael work, but certainly not the only one. There is a pervasive sense of well-being, of understanding, of tolerance, which is harder to describe, but tangible and vital to me, moment to moment. I am able to love more, in many different ways. I am more outgoing and appreciative of others from the most intimate relationships with my wife and son to casual encounters in the grocery store. My health is better, through Michael's specific instructions. Is it too simple-minded to say I am happier?

I could go on at length about all of this; it is probably (next to wood) my favorite subject. The truth is that my experience with Michael has changed everything for me, is really the center of my life, and gives me the confidence and focus I need to really get on with it.

YOUNG SAGE: I haven't been to many sessions, but they have been very interesting, at least what I've heard has been interesting. I think the people are very sincere without being stuffy about it, and they laugh a lot, which is reassuring. Most of the people I know who get involved in this kind of thing become deadly serious and they can't joke about their studies at all. In the Michael group, they like to make cracks and to tease each other and Michael. The mediums, too, are not what you might expect. They're sensible women—I understand one is a man, but I've never met him—who do real jobs in the real world and know what's going on in the world. They aren't what you might think a medium would be. Just watching Jessica sit there in a rocking chair in slacks and a bulky sweater while she works the board is an experience.

I don't know if the teaching has made that much difference to me. I keep thinking I've stumbled on someone who has monumental significance in my life and Michael tells me that we have complimentary Overleaves or that body types attract.

I can't imagine what it would be like to meet someone where there is a very strong pull, if this is Michael's idea of something minor.

I don't think I'd want to attend sessions regularly. For one thing, they can get pretty intense, and for another, a lot of what's asked could get pretty boring on a twice-a-month basis.

It's good to know that Michael is there and that I can ask questions if I need to, but I think a steady diet of it would be a bit much.

MATURE SCHOLAR: Reading about Overleaves solved one of life's great mysteries for me. I had always been frustrated by the fact that I could never "see" into the minds of people around to understand their thought processes. Through the use of Overleaves I can reason out a person's thinking. It makes life more understandable for me, though not necessarily easier to deal with.

Secondly, a distinct mental sigh of relief swept over me when I learned to accept the strong pulls to various people as past-life associations or present-life Agreements. Previously, I had not been able to find a rational basis for this overwhelming feeling of closeness. Although I could not say that I am easily given to spiritualism or metaphysics, I have always been willing to try out new concepts in my life.

Years ago, reading Edgar Cayce books piqued my curiosity about reincarnation. Yet the actual Cayce writing was difficult for me to understand with its archaic style. Then the series of Seth books, which have stopped for some inexplicable reason [the medium Jane Roberts died the year before this commentary was written], rang true against the inner tuning fork that I use to evaluate philosophies. Seth managed to explain the way that I had felt since I was a child, but the material did more to reinforce my closely held beliefs than to insert radical new ones.

The Michael material has reintroduced me to the concept of karma, originally advanced in the Cayce works, and it has made me realize the necessity of working things out with my fellow beings.

The danger that I see in the Michael teaching and the Overleaves information is that the readers will tend to categorize people and treat them differently somehow. I try to use the material to understand why someone responds in a certain way. I do not say, however, "Well, what would you expect from a Young Sage who is obviously in the Passion Mode!" I want to treat people as people, not as Cycles or Roles. Lastly, and perhaps most importantly, I am beginning to realize that, despite my natural inclination (as a Scholar) to hibernate, no one need stand alone. I had always known that it was acceptable to ask a friend for aid, perhaps advice, and even a loan of money occasionally, but I had never, ever considered asking for energy. I feel now that it is proper to do so and very probably necessary in the complex society in which we live.

YOUNG WARRIOR: I've only attended three Michael sessions, and that was some time ago. My cousin took me to them, thinking that they could help me learn to deal with my handicap. I lost a foot and most of my right arm in VietNam, and it took me a long time to come to terms with it.

Most people confronted with an amputee feel either that they must ignore the condition entirely or treat you as if you were in a wheel chair. The people in the Michael group weren't like that at all. They were aware of what had happened to me, and one of them actually made a joke about my hand. That floored me. I'd never had anyone, outside of the guys in the hospital, make jokes about losing limbs. And there wasn't any malice in the joke, it was just a joke. It shocked me that they could feel this way. I didn't think I was a freak to them, just a guy with one set of metal fingers.

Frankly, what Michael said didn't make a lot of difference to me, and even though my cousin was disappointed, I didn't want to keep on with the group. I know that I've been learning something about living this way. So what? But the thing that really mattered to me was the way the group accepted me, didn't cater to me or ignore me, and never pitied me. It felt great not to have anyone pity me. And I have the feeling that even though they might not understand how I felt, they were willing to let me handle things my way, and not try to get along by their rules, which was great, too. That Jessica was as friendly as anyone I've ever met, and I think that Camille is gorgeous. She even shook my prosthetic when I left. I offer that to people, sometimes, just to see what they'll do. Camille took it without batting an eye.

I know this is supposed to be about Michael. But the thing is, when I think about Michael, the only thing that really comes to mind is the group, and how much I liked them. Sorry I can't come up with anything better.

MATURE SCHOLAR: I'm more convinced than ever that nothing is wasted (though I often have to remind myself of this conviction); that all experience teaches something worthwhile. I'm more inclined to believe that other people are doing what is theirs to do, or trying to, no matter how bizarre it may seem to me; and that I have no business telling them what they should be doing. There is a very calming feeling that I don't have to hurry up and do everything in this one lifetime; there's time for it all.

I find I can more easily turn away and say, not now, maybe later—a concert career, a life as a painter or horse breeder or professor of languages—and be less inclined to diffuse my energy in dilettantism in everything.

I think I'm more willing than I was to stick with potentially troublesome or difficult situations if I feel potentialities for growth in them for me, instead of playing it safe all the time in the hope that everything will go smoothly. On the other hand, I'm more likely to avoid something that just looks like lots of trouble and eaten up time. That is, I think I trust my own judgment more about people and situations. There's a pleasing feeling of being in a world full of friends, known or unknown in this life—so far—instead of strangers. I like the idea that wherever I go, I may find an old friend, and I think I'm more interested in other people than I was, less self-centered and self-focused, with more willingness to reach out to strangers.

I'm more relaxed about the idea of death, my own and others', which I think sometimes makes me appear uncaring. On the other hand, having set this life up pretty solidly for myself, I'm determined not to lose it before I can wring out of it everything I can. Once you know you've deliberately set up all sorts of opportunities for yourself, you don't want to let any slip by you. I do get very irritated by behavior I identify as a product (troublesome to others) of soul-youth. But then I always was irritated by it; only now I know I ought to be more tolerant (having been the equivalent of a Hell's Angel many times myself), and I'm not.

The confirmation that there really are other species scooting around out there in the universe relieves a certain tendency toward romantic despair and that sense of vast isolation that I sometimes indulged in when I was younger (in this lifetime—and probably others, come to think of it). I love the idea that someday we'll make contact, and that I won't miss it; sooner or later, I'll be there.

The recognition of contact with old friends is sometimes a source of problems. If I acknowledge and act on the pull felt to a comparative stranger, they don't know what's going on (I can scarcely start off by telling them) and often react quite skittishly, for which you can't blame them. (Who is this strange woman? Is she after my body? If not, what is she after? And why am I interested in this person who is definitely not my type at all? What is going on here?) There's a lot of discomfort where one wishes only to share the pleasure of mutual recognition. Occasionally, just as I'm about to quit in exasperation, I will have a validation, often very brief, and it will keep me trying. This part is definitely stressful and non-jolly.

And then there's the fun part. I like having a bunch of rather far-flung friends all loosely knit together by their Michael-concerns. I like the diversity of the group, which includes people in occupations I normally wouldn't encounter socially, at least not on any level deeper than the very superficial. I like hearing what kinds of questions other people ask, and what kind of answers they get, and the sometimes rather hilarious camaraderie of sessions or even meetings outside of sessions. This is good for a natural loner like me, and I appreciate it.

There's this definite feeling of being involved in a life that is being helped to be pretty well focused, at least recently, instead of just floating along wondering what hit me all the time. Something else just occurred to me—that is that formulating questions for Michael helps, I think, in training a person to think about their life in a useful way. Knowing that there's someone to ask has accustomed me to look for helpful questions, and maybe to identify and analyze issues in my life that might otherwise have remained a lot hazier and more confused.

Now, about being married to my TC. In the most practical terms, this means and has meant that when he has something to offer concerning my work—criticism, advice—I listen very carefully because I know that his natural bent is to help me further my work. Similarly, I am more forthcoming with comments about his work than I might be otherwise. I have the sense that if we just keep moving together, keeping a sharp lookout for the feedback we give each other all the time, we can accomplish a great deal, either outwardly or inwardly or both.

It's strange sometimes to find myself living with a person who can remind me now and then just by the reactions between us of that underlying constant: that whatever the surface does, the basic commitment goes on forever. Mostly I forget about this, or rather it sinks into the background. On the most personal level, it's a matter of having the firm security of knowing that I'm living with the "right" person; the person who is basically on my side and whose side I am on;

the person with whom I can do my most effective work and growing and who can do his with me; the person with whom I have an old and solid relationship of mutual knowledge and trust.

Not that this means I can or do take him for granted. We can always go ahead and screw things up for ourselves, after all. Michael says, yes, of course, we've held each other back in past lives and "it would be surprising if you had not". But I don't go around looking longingly at other men, wondering if I might have done better with that one or another one. I don't have to waste my time or energy in that kind of doubt and fantasizing. I've connected up with the person I want and need, and it's up to me to make the most of this opportunity, which I gather is not so easy to come by. I know I'm married to my true best friend, best lover, best colleague, and that this is for a purpose—both of our purposes—which we can figure out by what we do as we go along. Though nothing is certain, it looks like a pretty well-designed life for both of us, and I certainly have more confidence in it than I would trying to work it out on my own. And more joy because we're awfully good at working and playing together. And more responsibility, because if we louse this up, what a pair of dopes we'll be! Or is this attitude itself a product of a life designed to be lived together with one's TC?

MATURE WARRIOR: What my TC wife writes is so eloquent and perceptive that I am reluctant to comment. However, I would place the emphasis differently in certain areas, especially those having to do with relations with others. My office life is important. Those relationships, some of them new and rich, and some reflecting past associations, complement the TC relationship. The TC relationship does not override them.

Often my TC has good political suggestions about the office, but in office matters I depend more on advice from professional colleagues I trust. My TC wife describes the feedback we give each other, but sometimes the focus goes phlooey, as in a recent project of hers when I was enthusiastic and supportive and entirely missed the problems correctly identified by several of her colleagues. As a TC, I'm no substitute for a colleague with ten years' professional experience. (Watch it, fella: your secondary Chief Feature is Self-Deprecation.) My TC wife notes that we have recently begun to consider the difference between us. "Consider" is a Scholar's word.

Those differences came into sharp focus while we were traveling recently, surprised us both, unpleasantly, and caused resentment and frustration. Sure, we're learning how to deal with that together, but meanwhile, the pain was real.

Addendum for **MATURE SCHOLAR:** Yes. The Task Companion bond includes its own difficulties. I think that having come to expect a high degree of "matching" and mutual reinforcement from each other, we found these surfacing differences more jarring than a non-TC couple might.

OLD SAGE: Michael has made me aware that I am truly and completely my own boss, that I must answer to no one but myself, and that what happens to me happens to me, not to anyone else. This has given me a sense of responsibility that surprises me at times, but also results in a great sense of freedom. I do not have to answer to anyone but me. No one is keeping score, no one is making or changing the rules for me but me. Michael has told Sages that there is a real danger for those on the Expression Polarity in general and Sages in particular to perform a life rather than live it. That comment has been very useful to me on many occasions and has helped me to understand where I have blown it for myself before, and what is often misunderstood by others. Another useful, but not very pleasant lesson that Michael has pointed out to me has been learning to be loyal. Until Michael explained to me how Sages and Artisans perceive relationships, I had never figured out what was going on in some of the relationships I had had, both as friendships and more intimately. Learning about loyalty, what it really is and how it works, has taught me a lot. It also helped me to be of use to my Warrior brother when his marriage ran into trouble. Just as I did not always show enough loyalty, he tended to show too much, doing what Michael called "holding the line until the bitter end". He did not find it easy to accept his separation, but I think that through Michael I was able to give him some real understanding and sympathy, and that counts for a lot.

MATURE SLAVE: What Michael has been most helpful with for me has been in dealing with my three kids. I have a Young Artisan, a boy age fifteen, a Mature King, a boy age thirteen, and an Old Warrior, a girl age nine. They were baffling to me, and I could sense that I was managing them badly in some way, and that no matter how much I did for them, it didn't seem to be the right thing. My neighbor [the male half of "Leslie Adams"] introduced me to Michael after his kids and mine had spent most of a summer playing together. He brought me into the group, and Michael explained to me about the King-thing, as the members of the group called it. I can tell now that in helping the Mature King, I was not giving him the sense of responsibility that a King has to have if he isn't going to turn out to be a despot of one sort or another. Since my King boy is very good at taking over everything, and the Warrior girl just loves it when he does, I developed an entirely different way of dealing with them. I let them, and encourage them, to do things together, but I don't help them out with everything the way I'd done before. Now they have to fend for themselves, and because my daughter is much younger, I make sure my King son is aware that he has an obligation to make sure she doesn't get harmed in any way. He's handled this very well, and in the last several months, the difference has been remarkable. I know that some of that is simply a matter of growing up more, and I am aware that it isn't always going to be smooth sailing just because I'm willing to work with their Essences rather than against them. As a single parent, I've been very aware of the pitfalls, and I can see that they'll be with me for a long time. For example, I haven't found a way to help my oldest boy deal with his resentment toward his father for leaving us. Michael has helped me see how the resentment is expressed (often very indirectly and in strange ways) but so far there's been little I can do with him for it. These things take time, I know, and heaven knows I've made more progress in the last year than I'd made in the previous four or five, but there's still a long way to go and many, many things to deal with along the way. Michael can help deal with them, but there's no way to avoid them.

MATURE SCHOLAR: At this time of my life, the Michael material has been more helpful than I can say, both in understanding myself and my wife, and those around me, but it has also answered many questions that have haunted me for most of my life. Michael has helped me to see that others are not like me, and that they are pursuing their lives in their ways as I am pursuing mine. Because they have chosen another way does not mean that they are on the wrong path or have erred in choosing their own way to go. This has been the most important understanding for me at this time, professionally and personally, and it has shown me the way to understand this and accept it.

Because of what Michael has taught me, I think I'm more understanding and more able to love those around me without putting conditions or restrictions on that love, so that fewer doors are shut and more are open. To say that Michael has given me an unrepayable gift is not putting it too strongly. Both my wife and I have benefited more than we can say from what Michael has taught, starting with learning to recognize the Chief Feature and what it does, to dealing with the day-to-day problems we all confront. I'm grateful for the insight, and for the concern. Thanks, Michael.

MATURE PRIEST: As a professional astrologer, I came to the Michael material with a great deal of interest mixed with skepticism. Anyone dealing in these areas of study comes up against a lot of information that is suspect, to say the least. Michael's teaching was more in tune with what I had come to regard as reliable information than much of what I had read, and at the time I decided that I wanted to do some research, comparing Overleaves and charts to determine the similarities if there were any.

Because of problems in my own life, that study, as it turns out, was almost a life-saver, and I mean that literally. In the midst of serious and very difficult crises, the Michael material gave me a positive focus that not only gave me some respite from what I was enduring day-to-day, but permitted me to keep my perspective on my life and the lives of my family. The studies I made at that time formed the basis for a continuing comparison of charts to Overleaves, and has shown some very interesting patterns.

Often in charts it is not always possible to determine what particular effect a transit or an aspect is likely to have on an individual. For example, it is possible to determine that the person who is the subject of the chart might have some serious difficulties with partnerships, but what that may mean beyond that is hard to see, if there are no other clues in the chart. With Overleaves, knowledge of the Goal and the Chief Feature often enables me to be more specific about where the stresses are likely to occur, and what they are apt to be like. This, in turn, has made me a more attentive astrologer, because I have the advantage of the added dimension of the Michael material to enhance the charts I prepare. During the crises I've already mentioned, the awareness that the problems encountered did not arise from karma helped me to release the hold that the circumstances had on me. I could be content with the pain and the separation as well as the termination of my marriage and the other attendant problems, since it was apparent that I had not avoided any binding reasons to continue in the difficult relationship—just as I found that putting the entire marriage into perspective kept me from giving way to despair when things were at their worst.

I think that there are many people out there who put themselves through needless anguish and even physical danger because they're convinced that it all can reach a magic point where everything turns around just because of their individual tenacity. That isn't true, of course, and most of us realize it, whether we like to admit it or not. With Michael's comments, I know I avoided many complications that I might otherwise have assumed I had to handle.

Few of the clients I have done charts for have been uninterested in the Michael material. Most of them are filled with questions, many evolving from their questions about their charts. Since I can't take them along to sessions, I'm glad that there's going to be a second book I can give them so that they can have access to more of the material.

Along those lines, I occasionally have clients who have obtained their Overleaves from other sources, and many times it is apparent to me, when I compare what they have to their charts (and I have quite a sizable file for the purposes of comparison at this time), that they have not been provided accurate information. I might not be able to determine precisely what the true Overleaves are, but I'm certain that they do not have the Overleaves they suppose. It might be a good idea for people who are in doubt about their Overleaves to consult a good astrologer with some background in the Michael material, particularly one who also does numerology, since Michael and numerology appear to have a great deal in common.

Michael has provided me with many useful insights in the past, and I've learned a great deal from everything he's taught. I hope that I'll be able to continue to learn from him, and to use what I learn not only for my own benefit, but for the benefit of my family and friends as well as my clients. It hasn't always been possible for me to feel positive about myself or about what I've been doing, but my own discipline has given me a worthwhile tool to aid me in my life, and the Michael material is an added depth and perspective for me.

I'm aware of how difficult channeling is, and I think that all the mediums—Jessica, Camille and both mediums in "Leslie Adams"— are to be thanked for giving so much energy to Michael and to us in getting this information.

OLD ARTISAN: I was in the Michael group at Jessica's for about two years, and it was interesting, but it's not really anything that I want to keep active with for very long. Michael said that most of the students who keep with this kind of teaching are Scholars, Warriors, Priests and Sages, and it looked that way to me, back then.

For the most part, I think I can figure things out for myself, and I really don't care where I died the last time around, or how. Much of that kind of question seems to be a waste of time to me, and I can't keep taking down all that dictation about a subject that really hasn't any bearing on what I'm doing now, and where I want to go.

I like the people in the group, don't get that wrong. Jessica's a wonderful woman, and Milly's not bad herself. They're very good at what they do, and I don't doubt they're legitimate.

But I want to get on with what I'm doing, and the rest is almost a waste of time. I might come back to it some day, but I can't see that happening for a long time yet. You could say that I'm not much of a candidate for enlightenment. Probably not. It's got to happen sometime, later on. I'll wait until it does.

MATURE SAGE: I've checked out everything Michael's told me as closely as I can, and I'm still astounded at how right he can be. In all the years I've been asking questions, and it's going on seven now, the matters that have been validatable (a Michael word) turned out very high on the reliability scale. Not that I ask questions all that much, especially since I've moved away from the Bay Area. Maybe four times a year I'll call something in to Jessica, and she gets back to me within two weeks, since the sessions are every two weeks, and then I do everything I can to check out what Michael has said. I don't really approve of the people in the group who come to Michael with every little thing. I think that this isn't what Michael's all about. Michael probably won't agree with me, because I know Michael says he doesn't care. Or they don't care. That's probably true, but it bothers me. Besides, eventually you have to choose for yourself in any case, so you might as well choose and be done with it. I like to save Michael for those situations where I know I don't have enough information to make a good decision, and there's no reasonable way I can get the information from a different source, or when the information I do have isn't trustworthy.

I will say that I've been using some of Michael's insights in my private teaching, and that it usually works out very well. I've also been making an effort to do more public speaking because it satisfies my need for an audience and the organization I work for knows that I'm good at it. For the last year or so I've been in therapy. The death of my parents was more difficult than I would have thought it could be, and for that reason, I wanted to straighten out some of my feelings. Between my therapist and Michael, I believe I'm starting to come out of the woods on this, and I hope that in the next year or so, I'll be able to stop the therapy. I might even stop asking questions of Michael. Just as I don't want to become dependent on my shrink, I don't want to get too dependent on Michael.

Still, seeing Jessica and some of the others at a wedding last spring brought back a lot of good memories and I think that I miss them as much or more than I miss what Michael has to say about the world. Jessica looked great, so did Lizzy and Alex. And I got to meet "Leslie Adams," at least half of him, at last. I'd hate to think that I could ever lose touch with all those wonderful people. It's so reassuring to know that, no matter what, I have friends like that. Even if we don't talk Michael, we've got so many interests in common, and there're so many intelligent people in the group who are willing to share what they do, that there are times that Michael is superfluous. I've had contact with three members of my sextant, by the way, and in the last three years, we've worked together twice on various projects. I'd like working with them no matter what, but knowing that there's another level to what we're accomplishing is very exciting. We're very good at communicating what it is we want to do, and everyone says that we generate real enthusiasm. I didn't bother to ask Michael about that. I would have had to have been unconscious not to recognize what was happening.

Don't get me wrong: I'm very much aware of the difference that Michael has made in my life, and I know I wouldn't have done half of what I've done if Michael's information hadn't encouraged me to follow up on hunches. I know I would have handled certain situations far less successfully without the insight that Michael provides. But at the same time, I want to be sure that I don't let Michael become a habit. I'd rather have too little of Michael than too much.

MATURE SCHOLAR: When someone asks what difference Michael makes, I don't think difference is the right word. It's like having the world turn around; anyone who has been asking questions for a long time is on the lookout for answers and I think that this frame of mind helps when coming to the Michael work. I had spent many years trying to find answers and had been pretty consistently disappointed, especially with the more conventional answers and methods that I found in my life.

About cardinality: I'm a Mature Scholar with a Goal of Submission, and this would lead you to assume that I'm a quiet person, wanting to get away from the world, and for years I've told my friends that is what I want to do. But since the time I was first aware of such things, I found that I've always been in the middle of activity, that people keep coming to me for projects and advice and organization, and God knows what else. As a result, I've spent my life between desires or forces. When I came into the Michael group, one of the first things I asked about was this dichotomy in my life, and at that time I was told that I am the cardinal-most Scholar of my Entity currently on the Physical Plane, which means that I am often being thrown into leadership roles simply by the nature of cardinality (that's paraphrasing Michael). I don't fight it anymore.

One of the things that convinced me that Michael was on to something was that there was none of this fantasy about everyone being kings and queens and popes and famous artists. Most of us learn that we pass very ordinary lives doing very ordinary things and dealing with very ordinary problems in fairly ordinary ways. That made sense to me from the start.

Thinking about what the information has helped me to do more effectively, I believe that my dealing with a very talented young man I met some time ago is about the clearest example I can give. I admired his work very much, and felt drawn to do something to help him advance in his work. This is not at all a usual reaction for me, incidentally. While this person's talent is indisputable, he behaved irresponsibly and unpleasantly, and this led me to ask Michael what was going on. I had tried several times to give up on the work relationship, but kept coming back to it. Michael indicated that we were involved in a working Monad and that this was the fifth attempt we had made at finishing it. With this information and a few insights, I decided to hang in there until the work got done, bad manners and strange behavior and all. It took well over two years to complete the Monadal work, and the process wasn't all that easy, but it finally got done.

Now that it's over, we're better friends than we were while we were working together, in part because the tension between us has gone. I've come to appreciate him in a different way, and he has accepted that, in spite of the fact that I'm not the same race or sex that he is, I still know how to do certain kinds of business better than he does, and that I can deal with contracts more effectively than he can. In fact, that is the one thing that lingers—he still discusses his contracts with me and occasionally actually listens to my advice.

Recently I've been involved in a project with a large number of people, many of whom are friends from the past. It's been difficult, with more pressure than any one of us imagined we'd have at the beginning. Occasionally someone will ask aloud what the hell we're all doing here, and usually I answer by quoting Michael: "Hanging out with old friends in difficult circumstances".

CHELSEA QUINN YARBRO: For myself, the Michael material has been a source of information in many ways. As a novelist, I've found that Michael has been very useful in my research, not in giving me actual data, but in telling me where I can find those data. At times, when accounts differ, I will ask Michael which account is correct, or if either account is, and if so, where and how do they err. When Michael answers such queries, I've done what I can to verify the material they have supplied.

On a more personal level, Michael's information has been useful and trustworthy, and while I probably have made as many mistakes with Michael material as I would without, I find I can recognize the errors and see what has caused them more clearly than I would have done if I had no information from Michael. Particularly, I have a better understanding of how much the Chief Feature controls and distorts all perceptions. That alone is worth all the hours I've spent transcribing dictation. As several of the others in the group have commented, the friendships that come from the Michael sessions are among the most valuable gifts of the teaching; I know my life would be poorer for the lack of them. If the friendships were all that the Michael material offered, it would be more than worth it. The insight and compassion and endless information that are included with the people who ask the questions puts the Michael teaching right up there with opera and horses.

The Michael group is into its second decade, which means that, before too many more years go by, it will be possible to see what the long-range aspects of these teachings are, if any. No matter what develops, my life has an added dimension through the Michael teaching which makes living richer. What more can anyone ask of any teaching?

Post Script in 2009

To answer some frequently asked questions . . .

Does the group still exist? Yes it does.

Is it still closed? Yes it is.

Have any interesting long-term results been seen? Most of the continuing group members seem to think so. I know the information I've received over time has been and continues to be valuable. Some of what they have communicated is very practical. Several group members report they have been more able to deal with allergies, menopause, and similar chronic problems. I know also one group member has said that Michael's information has helped her to successfully battle a serious chronic disease for more than fifteen years. And the group members continue to be some of my dearest friends.

Is there anyone in the original group still in it? A few people, and more than ten in the extended group, meaning those who are no longer living in the Bay Area, have been part of it for more than thirty years.

Are any of the original mediums still working with the group? One is; the other medium presently channeling has been at it for about a decade.

How has the information changed? In substance and style, it hasn't changed at all. Michael's syntax is still uniquely his own. Topically, Michael has expanded some of his areas of discussion, particularly into mathematical theory, just as the questions being asked have altered over time.

How many people have left the group and how many others have arrived? Five group members, including "Jessica and Walter Lansing" have died since this book was originally published; over the years more than two dozen members have left the group for a variety of reasons, and over the same period of time about twenty have taken their places.

Do you still attend meetings? Almost all of them.

Do you still find it worthwhile? Yes I do.

Who shows up? Typically we have a King, a Priest, three or four Scholars, three Warriors, two Artisans, and two Slaves. Three of these are Old, the rest are Mature, except for one seventh Level Young. For a while we had a couple of Sages, but one moved across country and one went on to other studies. Our phone-in and e-mail members are about a dozen regulars, and another five occasionals; three of them are in Europe. Two of the phone-ins have been asking questions for a quarter century.

How many pages of transcripts are there now? In excess of seven thousand single-spaced pages, and more coming along every month.

Will there ever be another Michael book? If I can find the right publisher, there will be.

Will Caelum Press reprint the remaining two Michael books? I hope so, but you'll have to ask them. If nothing else, Caelum deserves a huge amount of thanks for making the first two books, with additional material, available again. They've done the group a real service.

- THE END -

LaVergne, TN USA
03 March 2010
174599LV00002BA/33/P